P9-BAU-549

Raising Freethinkers
A Practical Guide for Parenting Beyond Belief

Dale McGowan

Molleen Matsumura

Amanda Metskas

Jan Devor

NOT FOR RESALE
This is a Free Book
Bookthing.org

American Management Association
New York ◆ Atlanta ◆ Brussels ◆ Chicago ◆ Mexico City ◆ San Francisco
Shanghai ◆ Tokyo ◆ Toronto ◆ Washington, D.C.

Special discounts on bulk quantities of AMACOM books are available to corporations, professional associations, and other organizations. For details, contact Special Sales Department, AMACOM, a division of American Management Association, 1601 Broadway, New York, NY 10019.
Tel: 800-250-5308. Fax: 518-891-2372.
E-mail: *specialsls@amanet.org*
Website: *www.amacombooks.org/go/specialsales*
To view all AMACOM titles go to: *www.amacombooks.org*

This publication is designed to provide accurate and authoritative information in regard to the subject matter covered. It is sold with the understanding that the publisher is not engaged in rendering legal, accounting, or other professional service. If legal advice or other expert assistance is required, the services of a competent professional person should be sought.

Library of Congress Cataloging-in-Publication Data

McGowan, Dale.
   Raising freethinkers : a practical guide for parenting beyond belief / Dale McGowan . . . [et al.].
      p. cm.
   Includes index.
   ISBN-13: 978-0-8144-1096-7 (pbk.)
   ISBN-10: 0-8144-1096-0 (pbk.)
   1. Religious education of children. 2. Parenting—Religious aspects 3. Free thought. I. Title.

BL2777.R4M34 2009
649'.7—dc22

                                                              2008042205

© 2009 Dale McGowan
All rights reserved.
Printed in the United States of America.

This publication may not be reproduced, stored in a retrieval system, or transmitted in whole or in part, in any form or by any means, electronic, mechanical, photocopying, recording, or otherwise, without the prior written permission of AMACOM, a division of American Management Association, 1601 Broadway, New York, NY 10019.

Printing number
11

Contents

Contents

Preface

In April 2007, *Parenting Beyond Belief: On Raising Ethical, Caring Kids Without Religion* was released. The first comprehensive book for nonreligious parents, *PBB* laid out a basic philosophy for nonreligious parenting in a wide variety of voices. The book fulfilled the promise of its preface to support and encourage nonreligious parents, but (also as promised) included relatively little in the way of practical advice.

The sound you heard upon opening this book was the other shoe dropping. *Raising Freethinkers: A Practical Guide for Parenting Beyond Belief* is just that—a practical guide. You'll find ideas and ponderings in these pages, but also specific answers to common questions and hundreds of activities and resources to make those ideas come alive.

Along the way we will also address some of the larger questions about nonreligious parenting that have surfaced since the release of *PBB,* including the first and foremost: What exactly *is* nonreligious parenting?

Vive la Différence—and the Common Ground

Not long after the release of *Parenting Beyond Belief,* I received an email from a liberal Christian. She was a regular reader of my secular parenting blog, The Meming of Life, and she'd had it with me.

Why, she asked, do I draw a line between "religious parenting" and "nonreligious parenting"? Isn't the kind of parenting I advocate—unbounded questioning, a scientifically informed, evidence-based worldview, questioning of authority, rejecting the notion of "sinful thoughts," developing moral judgment instead of simple rule following—isn't all that just "good parenting"? Am I *really* saying that religious parents can't do these things?

There is *nothing* secular parents can do that religious parents positively cannot do, I replied, just as there is nothing that religious parents can achieve that *we* can't.

"So why make the distinction at all?" she asked. "Why describe something called 'nonreligious parenting' if it's pretty much the same as good religious parenting?"

The answer is this: Even though we can and often do end up pursuing the same ends, religious and nonreligious parenting really *aren't* the same. There is a profound difference in the context, the space in which religious parenting and nonreligious parenting happen.

Both secular and religious parents *can* raise kids to value fearless questioning, think critically, question authority, and reject the idea of sin and the demonization of doubt. But the core principles of freethought encourage and support those values, while the core principles of religion discourage them. One lends itself to them; the other chafes against them.

My hat is off to religious parents who encourage unrestrained doubt, applaud fearless questioning, and reject appeals to authority. I admire their willingness to dissent from their group's majority. Considering the current growth in Christian fundamentalism at the expense of more moderate versions, such religious parents are salmon swimming against a mighty current. At the core of traditional monotheistic religion are the ideas that doubt is bad, that certain questions are not to be asked, and that church and scripture carry some degree of inherent authority.

But the most important message in her email is one too often overlooked by nonreligious and religious people alike: the fact that followers of progressive religion have far more in common with the nonreligious than they do with their more conservative and literalist coreligionists. Every time we distinguish between ourselves and those conservative religious practitioners, we should make an equal effort to recognize our substantial common ground with those progressives.

A particular strength of nonreligious parenting is that it can embrace several key human values without apology, values that religion has traditionally suppressed and feared. This embrace allows parents—gay or straight, single or partnered—to turn away from the dissonance of religion, to dance with their children in the light of knowledge, and to revel in questioning and doubting as the highest human callings, rivaled only by love.

Finding Our Voice—and Each Other

When I first approached agents and publishers with the idea of a book on non-religious parenting in 2003, I was confidently informed that no real audience existed for such a book. There was a book titled *How to Be a Jewish Parent,* serving the 2.5 percent of the U.S. population that is Jewish; another titled *Effective Islamic Parenting* for the 1 percent that is Islamic; and even one called *Raising Witches: Teaching the Wiccan Faith to Children* for that 0.004 percent slice of the U.S. pie. But the 14.1 percent of the U.S. population that identify as nonreligious[1] was still relatively invisible just a few years ago.

That changed in October 2005 when Sam Harris's *The End of Faith* hit number 4 on the *New York Times* Best Seller list. Six months later, there was little difficulty in finding a publisher for *Parenting Beyond Belief.* The book has found a large and receptive audience of parents, often grateful and surprised to find that they were not alone after all.

I've heard it claimed that we're in the midst of a "secular parenting renaissance." Dozens of new nonreligious parenting resources have come into being since the release of *PBB* in April 2007, including discussion forums, blogs, and local nonreligious parenting groups in cities including New York, Washington, DC, Raleigh, Portland (OR), Palo Alto (CA), Austin, Albuquerque, and Colorado Springs.

But "renaissance" isn't quite right. A renaissance is a *re*birth—and non-religious parenting is not born again by either definition. It's the *birth* of a nonreligious parenting movement we are witnessing. It's not that nonreligious parenting is new, of course, but it's only now that we are finding each other, forming a movement and a community, learning that we've been living all along in neighborhoods and cities filled with parents who are grappling with precisely the same questions we are. Even better, we're finding a consensus on how best to answer those questions.

The "Best Practices" Model

Religion provides parents with answers. But on one parenting topic after another—moral development, sexuality, dealing with death, child discipline, avoiding substance abuse, and more—a growing body of research across multiple disciplines shows that traditional religious answers often get it precisely wrong. It isn't just a matter of "different strokes"—ignoring the best of our knowledge in favor of conservative religious practice often results in impaired moral development,[2] more dysfunctional behavior,[3] equal or greater rates of teen pregnancy,[4] a more confused attitude toward death,[5] and equal or greater alcohol and drug abuse[6] than scientifically informed secular approaches—a sobering pattern explored throughout this book.

So it isn't surprising that so many religious and nonreligious parents alike are walking away from these counterproductive ideas. But even as bad answers are discarded, the questions remain. In addition to searching out the best insights from research, nonreligious parents are turning to each other, building an informed and continuously tested consensus on the best practices for nonreligious parenting.

"Best practices" are practices that have been found most effective in a given field. In the absence of a single authority, nonreligious parents are developing their own set of best practices, informed by scientific research and shaped by their own experiences.

Perhaps most important of all, best practices are not commandments carved in stone but an evolving set of guidelines—a kind of cultural Wiki, continuously edited and re-edited by those who are testing its assumptions on a daily basis.

After nearly three years of research, travel, teaching, and discussion, I offer the following evolving list of nine best practices for nonreligious parenting:

1. *Encourage ever-wider circles of empathy.* Worldview, race, nationalism, and various other chauvinisms cut us off from empathy with the rest of humanity. Nonreligious parents should encourage their children to reach beyond such artificial boundaries.

2. *Encourage active moral development.* Children can and should be encouraged to develop *active* moral reasoning by understanding the reasons to be and do good.

3. *Promote ravenous curiosity.* An active and insatiable curiosity is the key to learning and the engine of a productive and engaged life.

4. *Teach engaged coexistence.* Religion in some form will always be with us. Our job is to raise kids to coexist with religion while engaging and challenging its adherents to make its effects more humane—*and* inviting the same in return.

5. *Encourage religious literacy.* Children must be made knowledgeable *about* religion without being indoctrinated *into* religion.

6. *Leave kids unlabeled.* Calling a child a "Christian" or an "atheist" is counterproductive to encouraging genuine freethought. It is just as dishonest

to label a child with a complex worldview as to call her a "Republican" or a "Marxist."

7. ***Make death natural and familiar.*** By shielding our children too completely from the contemplation of death, we set them up for a much more difficult and dysfunctional adult relationship with mortality.

8. ***Invite the questioning of authority.*** At the heart of freethought is the rejection of the argument from authority. Encourage children to ask for the reasons behind rules and the reasoning behind answers.

9. ***Normalize disbelief.*** There is no greater contribution nonreligious parents can make to their children's future as freethinkers than to make religious disbelief a normal, unexceptional option in our culture.

These practices require a guiding philosophy as well—the philosophy of humanism, one rooted in the dual principles of love and reason so beautifully captured by the Bertrand Russell quote that begins *Parenting Beyond Belief.* "The good life," Russell noted, "is one inspired by love and guided by knowledge." Freethought, in its pursuit of knowledge, too often leaves the principles of love and compassion to fend for themselves. This is the point at which science and reason become unmoored and alienating. Without compassion and a deep-seated empathy, our freethinking principles become too detached from our humanity to do us any good.

Even a parent who agrees that the practices are sound will have countless questions about how to actually achieve them: *How* can I teach my kids to engage religion productively? *How* can I make them literate without indoctrinating them? *How* can I engender that ravenous curiosity, comfort them in the face of death, push out the boundaries of empathy? These and over 100 other questions form the backbone of this book. Each chapter begins with an introduction to frame the chapter topic, followed by "Questions and Answers" featuring many of the most common questions voiced by nonreligious parents. Each then concludes with specific activities to engage the topic with your kids and/or partner, and a carefully selected list of resources for further exploration.

The Contributors

As with *PBB*, I knew that a collaboration would produce a far better result than anything I could achieve on my own. After much consideration and consultation, I invited three co-authors with deep knowledge and experience in practical freethought education. All three are wonderful writers and thinkers, and each has brought unique strengths and perspective to the project. In bringing this book about, the three best decisions I made are named Molleen, Amanda, and Jan:

Molleen Matsumura has been a humanist activist and writer for over twenty years. She has worked to defend reproductive freedom, separation of religion and government, evolution education, and marriage equality. Her writing has appeared in *Free Inquiry*, *New Humanist* (UK), *Humanistic Judaism*, and *Reports of the National Center for Science Education*, among other publications. Molleen has been a project director for the National Center for Science Education and currently serves on the advisory boards of the Secular Student Alliance and Americans United for Separation of Church and State. She writes the humanist advice column, *Sweet Reason;* some past columns can be found at *www.sweetreason.org* or in the Parenting section of the website of the Institute for Humanist Studies (*www.humanist studies.org*).

Amanda Metskas is the Executive Director of Camp Quest, Inc. (*www .camp-quest.org*). She has been involved with Camp Quest since 2003 and served on the board of directors since 2004. Amanda has been a counselor at Camp Quest Ohio, Camp Quest Michigan, Camp Quest West, Camp Quest Smoky Mountains, and Camp Quest Minnesota. While at camp, Amanda leads educational activities on critical thinking, debate, and international relations. During the rest of the year, she works on coordinating and promoting Camp Quest programs from her office at the Camp Quest headquarters in the Institute for Humanist Studies. Amanda holds a BA from Brown University in international relations and psychology and an MA in political science from Ohio State University. Her co-authored essay about Camp Quest appears in *Parenting Beyond Belief.*

Jan Devor holds a BA and MA in education from the University of Michigan. She taught middle school for thirteen years and then embarked on a seventeen year career as Director of Religious Education with Unitarian Universalist congregations in Concord, MA, and Minneapolis, MN, where she is currently serving the First Unitarian Society. Jan has been credentialed at the Master's Level in religious education by the Unitarian Universalist Association and has co-taught a graduate-level class at United Theological Seminary in religious education theory, philosophy, and practice. She and her husband have raised two Unitarian Universalist freethinkers.

Dale McGowan left a fifteen-year career as a college professor in 2006 to pursue writing full-time. In addition to editing and co-authoring *Parenting Beyond Belief*, he writes the secular parenting blog The Meming of Life and teaches nonreligious parenting seminars around the United States. He holds degrees in physical anthropology and music theory from UC Berkeley as well as a PhD in composition from the University of Minnesota. Dale lives with his wife Becca and their three children near Atlanta, Georgia.

Although each of us offered input and material for the entire book, each had primary responsibility for two chapters, as indicated in the Contents. Any first-person references within a given chapter can generally be attributed to the author of that chapter. As editor of the book overall, all errors can be safely attributed to me.

Add Your Voice!

It's such an exciting time to be a nonreligious parent. We have more resources, a more tangible sense of community, and better ways to share ideas than ever before. Drop by *www.ParentingBeyondBelief.com* to join the *PBB* discussion forum, to follow my parental grapplings at The Meming of Life, and to keep up with the latest news in the world of parenting without religion. We hope you'll add your voice as we continue to explore, invent, and shape our collective understanding of the best practices for raising happy, curious, ethical, and productive kids without religion.

Dale McGowan
dale@ParentingBeyondBelief.com

Notes

1. In 2001, according to CUNY's American Religious Identification Survey (ARIS). Current estimates put the number between 16 and 18 percent.

2. Including research by Nucci, et al., quoted in Pearson, Beth, "The art of creating ethics man," *The Herald* (Scotland), January 23, 2006. See Chapter 2.

3. "Is Corporal Punishment an Effective Means of Discipline?" American Psychological Association, *www.apa.org/releases/spanking.html*. See also Chapter 9. Accessed May 4, 2008.

4. "Abstinence Education Faces an Uncertain Future," *New York Times*, July 18, 2007; Bearman, Peter, and Hannah Brückner: "Promising the Future: Virginity Pledges and First Intercourse." *American Journal of Sociology*, *106*, (4) (January 2001), 859–912. See also Chapter 4.

5. See Chapter 7.

6. Valliant, George E. *The Natural History of Alcoholism* (Cambridge, MA: Harvard University Press, 1983). See also Chapter 4.

Acknowledgments

Molleen Matsumura

Next to parenthood, writing the "Sweet Reason" advice column was the best preparation for contributing to this book. So, deepest thanks to Matt Cherry for inviting me to launch it; sometimes our friends know us better than we know ourselves. Elaine Friedman and Ruth Geller have been friendly and thoughtful editors. So has Duncan Crary, who goes the extra ten miles in giving support.

Jone Johnson-Lewis, Don Montagna, and Lois Kellerman gave permission to include "Steps to Seeking Forgiveness"; Jone and Lois offered additional advice and support. Kate Lovelady obtained permission to use the St. Louis Ethical Society Sunday School's "Core Values." Arthur Dobrin generously gave permission to quote extensively from his book. Chris Lindstrom, Susan Rose, Bobbie Kirkhart, Cleo Kocol, John "The" King and many more people have also been helpful. Tim Madigan introduced me to the research on flow and has been a source of constant encouragement through the years.

Thanks to Elly Matsumura, Maja Marjanovic, Janelle Ishida, Adi Wise, Robyn Gregg, and Caitlin Nye—I can say from experience that our children are our best teachers.

Even a writer has no words for how supportive and inspirational Ken Matsumura has been.

Jan Devor

I would like to acknowledge the Unitarian Universalist religion for being a place where people search for answers to religious questions and are not given the answers to swallow whole. It is a place where acceptance and respect are taught as the guide words for living in this diverse world of ours. It has been a haven for me as an agnostic, a place to raise my family in community and to find friends who have supported me in this journey we call life.

Thanks to Rev. Dr. Kendyl Gibbons for her inspiration and friendship, to my kids who make me stretch, and to my husband who has made this life meaningful, loving, and fun.

Amanda Metskas

Thank you to Dale McGowan, for inviting me to be a part of this amazing project. Your humor and wisdom made working on this book a joy.

Thank you to all the parents, campers, and volunteers of Camp Quest. Much of my contribution here I owe to working with and learning from all of you.

Thank you to my husband, August E. Brunsman IV. I'd been a humanist for a long time, but I didn't know the word or find the community until I met you. Thanks for leading me down the rabbit hole and for your support, insights, and encouragement along the way.

And last and most of all, thank you to my parents, who raised a freethinker despite the consequences. Your willingness to discuss and debate rather than simply demand required a patience that I'm sure I'm only beginning to understand.

Dale McGowan

Thanks first and foremost to the hundreds of nonreligious parents around the world for asking the questions and suggesting the answers from which this book was spun. A special wave to everyone at the Parenting Beyond Belief Discussion Forum, the readers and commenters on the Meming of Life blog, and participants in the *PBB* Seminar Tour. This one's for you.

Thanks to my agent Uwe Stender and to Christina Parisi and Kama Timbrell at AMACOM for patiently enduring all of my ongoing nonsense.

Heartfelt thanks to Molleen, Jan, and Amanda for their easygoing brilliance and levelheadedness. You've ruined me for all future collaborations. Thanks also to Louise Mead at the National Center for Science Education; Matt Cherry at the Institute for Humanist Studies; and Nica Lalli, Susan Wurzer, and Chris Lindstrom of Camp Quest West.

Deepest gratitude to my parents, Carol and David, for raising freethinkers, which made it all the easier for me to do the same. Finally, a huge squeeze to Becca, Erin, Delaney, and Connor. What an incredible privilege it is to be your husband and dad. Respectively.

The choices of pull quotes and statistics scattered throughout the book were almost entirely mine, as is the book's Preface. Any lapse of judgment or errors in those materials should be charged to my account. It also goes without saying that none of those who have helped the four of us in the creation of this book shall be held responsible for any errors without the express written consent of Major League Baseball.

CHAPTER 1

The Inquiring Mind

Dale McGowan

How does white milk come from a red cow?
Why doesn't the sun fall down?
How is it that all rivers flow into the ocean without ever filling it?

These questions, which could have come from any child today, are from the Rig Veda, a 3000-year-old Hindu text—and wondering and questioning are surely much older still. Early *Homo sapiens*, endowed with the same cranial capacity as your Aunt Diane,[1] had to be asking similar questions 125,000 years ago. And once oral language developed sufficiently to share these thoughts, parents and others around a child would have had to respond, one way or another, to the endless stream of questions.

It's the human impulse to wonder and ask questions that eventually gave birth to both religion and science, two different ways of responding to the same challenge: an overdeveloped neocortex hungry for answers.

In preparing to write this book, I plunged into the current parenting literature from many perspectives, including religious parenting books. Some are very sound, like the well-grounded work of Christian parenting author Dr. William Sears. Some are mixed, including (to my admitted surprise) James Dobson, who serves up some solid parenting advice along with his unfortunate enthusiasm for corporal punishment, gender stereotypes, and homophobia.

But if book sales and general prominence are any measure, one parenting author has had more to say about questioning and the life of the mind than any other: author and televangelist Joyce Meyer. Meyer has sold over a million copies of a book called *Battlefield of the Mind: Winning the Battle in Your Mind*, for which this passage can serve as an encapsulation:

> I once asked the Lord why so many people are confused and He said to me, "Tell them to stop trying to figure everything out, and they will stop being confused." I have found it to be absolutely true. Reasoning and confusion go together.

In 2006, Meyer issued a version of *Battlefield of the Mind* for teens, including passages like this:

> I was totally confused about everything, and I didn't know why. One thing that added to my confusion was too much reasoning.

This mantra comes back again and again in her advice, in millions of books and throughout her broadcasting empire: *Don't even **start** thinking*. Most troubling of all is the attempt to make kids fear their own thoughts—right at the age they *should* be challenging and questioning in order to become autonomous adults:

> Ask yourself, continually, "WWJT?" [What Would Jesus Think?] Remember, if He wouldn't think about something, you shouldn't either. . . . By keeping continual watch over your thoughts, you can ensure that no damaging enemy thoughts creep into your mind. (from *Battlefield of the Mind for Teens*)

Many progressive religious parents are outraged by Meyer's "fearthought" approach. But even those of us who don't consciously

> 66 When University of Texas sociologists John P. Bartkowski and Christopher G. Ellison compared dozens of secular parenting books with conservative Protestant parenting manuals, they found that a literal interpretation of the Bible's childrearing advice contributed directly to a worship of authority in all spheres of life, including the political. . . . They also found that conservative evangelical parenting gurus disagreed with mainstream counterparts on virtually every issue. According to their study, secular, science-based parenting advice emphasizes personality adjustment, empathy, cooperation, creativity, curiosity, egalitarian relations between parents, nonviolent discipline, and self-direction. Conservative Protestants, on the other hand, stress a tightly hierarchical family structure and a gendered division of labor, with a breadwinning father at the top of the pyramid and children at the bottom. 99
>
> —Jeremy Adam Smith, senior editor, *Greater Good* magazine[2]

sign on to this kind of thinking must look it squarely in the eye—because it's in our cultural blood. Most of us were raised in homes that were religious to some degree, and many of us carry remnants of these fearful ideologies into our own parenting. Whether we are religious or nonreligious, our attitudes toward questioning and moral development too often include some undercurrent of anxiety and mistrust, the unspoken feeling that our primary job as parents is to stave off a bubbling depravity that lurks just below the surface of our children.

> " Fear believes—courage doubts. Fear falls upon the earth and prays—courage stands erect and thinks. Fear is barbarism—courage is civilization. Fear believes in witchcraft, in devils and in ghosts. Fear is religion, courage is science. "
>
> —Robert Ingersoll, nineteenth-century U.S. orator

In this chapter, I hope to make the case that this trembling view of human nature is simply not borne out by the best of our knowledge. We will focus on the moment of the question, a moment that is the foundation of freethought parenting, encouraging an approach that holds no question unaskable and no thought unthinkable.

I want the idea that questions can be feared because of the answers they might produce to baffle my kids. I want them to find *hilariously silly* the idea that certain lines of thought cannot even be pursued, lest they be caught. That requires a certain amount of parental self-discipline. It requires the ability, for example, to not paint the far wall with soup when the 5-year-old asks if monkeys have vaginas, or why black people have big lips, or who will put her blankie on her grave when she dies—all three of which have come up at our dinner table. It requires a firm conviction that there is no rock that can't be upended if you think there might be something under it. And, of course, there always, always might.

Let's begin with a conversation about wonder and curiosity, the incentives that drive questioning, then dive into the art, science, and joy of questioning itself.

Questions and Answers

Q: I remember my own childhood as a time of wonder, but I sometimes worry that my own children are missing out on that. How can I instill a sense of wonder in my kids?

A: Ideally, it isn't something to be instilled from the outside. What a parent can do is facilitate natural wonder by simply removing obstacles to it.

The tendency toward wonder comes prepackaged. But like many other developmental windows that are open wide during childhood—languages, musical abilities, and more—a sense of wonder usually diminishes over time, until we begin to see things like spiderwebs, telephones, and our own bodies as everyday objects instead of the wonders they are.

Developing and keeping a sense of wonder requires time, opportunity, and practice. Some tips:

1. *Allow unstructured time.* Most people today are the victims of wall-to-wall structure. Wondering, creativity, independence, and a host of other assets require regular opportunities for completely unstructured time. That's time with no instructions, no screen of any kind (expect maybe sunscreen), and *no script.*

   If you're starting late, and your kids are accustomed to constant structure, the lack of a script will lead to an immediate and familiar protest: "I'm bored!" Lead them not into the TV room or yet another group sport, but deliver them from structure. Depending on the age of the child, you can point them to a box of sidewalk chalk, a sandbox, a patch of woods, a magnifying glass, a microscope, a telescope, an aquarium, a tidepool, the sky—all of which are invitations for kids to engage their *own* creativity, reflection, and wonder.

   One of the best opportunities for unstructured wondering is the family car trip. For the love of wonder, DO NOT turn on the DVD player! One philosopher I know credits staring out the window on long car trips as her first invitation to philosophical wondering.

2. *Choose wonder-inducing family activities.* The occasional trip to the zoo, the aquarium, the science museum, the planetarium, or even a simple walk in the woods can provide an unparalleled opportunity to ponder things beyond the everyday. It's in places like these that kids can learn to see the world in a wholly different way.

3. *Shake up the familiar.* Help kids shake themselves free of numbing familiarity by changing one or more points of reference in time or space. Zoom in on the everyday with a microscope, turning salt into boulders and a drop of water into an aquarium of life. Zoom out from the roof of your own house and into space with Google Earth or with a telescope or binoculars. Search the phrases "slow motion" and "time lapse" on YouTube to see how changing the speed of time reveals the incredible natural processes around us.

4. *Point out the wonder in the everyday.* You don't have to stand on the edge of the Grand Canyon or go skydiving to experience wonder. You don't even have to pick up a microscope or a time-lapse camera. Everyday things get more wonderfully strange the more you look and learn. Watch a hummingbird at a feeder. Stay up late for a meteor shower. Get yourself a Venus flytrap. Magazines like *National Geographic Kids* and programs like *Nova* and the Discovery Channel lineup can provide a peek behind the curtain of the natural world.

Take opportunities to add wonder-inducing information to an everyday moment. Referring to a beautiful sunset as a "beautiful earthturn" or telling kids to put on starblock before they go out in the starshine can further shake up the familiar. While looking at the night sky, mention that light takes one second to get to our eyes from the moon, eight minutes from the sun, and over four years from the nearest star. To underline our ancestry, my family sometimes refers to our dog as "the wolf" and ourselves as her monkeys. These are all ways to transform the everyday.

> I can live with doubt and uncertainty and not knowing. I think it's much more interesting to live not knowing than to have answers which might be wrong. I have approximate answers and possible beliefs and different degrees of certainty about different things, but I'm not absolutely sure of anything and there are many things I don't know anything about, such as whether it means anything to ask why we're here. I don't have to know the answer. I don't feel frightened by not knowing things, by being lost in a mysterious universe without any purpose, which is the way it really is as far as I can tell. It doesn't frighten me.
>
> —Richard Feynman, Nobel Laureate in Physics

Once kids get a taste of the wonder that's just below the surface of the everyday world, you won't have to prompt them a bit—they'll lead the way. But parents have to get the ball rolling by giving them the three things they need—time, opportunity, and practice.

Q: How can I encourage ravenous curiosity in my kids?

A: Think of curiosity as the link between wonder and understanding. Wonder is the "wow" moment: "Wow, look at all the stars!" "Wow, look at the way that chameleon changes colors!" Curiosity is the next step—the desire to understand: "How do the stars keep burning?" "How many stars are there?" "How does the chameleon do that?"

If curiosity is what you're after, your main goal in responding to a question shouldn't be giving the answer. In some cases, an immediate answer can even *extinguish* curiosity. What you want is to keep the questions coming, day after day, year after year. To do that, you want first and foremost to make the child feel that questioning itself is a fun and rewarding thing to do. Adding some appropriate praise—"What a great question!"—makes it clear that you see questioning itself as a neat thing to do.

> " I have no doubt that in reality the future will be vastly more surprising than anything I can imagine. Now my own suspicion is that the Universe is not only queerer than we suppose, but queerer than we *can* suppose. "
>
> —J.B.S. Haldane,
> in *Possible Worlds*
> *and Other Papers* (1927)

If you don't know the answer, leap on the opportunity to say so! In so doing, you can *join* the child in the search for an answer, modeling curiosity at every step. Tell her that you'd like to know the answer yourself. Ask if she has any guesses and offer some of your own before you look it up.

Best of all, model your own curiosity: "I wonder if fish sleep." "I wonder why light goes faster than sound." "I wonder what it's like outside of the universe." Doesn't matter whether you have the answers or even whether there *are* answers. Just let your kids catch you being curious and they'll surely follow your lead.

(See the Activities section of this chapter for some specific curiosity boosters.)

Q: I want to encourage my kids to be critical thinkers, but not cynics. Where is the line between healthy skepticism and unhealthy cynicism?

A: Even healthy skeptics will often hear the accusation that they are, as Spiro Agnew put it, nothing more than "nattering nabobs of negativism." Kids need to know that they'll hear this kind of accusation often, especially from those whose favorite ideas are squirming under the microscope.

> " My practice as a scientist is atheistic. That is to say, when I set up an experiment I assume that no god, angel, or devil is going to interfere with its course; and this assumption has been justified by such success as I have achieved in my professional career. I should therefore be intellectually dishonest if I were not also atheistic in the affairs of the world. "
>
> —J.B.S. Haldane, in *Fact and*
> *Faith* (1934)

Skepticism—the simple request for reasoning or evidence before accepting a proposition—is a virtue to treasure and cultivate in our kids. But cynicism[3] is something quite different. A cynical position makes negative assumptions as a matter of course, not as a result of the evidence, so a cynic is as uncritical as a dewy-eyed believer. One accepts without thinking; the other rejects without thinking. Both postures are obstacles to critical thinking, and both should be actively avoided.

The key to avoiding cynicism is to teach the value of critical thinking from a very young age. If you begin to see a pattern of unthinking cynicism, this value can be called upon to place a child's developing inquiry back on track.

Whenever you hear the too-confident, cynical dismissal of an idea, play devil's advocate, articulating the best arguments on the other side or asking your child to do so. It's easy to build a confident house of cards if you don't bother to hear the best of the other side. (We've all been on both sides of that one, eh?) Seeking out the most reasonable advocates of opposing viewpoints is one of the "best practices" for critical thinking.

And oh, let's not forget the old peek in the mirror. If you've been known to strike a fashionably cynical pose once in a while, don't be surprised to see the kids trying it out.

> " The process of acceptance [of a new idea] will pass through the usual four stages:
>
> (1) this is worthless nonsense;
> (2) this is an interesting, but perverse, point of view;
> (3) this is true, but quite unimportant;
> (4) I always said so. "
>
> —J.B.S. Haldane, writing in *Journal of Genetics* (1963)

Q: I want my kids to be fearless inquirers, willing to overturn assumptions and to challenge ideas and beliefs in their search for the truth. But I also want to teach them to be respectful. These two things often seem to be in conflict. How do I help my children learn to balance the search for truth with the need to respect others?

A: The respect question is another that strikes at the heart of critical thinking—especially when the topic is religion. The key is to distinguish between several different categories of respect. Respect for individuals and respect for their ideas are quite different and must be separated.

People are inherently deserving of respect as human beings, and no one can be faulted for shutting you out if you declare disrespect for their very personhood. Ideas are another matter. I feel too much *respect* for the idea of respect to grant it automatically to all ideas.

Even if I disagree with it, I can respect an opinion if it is founded on something meaningful, like rational argument or careful, repeatable observation. The other person may have interpreted the information differently, but I can still respect the way she's going about it. Suppose on the other hand that someone says Elvis and JFK are working at a laundromat in Fargo and offers a dream or tea leaves or a palm reading as evidence. It would render the word "respect" meaningless to say I respect that opinion. I both disagree with it *and* withhold my respect for it. And that's okay. No need to degrade the other person. I know all sorts of lovely, respectable people who hold a silly belief or two—including myself, no doubt—and wouldn't think of judging them, or me, less respectable for it.

If your kids develop critical thinking as an active habit, they need to learn and practice this distinction and be able to explain it to others. It makes the path of the critical thinker smoother to disentangle the respect question—though never *completely* smooth.

> 66 Ever since puberty I have believed in the value of two things: kindness and clear thinking. At first these two remained more or less distinct; when I felt triumphant I believed most in clear thinking, and in the opposite mood I believed most in kindness. 99
>
> —Bertrand Russell, philosopher, from his *Autobiography* (v. 2, p. 232)

Q: When it comes to free inquiry, is *anything* "sacred"?

A: Yes and no. Don't you just hate that answer?

The word "sacred" has two different major meanings. *Sacred* is used to denote specialness, to mark something as awe-inspiring, worthy of veneration or deserving of respect. In this first sense, the nonreligious tend to hold many things sacred—life, integrity, knowledge, love, a sense of purpose, freedom of conscience, and much more. One might even hold sacred our right and duty to reject the *second* meaning of sacred: something inviolable, unquestionable, immune from challenge.

This second definition of sacredness is much like the concept of hell—it exists primarily as a thoughtstopper. As such, it has no place in a home energized by freethought. One of the most sacred (def. 1) principles of freethought is that no question is unaskable. Encouraging reckless inquiry in your kids means laughing the second definition of "sacred" straight out the door.

Given that understanding of the dual meaning of sacredness, it should now make sense that I consider it a sacred duty to hold nothing sacred.

Q: If you were to choose one story from children's literature that our kids should hear to encourage independent thinking, what would it be?

A: There are so many—Philip Pullman's *His Dark Materials*, for example, or *Huck Finn*— but it's hard to beat the power and message of *The Emperor's New Clothes* by Hans Christian Andersen. It's easy to lose sight of the unique power of a story as familiar as this one, so it's worth retelling:

An emperor, overly obsessed with clothes, hires a pair of tailors who promise to make him the finest clothes imaginable from a bolt of magic cloth. The tailors—who are actually just a couple of swindlers—claim the cloth cannot be seen by anyone who is stupid or unworthy of his position. In fact, there is no cloth at all.

The emperor sends his courtiers one by one to see the work in progress. Each sees nothing on the loom but is too terrified to say so for fear of proving himself stupid or unworthy and so praises the beauty of it to the emperor. At last the tailors bring the "finished" suit to the emperor, who (unable to admit to not seeing something his underlings *have* seen) immediately dons the clothes for a parade through town, during which the crowd pretends to marvel at the clothes. Suddenly a young child, unhindered by the nonsense that ties the tongues of the adults, blurts out, "But he has nothing on at all!" The crowd, validated in their own perceptions by the child's honesty, laughs the naked emperor back to his palace.

In a few short pages, the story satirizes vanity, power, conformity, self-doubt, and human gullibility while praising evidence, courage, and honest dissent. If you can find a tale that more neatly captures the values of freethought, I'll eat my miter.

Q: What are the attributes that encourage an inquiring mind, and how are they developed?

A: I think there are three main requirements for an inquiring mind: (1) self-confidence, (2) curiosity, and (3) an unconditional love of reality.

1. **Self-confidence.** The best way to instill confidence is to encourage autonomy. We parents often intervene too much to spare our kids a moment's frustration, uncertainty, or failure. An infant crawls under the legs of the dining room chair and becomes momentarily uncertain how to get out. She cries, and Mom leaps to her feet, ushering the baby into the open. A first grader struggles with his seat belt—Dad clicks it into place. A middle schooler gives up on a math problem after 30 seconds, asks for help, and gets it.

These rescues add up, and eventually the child sees a moment's frustration as a brick wall and looks to someone else for help. Who can blame him if he never had the opportunity to struggle and sweat and muscle through those walls on his own?

Inquiry is the act of a confident, autonomous mind. It's the act of someone who believes she *can* break through the walls between ignorance and knowledge. If you want inquiring kids, work on confidence—and confidence starts with autonomy.

2. **Curiosity.** The value of curiosity is addressed elsewhere in this chapter, but it's important to underline the link here to the inquiring mind. No one asks questions if he isn't curious about the answers. The parent of a ravenously curious little boy once told me that the boy's grandmother, exasperated at the child's endless questions, once said, "You don't have to know *everything!*" Yes, it's sometimes hard to stay patient and engaged, but you might want to avoid such sentiments. Indifference overtakes us soon enough. Nurture curiosity while it's natural and wild.

> ❝ Doubt everything. Find your own light. ❞
>
> —Last words of Gautama Buddha, in Theravada tradition

3. **The unconditional love of reality.** The *conditional* love of reality is at play whenever a healthy, well-fed, well-educated person looks me in the eye and says, "Without God, life would be hopeless, pointless, devoid of meaning and beauty." Whenever I hear someone say, "I am only happy *because* . . ." or "Life is only bearable *if* . . . ," I want to take a white riding glove, strike him across the face, and challenge him to a duel in the name of reality.

I want my kids to see the universe as an astonishing, thrilling place to be *no matter what*, whether God exists or does not exist, whether we are permanent or temporary. I want them to feel unconditional love and joy at being alive, conscious, and wondering. Like the passionate love of anything, an unconditional love of reality breeds a voracious hunger to experience it directly, to embrace it, whatever form it may take.

Children with that exciting combination of love and hunger will not stand for anything that gets in the way of that clarity. Their minds become thirsty for genuine understanding, and the best we can do is stand back. If religious ideas seem to illuminate reality, kids with that combination will embrace those ideas. If instead such ideas seem to obscure reality, kids with that love and hunger will bat the damn things aside.

Q: My son is described as "offbeat" or "weird" because he likes to think outside the box and often holds opinions that are different from his peers'. I like this about him but am afraid that he will get beaten down. Am I right to encourage this in him, or am I just making things more difficult for him?

A: Robert Heinlein once said, "Don't handicap your children by making their lives easy." Sometimes making things easier is the wrong thing for parents to do.

One of the most soul-crushing pressures on our kids is the pressure to conform. Clothes, posture, speech, attitudes—everything seems to go into the sausage grinder at some point as kids flock to conform to their peers. And that herd mentality is not only sad—it's dangerous. I'm not just talking about the dangers of sex and drugs here—those are serious concerns, of course, and a nonconformist spirit can help kids resist these pressures as well. But there's also damage done on a much larger scale when teenage sheep become adult sheep, and "United We Stand" becomes a way of life.

Why Societies Need Dissent by Cass Sunstein lays out a solid defense of dissent and nonconformity as genuine assets. Organizations and nations are historically much more likely to prosper if they welcome dissent and promote openness. When dissent is silenced, both the good and bad ideas of the majority survive unchallenged. But when dissent is allowed to thrive, bad ideas stand some chance of being found out and eliminated.

Research, including the Solomon Asch studies (in which many subjects ignored the clear evidence in a simple perception test to conform to the incorrect majority) and the frightening Milgram experiments (in which everyday folks showed a willingness to inflict pain or even death on an innocent person if they were ordered to do so by an authority figure), powerfully demonstrates the tragic consequences of the love of conformity.

A variation in the design of the Asch study provides a profound lesson about dissent. The same study was run with groups of various sizes. In each group, a single confederate served as a lone dissenter, identifying the correct line segment against as many as twelve others giving the wrong answer. In these cases, the presence of that lone dissenter reduced the error rates of subjects by 75 percent. This is a crucial realization: **If a group is embarking on an unfortunate course of action, a lone dissenter may turn it around by energizing ambivalent group members to join the dissent instead of following the crowd into error.** Think of Henry Fonda in *Twelve Angry Men*. Think of the Bay of Pigs and what might have been accomplished by a single dissenter.

Talk to your kids about valuing nonconformity/diversity, the outright dangers of conformity, the importance of dissent. Offer nonconformist role models like Copernicus, Mandela, Darwin, Gandhi, and King. And Jesus, for that matter. To bring the message home another way, sing Malvina Reynolds's "Little Boxes" as a lullaby.

Q: I want to encourage my daughter to ask a lot of questions, but I can't figure out how. She asks a question, I answer, and we're done! How can I get her to ask the next question, and the next, and the next?

A: It seems obvious that the best thing to do when asked a question is to answer it. But when it comes to encouraging inquiry, it's actually one of the least helpful things a parent can do: "Mom, how far away is the sun?" "Ninety-three million miles." *Clunk! The inquiry is closed! Elvis has left the building!*

Many nonreligious parents I've talked to seem to want to fill their kids' heads with as many right answers as quickly as possible, as if that will keep incoming nonsense from squeezing into the elevator: "Sorry, all full of true stuff. Take the next child."

The idea is not to pack them with answers, but to make questioning itself a pleasurable habit. By focusing on making the process itself positive, you will virtually guarantee the next question. And the next.

Q: So if I'm not supposed to answer her questions, what am I supposed to do?

A: First of all, it's fine to give a straightforward answer much of the time. Just mix it up with some of these:

INVITE A GUESS

KID: "How far away is the sun?"

MOM: "What would you guess?"

KID: "100 miles!"

MOM: "Good guess! That's what people thought a long time ago. They thought it was attached to the sky about 100 miles away, but now we know it's a star out in space. Okay now. Grandma's house is 700 miles away. Do you think the sun is closer than that?"

FIND OUT TOGETHER

"How far away is the sun?"

"I dunno. Let's get a tape measure and find out!"

"Dad!! You're such a dork."

"Well, how can we find out then, smarty pants?"

"Google it!"

(After Googling it . . .) "Now I wonder how they figured that out without a tape measure?"

THE OBVIOUS FIB

"How far away is the sun?"

"About 20 feet."

"No, it isn't!"

"I'm pretty sure it is. Maybe 21."

"It's MUCH more than that!"

"Well, how far do YOU think it is?"

VALUE-ADDED ANSWER

"How far away is the sun?"

"93 million miles."

"Wow, that's far!"

"Wouldn't want to walk it. Hey, you know how they figured that out? It's the most amazing story . . ."[4]

THE QUESTION CHAIN

Eventually, the child will pick up the rhythm herself and provide the next question herself:

"How far away is the sun?"

"93 million miles."

"Wow, that's far! **How did they figure that out?**"

"You know, it's the most amazing story . . ."

I've used an empirical question here—one for which there is a single verifiable answer—but the same techniques work to keep nonempirical or "values" questions going.

If you want to encourage a child to continue asking questions, the single biggest mistake you can make is something freethought parents do way too much: Offer uninvited corrections. If a 6-year-old child makes a guess that's wrong, resist as often as possible the urge to correct it. This advice galls many freethinkers: "Let a wrong answer go unchallenged?! But, but, but . . . *What if it gets stuck in there?*"

Relax. Remember, you want questioning itself to be pleasurable, and constant correction at an early age does not achieve this. If you are teaching critical thinking as a value, the child will quickly develop the urge to self-correct and to invite your help.

A sample conversation with a 6-year-old:

KID: I think Bowser can read my mind.

DAD: Oh? Why do you think that?

KID: I was gonna give her a crust of bread, and she started wagging her tail as soon as I thought of it!

> *(Here's the moment we typically wind up the correction machine, making sure the child knows that there's a nonparanormal explanation. Resist!)*

DAD: Hmm. Well, we better watch what we're thinking, then!

Good Dad! I'm so proud of you. You didn't say it was true *or* false, and she didn't ask you to (yet). You simply made her feel good for thinking and guessing and inquiring about the world. *There's plenty of time for insisting on the right answers.* First, we need to build the desire and the tools to find them on her own.

There comes a time (generally age 8 to 10) when the child will recognize that you have not weighed in on a hypothesis and begin inviting you to do so:

DAD: Hmm. Well, we better watch what we're thinking, then!

KID: So do you think she can really read our minds?

> *(Now instead of stomping on it, draw out her own thinking . . .)*

DAD: I don't know. . . . Can you think of any other explanation?

Around age 13, kids will generally *stop* inviting you to weigh in—a natural part of finding their own identity. But if you established yourself as a facilitator of thinking instead of The Guy with the Big Red Pen, you just may be invited to continue the inquiries together after all.

Q: I'm uneasy with the "obvious fib." We must never lie to our children.

A: I've heard this assertion that "we must never lie to our children" from many nonreligious parents, always intoned in the kind of hushed voice usually reserved for sacred pronouncements. Although I don't advocate outright lying, the playful fib can work wonders for the development of critical thinking.

Many nonreligious parents, in the admirable name of high integrity, set themselves up as infallible authorities. And since (like it or not) we are the first and most potent authority figures in our kids' lives, turning ourselves into benevolent oracles of truth can teach our kids to passively receive the pronouncements of authority. I would rather, in a low-key and fun fashion, encourage them to constantly take whatever I say and run it through the baloney meter.

I tell them "The sun is twenty feet away" precisely so they will look at me and say, "Dad, you dork!!" When they ask what's for dinner, I say, "Monkey lungs, go wash up." When the fourth grader doing her homework asks what 7 times 7 is, I say 47, because she should (a) know that on her own by now and, equally important, (b) know the wrong answer when she hears it.

Yes, I make sure they end up with the right answer when it matters, and *no,* I don't do this all the time. They'd kill me. But pulling our kids' legs once in a while is more than just fun and games. Knowing that Dad sometimes talks nonsense can prepare them to expect and challenge the occasional bit of nonsense, intentional or otherwise, from peers, ministers, and presidents.

Q: You suggested letting our children "run with ideas" instead of making constant corrections. But what about religious questions? I don't want to force my views on my child, but at the same time I feel the need to be a little more proactive in that area. I can't sit still while she runs with some religious notion, can I?

A: Depends. Are you trying to get her head full of the right answers, or trying to raise a powerful, autonomous thinker? "With questions of belief," someone once said, "you have three choices: feed the child a confirmation, feed the child a disconfirmation–or teach the child to fish."[5]

Religion has no magical powers to seduce our children. Yes, it comes with emotional lures that can subvert reasoning, but the proper response is to strengthen reasoning by building critical thinking skills, not hide the lures. Religion loses its power to emotionally hijack the mind when you take it out of the singular and into the plural. If a child is raised hearing only one religious perspective—orthodox Islam, let's say, or Hasidic Judaism, or evangelical Christianity—the potential for emotional hijacking is very real. But if the child is allowed to consider several different possibilities without fear, each one loses any emotional monopoly, and the child can turn to reason to sort it out.

Ideally, your kids will try on many different religious hats along the way. My daughter Delaney came to me at age 4 and announced that she had finally figured out, as she put it, "the God and Jesus thing." Jesus, she said, made all the good things in the world, and God made all the bad and scary things.

Few religious parents would be able to let this rest, to let their child sleep on the hypothesis that God is the source of all evil. But many nonreligious parents do little better when they say, "No, no—God isn't real." In the process, both sets of parents will have substituted their authority for the child's autonomous thought. I've always preferred to praise the independent thought and let the child run with it. It's good practice. "Cool," I said to Delaney. "I never thought of it like that."

The next week, she had a new theology: God, she said, makes all the things for grownups, and Jesus makes the things for kids. My favorite example: God made the deep end of the pool, and Jesus made the shallow end, for her.

I hugged her. "So God for me and Jesus for you, eh?"

"I guess so," she said. "I'm not sure. I'm still thinking about it."

And that's all I ask. More recently she's been trying on the glasses of secular humanism, but I fully expect her to continue trying on spectacles, going back and forth, back and forth, until she finds the pair that makes the most sense. So let your child hypothesize about the world without constraints and without fear in all areas, including religion.

Q: I still worry that the natural gullibility of childhood will do its work, and my child will end up unable to tell fantasy from reality unless I am vigilant.

A: It's very common to see our kids as suckers for a good fantasy, but there's increasingly strong evidence that we needn't be quite so concerned. A 2006 study in the journal *Child Development* suggests that young children, although certainly impressionable, are less gullible than many parents fear.

By age 4, children make consistent use of context to decide whether a new piece of information is likely to be fact or fantasy. In three separate studies, children between the ages of 3 and 6 were given information either in scientific terms ("Doctors use surnits to make medicine") or in fantastical terms ("Fairies use hercs to make fairy dust"). Children's ability to use contextual cues to decide the likely truth of a given statement proved higher than had previously been supposed and increases significantly between the ages of 3 and 5.

University of Texas professor Jacqueline Woolley, the lead author of the studies, put it this way: "It is clear from the present studies that young children do not believe everything they hear, and that they can use the context surrounding the presentation of a new entity to make inferences about the real versus fantastical nature of that entity."[6]

This is good news for parents wishing to protect their children from religious indoctrination and may partly explain why religion has found it necessary to back up even the most attractive religious claims with threats of hell. To counter a child's natural ability to use context to discriminate between reality and fantasy, religious indoctrination must construct multiple barriers and safeguards. Freethought simply requires the removal of these barriers and the encouragement of skills already present in the child.

Q: My 6-year-old is fascinated by the natural world. I've tried to introduce her to the idea of evolution, but when I say, "A long time ago, apes turned into humans," she squinches her face—and I know she's picturing something pretty funny. How can I help her understand the long, slow, fascinating process of evolution?

A: By teaching it the same way evolution happens—in small steps over many years:

1. **Draw her attention to adaptations.** If I'm out on a walk in the woods with my own daughter and we see a deer with protective coloration, I'll often say, "Look—you can barely see it! What if I was an animal trying to find a deer to eat? That one wouldn't be very easy to find. And its babies would have the same coloring, so I'll bet they'd be hard to find, too."

2. **Imagine a poor adaptation.** "Hey, what if it was bright pink? I think I'd have a pink one for supper every night, they'd be so easy to catch." I step on a twig and the deer bolts away. "Ooh, fast too! I'll bet I'd have to eat *slow* pink ones every night. Soon there wouldn't be any slow pink ones left because I'd have eaten them all!"

3. **Move to natural selection, using a nonhuman example and a shortened timescale.** Evolution itself requires thousands of generations and a massive timescale, so above the microbial level we can't see it in action. But we can study *natural selection*, the mechanism by which evolution occurs. Once natural selection is understood, evolution is an inevitable consequence of the passage of time. And one creature in particular is just waiting in the wings, so to speak, to explain natural selection to our kids: the peppered moth.[7] See the Activities section of this chapter for the story of the peppered moth, then tell it to your kids on your next walk in the woods.

4. **Use analogy to teach the otherwise unimaginable timescale.** Analogies can be difficult for very young kids, but once your child is able to handle that level of abstraction, there's no better way to render the inconceivable conceivable. Saying a million Earths would fit inside the sun is fine, but saying "If the sun were a soccer ball, Earth would be a peppercorn"—now I get it. Same goes for time. Use either Sagan's Cosmic Calendar or Dawkin's armspan analogy, both of which are described in the Activities section of this chapter.

Q: I want to try to answer all of my child's amazing and wonderful questions, but often my scientific literacy isn't good enough. I don't know why the sky is blue, but I know there is a reason! Are there good resources for parents like me that have kid-friendly answers to these questions?

A: Yes, there are, and you'll find several in the Resources section of the chapter—but that's a secondary concern. When it comes to encouraging wondering and questioning in children, remember that knowing the answers is the least important quality for a parent to have. *Caring* about the answer and caring even more about the process is much more important than the answer itself.

In *The Sense of Wonder,* Rachel Carson put it this way: "If a child is to keep his inborn sense of wonder, he needs the companionship of at least one adult who can share it, rediscovering with him the joy, excitement and mystery of the world we live in." I honestly feel sorry for the child who has never heard a parent say "Jeez, I don't know!" then drop everything in the excited rush to find out. Give your child the gift of seeing that knowledge is never complete, not even for Mom or Dad, and that a ravenous curiosity is always a thrilling bird to feed.

■ ■ ■ ■ ■

Freeing Our Kids from "Fearthought"

My daughter Erin went through a brief period at age 8 when she would literally dissolve into tears at bedtime but was unwilling to discuss it. The morning after one such nighttime session, we were lying on the trampoline together, looking at the sky, and I asked if she would tell me what was troubling her.

"Did you do something you feel bad about, or hurt somebody's feelings at school?" I asked. "There's always a way to fix that, you know."

"No," she said. "It isn't something I did."

"Something somebody else did? Did somebody hurt your feelings?"

"No." A long silence. I watched the clouds for awhile, knowing it would come.

At last she spoke. "It isn't anything I did. It's something . . . I *thought.*"

I turned to look at her. She was crying again.

"Something you thought? What is it, sweetie?"

"I don't want to say."

"That's OK, you don't have to say. But what's the problem with thinking this thing?"

"It's more than one thing." She looked at me with a worried forehead. "It's bad thoughts. I think about saying things or doing things that are bad. Like . . ."

I waited.

"Like bad words. That's one thing."

"You want to say bad words?"

"NO!!" she said, horrified. "I don't at ALL!! But I can't get my brain to stop thinking about this word I heard somebody say at school. It's a really nasty word and I don't like it. But it keeps popping into my brain, no matter what I do, and it makes me feel really, really bad!!"

She cried harder, and I hugged her. "Listen to me, Erin. You are never bad just for thinking about something. Never."

"What? But . . . if it's bad to say a bad word, then it's bad to think it!"

"But how can you decide whether it's bad if you don't even let yourself think it?"

She stopped crying in a single wet inhale, and furrowed her brow. "Then . . . It's OK to think bad things?"

"Yes. It is. It's fine. Erin, you can't stop your brain from thinking—especially a huge brain like yours. And you'll make yourself crazy if you even try."

"That's what I'm doing! I'm making myself crazy!"

"Well, don't. Listen to me now." We went forehead to forehead. "It is never bad to think something. You have permission to think about everything in the world. What comes after thinking is deciding whether to keep that thought or to throw it away. That's called your judgment. A lot of times it's wrong to act on certain thoughts, but it is never, ever wrong to let yourself think them." I pointed to her head. "That's your courtroom in there, and you're the judge."

The next morning she woke up excitedly and gave me a high-speed hug. Once she had permission to think the bad word, she said, it just went away. She was genuinely relieved.

Imagine if instead I had saddled her with traditional ideas of mind-policing, the insane practice of paralyzing guilt for what you cannot control—your very thoughts. Instead, I taught her what freethought really means.

In the years since that day, Erin has often mentioned that moment. She has said it's the best thing I ever did for her. As with most such moments, I had no idea at the time that I was giving her anything beyond the moment itself. I just wanted her to stop crying, to stop beating up on herself. But in the process, it seems, I genuinely set her free.

■ ■ ■ ■

Activities

There are scads of terrific published activities to promote curiosity, wonder, and questioning. I've chosen to highlight a few particular favorites of nonreligious parents, including some that have been kid-tested at Camp Quest and elsewhere. The Resources section includes books and sites that are brimming with more still more activities, ideas, and resources.

Analogy 1: The Cosmic Calendar

Ages 8+

Next time your child floats a question about the dinosaurs, or the age of the earth, or the Big Bang, or has a homework assignment that touches on deep time—try this simple, engaging activity.

> *Materials:* blank twelve-month calendar for each child (download free calendars at *www.office.microsoft.com* > templates > calendars)

Analogies can help kids grasp immense timescales. Carl Sagan suggested compressing the history of the universe to date into a single year.[8] On a blank calendar, write BIG BANG on January 1, and NOW in the lower right corner of December 31.

Somewhere between the Big Bang and today, all sorts of things happened. Everything, in fact. Ask your kids to estimate *when* on the compressed calendar you would put:

- The first dinosaurs
- The first plants
- The extinction of the dinosaurs
- The formation of the Milky Way galaxy
- The first humans
- Roman Empire
- The formation of the earth
- The formation of Earth's oxygen atmosphere
- The voyages of Columbus

Ask the questions out of order so kids can think about which had to come first, and next, and next (e.g., Milky Way before Earth, dinosaurs come and go before humans, plants before oxygen).

When I was a kid, I would probably have put the Milky Way somewhere in February, Earth in March, dinos in April, people in May—something like that. A certain kind of kid will be gobsmacked by the actual answers:

Milky Way forms:	May 1
Earth forms:	September 14
First (photosynthetic) plants:	November 12
Oxygen atmosphere:	December 1
Dinosaurs:	December 24
Extinction of dinosaurs:	December 28
First humans:	December 31 at 10:30 p.m.
Roman Empire:	Four seconds ago
Columbus:	One second ago

Analogy 2: The Span of Life

Ages 8+

Richard Dawkins created another spectacular time-grasping analogy that focuses on the last quarter of universal history: the history of life on Earth.

Materials: arms (human)

Stretch your arms out to represent the span of the history of life on Earth. From your left fingertip all the way across your middle to well past your right shoulder, life consists of nothing but bacteria. At your right wrist, the most complex form of life on Earth is worms. The dinosaurs appear in the middle of your right palm and go extinct around your last finger joint. The whole story of *Homo sapiens* is contained in the thickness of one slim fingernail clipping.

As for *recorded* history—the Sumerians and Babylonians, the Pharoahs of Egypt, Ancient Greece and Rome, Jesus, Napoleon and Hitler, the Beatles and Britney Spears—they and everyone else who has lived since the dawn of recorded history are blown away in the dust from one light stroke of a nail-file.

Simply knowing that 99.98 percent of the history of the universe happened before our species even arrived on the scene is the single most humbling earth-quake of perspective we can ever achieve.

But there's more . . .

Analogy 3: The Size of the Solar System
Ages 6+

> *Materials:* a soccer ball, several peppercorns, several pins (w/pinheads), a ping-pong ball, a marble, and an open field

It has been said, and rightly so, that people who see themselves in a human-centered universe "are able to do so largely in proportion to their inability to do math."[9] Even without much math, analogies can take us a long way. The immensity of space is difficult to grasp, but not as abstract as time, so even kindergarteners can give it a go. There are countless ways to help kids begin to grasp the size of the universe and our infinitesimal place in it. I offered this example in Parenting Beyond Belief:

Find a large open space. Put a soccer ball in the middle to represent the sun. Walk ten paces from the ball and stick a pin in the ground. That's Mercury. Take nine more full steps and drop a peppercorn for Venus. Seven more steps, drop another peppercorn for Earth. An inch away from Earth, stick another pin in the ground for the Moon, remembering that this inch is the furthest humans have been so far. Another fourteen steps, drop a very small peppercorn for Mars, then continue another 95 steps and drop Jupiter, a ping-pong ball. 112 paces further, place a large marble for Saturn. Uranus and Neptune are still further apart, and recently demoted Pluto would be a small pinhead about a half mile from the soccer ball.

So how far would you have to walk before you can put down another soccer ball for Proxima Centauri, the very nearest star to our Sun? Bring your good shoes—it's over 4000 miles away at this scale, New York to Berlin.[10] That's the *nearest star.* And there are about a trillion such stars in the Milky Way galaxy alone, and roughly a hundred billion such galaxies, arrayed through billions of those light years in every direction.

See also: An amazing video on YouTube comparing the relative sizes of planets and stars: *www.youtube.com/watch?v=Tfs1t-2rrOM* (or search for "relative size of planets").

Analogy 4: The Size of the Galaxy and the Universe
All Ages

Materials: one round sandbox, 20' in diameter—or a good imagination

How big is the Milky Way galaxy? First, remember that one million Earths would fit in the sun. Now imagine an enormous round sandbox, 20 feet across and a foot thick. If our sun were a single grain of sand in that sandbox, the sandbox would be the Milky Way galaxy, which is filled with as many stars as there are grains of sand in the sandbox.

Now shrink that entire *galaxy* down to a single grain of sand. The grains of sand in the sandbox now represent the number of galaxies in the universe.

Sit in the sandbox and run your fingers through the galaxies. Repeat.

See also: The Hubble Deep Field photo, which many have called "the most important photo ever taken" for its paradigm-rattling power: *http://hubblesite .org/newscenter/archive/releases/2004/07/* (accessed May 8, 2008).

Analogy 5: The Fantastic Voyage

Ages 6+

Don't neglect the microscopic world beneath our scale.

Materials: none

"If a golf ball could be magnified to the size of the whole earth, most of its atoms would be more or less the size of a golf ball."[11]

An atom is mostly empty space—a nucleus surrounded by electrons orbiting at a distance. If an atom were expanded to the size of a stadium, the nucleus would be the size of a grape on the 50-yard line.

Special peek into microworlds: "Cellular Visions: The Inner Life of a Cell" — animated short created by XVIVO Scientific Animation and available all over the Internet. Google "Cellular Visions" or "The Inner Life of a Cell." Ages 6+.

Telephone Detective
Ages 7+ for six or more players

Materials: index cards

This is the traditional game of telephone (a.k.a. Chinese whispers, Russian Scandal, or Grapevine) with a twist. Put a small dot on one index card.

Pass out cards to the entire circle. One person, designated the Source, starts a message around the circle, whispering from one person to the next. Whoever has the card with the dot is instructed to slightly change the message. The Source (first in the circle) then asks questions to determine where the message was changed.

One problem: Members of the circle can *lie*. Once the Source has asked (at most) one question per person, he or she points to the person he or she thinks has the dot. The accused shows his or her card. If there is no dot, the Source is out. If there is a dot, the holder is out.

The game then resumes with a new Source and continues until two winners remain.

Geomythology (Camp Quest)

Ages: 8-14

A terrific party game for creative and science-minded kids.

> *Materials:* a variety of dinosaur skeleton modeling kits, drawing paper, colored pencils

Many of the ancient stories of mythical beasts—such as dragons, gryphons, and the Cyclops—grew out of the attempts by people in Bronze Age cultures to explain fossilized bones found near their settlements.[12] This activity puts kids in the sandals of ancient people who attempted to make sense of found fossils—just one example of the human drive to understand.

1. Remove the kits from the boxes. Intermix the parts to resemble a site with mixed fossil deposits. *Do not allow the kids to see the pictures on the boxes or the kit instructions!*

2. Give each child or group a mixed selection of bones. Let them know that when people find fossils, skeletons are almost always incomplete. It's often hard to tell whether just one animal is present or if there are multiple animals in the fossil site.

3. Have each group assemble a creature or creatures out of their pieces.

4. Ask each child or group to draw what the living creature or creatures would have looked like. Did it have scales? Fur? Tusks? A long neck?

5. Have each child or group show off its skeleton model(s) and drawing(s), and explain its creature(s).

Not all myths are purely the product of imagination. Many originated in attempts to explain the evidence of our senses. Even when they weren't accurate, the people who created them may have had good reasons for believing them at the time. This activity also gives kids insight into science as a process of using the available evidence to come up with the best explanation we can. If later evidence changes what we know, we revise our explanations.

The Truth Is Out There (Camp Quest)

Ages 8–14

Materials: random household junk, digital camera(s)

Using digital cameras and ordinary objects (frisbees, pie pans, aluminum foil, etc.), have kids stage the best possible "UFO photos."

Invisible Unicorns (Camp Quest)

All ages

Materials: critical thinking skills

This critical thinking challenge asks campers to disprove the existence of the two invisible unicorns that live at Camp Quest. The camp has offered a prize of $100 to the first camper who can successfully prove that the unicorns don't exist—a prize still unclaimed after twelve years and counting. By trying to prove a negative, kids learn why the burden of proof must rest on those making spectacular claims.

Mothwalk

All ages

This activity is a story, best told while walking in the woods in the evening, just as the moths begin to emerge . . .

Materials: a lovely patch of woods

Two hundred years ago, there were moths in England called peppered moths. They were light gray with dots of black and brown all over them. They looked like somebody had peppered them, which worked out fine for the moths—it made them blend in with tree bark so it was hard for birds to find them and eat them.

But there were also a few peppered moths who didn't look peppered at all: They were completely black. But only a few. You can probably guess why: The black ones didn't blend in very well, so they were dinner for the birds. If someone has you for dinner, you aren't going to have too many babies, of course. And since the black moths were being eaten the most, there were never too many black baby moths being born.

Then something interesting happened. Big factories were built in the town near the moths' forest. Dark black smoke belched out of huge smokestacks, making the air near the town very dirty. In fact, the bark on the trees in the moths' forest turned completely black from the dirty factory smoke.

That made things a little different for the moths. What do you think changed? Now the *black* moths were almost invisible on the black tree trunks, and the light-colored peppered moths were so easy to see. Well, maybe you can guess what happened. Birds only eat what they can find, so who were they eating now? That's right: the *light-colored* ones! The black moths were probably pretty happy about this: Now more of their babies could be born and stay safely hidden from the birds on the black tree trunks.

About twenty years later, people noticed that almost *all* of the moths in the forest were black and only a few were light gray. The peppered moth had been changed, all because its environment changed.

Supplement with: "Camouflage Egg Hunt" on pp. 241–243 in *Parenting Beyond Belief*.[13]

(See the Resources section below for links to amazing websites with many more activities for the inquiring mind.)

Resources
Social/Cultural
Peace Corps / World Wise Schools

> *www.peacecorps.gov/wws*

An incredibly rich source for activities and lesson plans in science, the arts, environmental issues, cross-cultural understanding, and more—all with an internationalist flavor. Age 9+.

National Geographic Kids

> *www.kids.nationalgeographic.com*

A bottomless well of delights. Age 8+.

Free Rice

> *www.freerice.com*

Brilliant concept. Flex your vocabulary and end world hunger at the same time! Age 10+.

Lateral Thinking and Brain Teasers

Perry, Susan K. *Playing Smart: The Family Guide to Enriching, Offbeat Learning Activities for Ages 4–14,* revised ed. (Minneapolis, MN: Free Spirit Publishing, 2001). Now available at the author's website at *www.bunnyape.com/other_books .htm.* See longer review in Chapter 5 Resources. A simply amazing book.

The Impossible Quiz

A hilariously bizarre online quiz, loaded with opportunities for divergent thinking. Available on many sites. Google "The Impossible Quiz"—then cancel your pressing business for the day. Age 10+.

Fun Brain

> *www.funbrain.com*

"The Internet's #1 education site for K-8 kids and teachers."

SmartKit Brain Gym and Puzzle Playground

> *www.smart-kit.com*

Terrific variety of puzzles and games, including flash animations. *Personal favorite:* Mass Attack. Just try to stop playing it.

Discover Education's Brain Boosters

> *www.discoveryeducation.com* > School Resources > Brain Boosters

Over 200 puzzles and brain-teasers, including a large section on lateral thinking.

The Final Frontier

NASA and Associated Sites

> NASA *www.nasa.gov*
> NASA Education *www.education.nasa.gov*
> Jet Propulsion Laboratory *www.jpl.nasa.gov*

Your tax dollars beautifully at work! Three different amazing and multifaceted sites. Articles, games, puzzles, science news, videos, activities, and more. Click the links marked EDUCATION, STUDENTS, and FOR KIDS.

> ***See also:*** **NASA's Imagine the Universe**
> *http://imagine.gsfc.nasa.gov/index.html* > Teacher's Corner
> ***Special treat for high schoolers:*** "What Is Your Cosmic Connection to the Elements?" downloadable pdf in the Teacher's Corner.

Evolution and Genetics

Charlie's Playhouse

> *www.charliesplayhouse.com*

An exciting new company making clever toys and games that teach kids about evolution, from a 30-foot illustrated timeline of talking life forms to a fascinating and fun board game that illustrates how natural selection works.

Judgment Day: Intelligent Design on Trial

> *www.pbs.org/wgbh/nova/id/*

The brilliant PBS program detailing *Kitzmiller* v. *Dover,* the landmark trial that dealt the most serious blow yet to the creation science agenda. View the entire program online, or take advantage of terrific educational resources.

National Geographic Genographic Project

> *www.nationalgeographic.com/genographic*

A unique opportunity to be a part of cutting-edge research in human migration patterns. Order a DNA testing kit from the site, use the simple cheek scraper to harvest your cells, then send it in the tubes provided to the Genographic Project for analysis. By looking for marker mutations in your genome, the lab will trace your deep ancestry, showing the path and timing of your ancestors' exodus from Africa. Well worth the price ($99 per kit at this writing). Check out the website for more detailed information about this incredible project.

Miscellaneous Science
Science News for Kids

www.sciencenewsforkids.org

A gold mine of a website. Surf or subscribe.

The Exploratorium

www.exploratorium.edu

Special treats: *www.exploratorium.edu/brain_explorer* (puzzles, illusions, memory games, and more) and *www.exploratorium.edu/ronh/solar_system/all_bodies .html* to put in any size diameter for the sun, and get back the diameters of the other solar system bodies, and the radii of their orbits around the sun, so you can do this activity with a sun of any size and corresponding distances and sizes of other objects.

Philosophy/General
The Philosopher's Club/Socrates Café

www.philosopher.org

Click on the "Philosopher's Club" link for kids' activities.

Calkins, Lucy. *Raising Lifelong Learners* (New York: Da Capo, 1998). One of the truly great resources for parents wishing to raise children with a ravenous curiosity and the means of feeding it for a lifetime.

Zahler, Kathy. *50 Simple Things You Can Do to Raise a Child Who Loves to Read* (New York: Arco, 1997). A perfect practical adjunct to the Calkins book. Well worth seeking out.

Galens, Judy and Nancy Pear. *The Handy Answer Book for Kids (and Parents)* (Canton, MI: Visible Ink, 2002). Among the best of the general answer-to-everything references for kids. Well-organized, engaging, and both browsable and useful for specific reference. Everything from empirical science ("What is a black hole?" "Why does a skunk stink?" "How old is the Earth?"—and the right answer) to social science ("What is a homosexual?"—including an excellent slap at homophobes) to the big questions ("Where will I go when I die?" "Who is God?"). Age 10+.

Additional Resources

See also the following books and videos reviewed in *Parenting Beyond Belief*:

McNulty, Faith. *How Whales Walked into the Sea* (New York: Scholastic Press, 1999). Ages 6–12.

McCutcheon, Marc. *The Beast in You!–Activities & Questions to Explore Evolution* (Charlotte, VT: Williamson, 1999). Ages 8–12.

Lawson, Kristan. *Darwin and Evolution for Kids–His Life and Ideas with 21 Activities* (Chicago: Chicago Review Press, 2003). Age 12+.

Peters, Lisa Westerberg. *Our Family Tree: An Evolution Story* (New York: Harcourt Children's, 2003). Ages 4–9.

Gamlin, Linda. *Eyewitness: Evolution* (New York: DK Children, 2000). Ages 10–14.

Pfeffer, Wendy. *A Log's Life* (New York: Simon and Schuster Children's, 1997). Ages 4–8.

Couper, Heather, with Nigel Henbest. *Big Bang–The Story of the Universe* (New York: Dorling Kindersley, 1997). Ages 12–18.

Bailey, Jacqui. *The Birth of the Earth* from The Cartoon History of the Earth series (Tonawanda, NY: Kids Can Press, 2001). Ages 9–12.

Walking with Cavemen (London: BBC, 2003). Age 8+.

Walking with Dinosaurs (London: BBC, 1999). Age 10+.

Intimate Universe: The Human Body (London: BBC Warner, 1998). Age 6+.

Evolution, PBS series (Boston: Clear Blue Sky Productions, 2001). Age 12+.

Notes

1. Jurmain, Robert, et al., *Introduction to Physical Anthropology* (New York: Thompson Wadsworth, 2005), p. 374.

2. Smith, Jeremy Adam, "Households to the Right of Me: Going Behind Closed Doors in Christian Right Households," *www.AlterNet.org*, April 11,

2008. See also Smith's phenomenal blog Daddy Dialectic at *www.daddy-dialectic.blogspot.com*. Accessed May 2, 2008.

3. Used here in its modern sense. The ancient Greek philosophy of Cynicism has little in common with current usage.

4. Look into the absolutely heartbreaking story of French astronomer Guillaume Le Gentil, preferably as told by Bill Bryson in *A Short History of Nearly Everything* (New York: Broadway Books, 2003).

5. McGowan, Dale, "Santa Claus—The Ultimate Dry Run," in *Parenting Beyond Belief* (New York: AMACOM Books, 2007), p. 89.

6. Woolley, J.D. and J. Van Reet, "Effects of Context on Judgments Concerning the Reality Status of Novel Entities," *Child Development, 77*, (6) (2006), quoted at ScienceDaily. Accessed May 2, 2008, from *www.sciencedaily.com/releases/2006/11/061116114522.htm*

7. Creationists trumpet the supposed dethroning of the peppered moth as an illustration of natural selection, pointing to various errors found in early experiments. But subsequent experiments have confirmed the original hypothesis. In the book *Moths* (London, UK: Collins New Naturalist, 2002), Cambridge biologist Michael Majerus sums up the consensus in the field: "I believe that, without exception, it is our view that the case of melanism in the Peppered Moth still stands as one of the best examples of evolution, by natural selection, in action."

8. Although he often cited this analogy, its first mention was in *The Dragons of Eden* (New York: Ballantine Books, 1977).

9. Wingrove, Rick, "The Assertive Atheist." Accessed April 18, 2008, from *www.flamewarrior.com*

10. This marvelous exercise is adapted from Cassidy, John, *Earthsearch* (Palo Alto, CA: Klutz, 1994).

11. "Basics for the Non-Scientist," TRIUMF website, Canada's National Laboratory for Particle and Nuclear Physics. Accessed May 8, 2008, from *www.triumf.ca/welcome/basics.html*

12. See Mayor, Adrienne, *The First Fossil Hunters* (Princeton, NJ: Princeton University Press, 2000) for an excellent description of this phenomenon in Ancient Greece and Rome.

13. Originally in Chapter 6 of Kristan Lawson's *Darwin and Evolution for Kids* (Chicago: Chicago Review Press, 2003).

CHAPTER 2

Living and Teaching Ethics in Your Family

Molleen Matsumura

Ask Lois Kellerman, a longtime Ethical Culture Leader, what she's thinking when she creates moral education programs for children, and the first thing she says is, "You're creating more than a curriculum—you're building a culture that nurtures the growth of humane values. Even tiny details make a difference. For example, at the Humanist Community Sunday School in Palo Alto, we had kids take their shoes off for two reasons: It was a noncoercive but effective way to keep kids from running around and hurting themselves during quiet times, and it incorporated a habit familiar to the many Asian American kids in the group. Of course, once you set up the framework, you will have to sustain it." The same is true for families.

Freethinking parents generally hope to raise kids who are independent thinkers. They often remark, "Sure, I want to raise my kids to be moral. But I don't want to brainwash them." But not all teaching is brainwashing, and teaching is exactly what kids need from their parents. Home is where they learn important skills and attitudes—from language to self-care and social skills—well before the first day of school. Just remember, education (providing leadership for your kids as they learn life skills) is different from indoctrination (pouring ideas into their heads without inviting critical examination).

Extensive research has confirmed that parenting styles strongly affect children's ethical development. Authoritative (as opposed to authoritar*ian*) parenting, which combines responsiveness with high and clearly expressed expectations, is most successful.[1]

Researchers have found "a consistent picture of childrearing effects . . . [P]arents who tend to be harshly and arbitrarily authoritarian or power-assertive . . . are less likely to be successful than those who place substantial emphasis on induction or reasoning, presumably in an attempt to be responsive to and understanding of their child's point of view."[2]

> 66 Children's understanding of morality is the same whether they're of one religion, another religion or no religion. But if it's simply indoctrination, it's worse than doing nothing. It interferes with moral development. 99
>
> —Larry Nucci, director,
> Office for Studies
> in Moral Development,
> University of Illinois

An especially powerful example of the influence of parenting style on moral development is found in the book *The Altruistic Personality* by researchers Samuel and Pearl Oliner. The Oliners conducted over 700 interviews with survivors of Nazi-occupied Europe—both "rescuers" (those who actively rescued victims of Nazi persecution) and "non-rescuers" (those who were either passive in the face of the persecution or actively involved in it). The study revealed profound differences in the upbringing of the two groups—in both the language and practices that parents used to teach their values.

It likely comes as no surprise that the morality of adults reflects their moral education as children. What may surprise some, given traditional beliefs about moral education, is which kind of moral education leads to which result.

Non-rescuers were twenty-one times more likely than rescuers to have grown up in families that emphasized *obedience*—being given rules that were to be followed without question—while rescuers were over three times more likely than non-rescuers to identify "reasoning" as an element of their moral education. *"Explained,"* the authors note, "is the word most rescuers favored" in describing their parents' way of communicating rules and ethical concepts.[3]

Both the Oliners' results and the central role children play in their own moral development are underlined by cross-cultural research from the Office for Studies in Moral Development at the University of Illinois, Chicago. Children in cultures around the world tend to reach certain landmarks in moral development reliably and on time, according to lead researcher Larry Nucci, regardless of what their parents do or don't do. "Children's understanding of morality is the same whether they're of one religion, another religion or no religion," says Nucci.

There is just one major exception, one way in which parents can actually *impede* their children's moral growth: "If it's simply indoctrination," he says, "it's worse than doing nothing. It interferes with moral development."[4]

The one practice conservative religious thought insists is vitally important in moral education—teaching unquestioning obedience to "absolute" rules—turns out to be the single least productive thing we can do for our children's moral development.

Instead, the best thing we can do is to encourage our kids to actively engage in their own moral development—asking questions, challenging the answers they are given, and working hard to understand the *reasons* to be good. Marvin Berkowitz, professor of character education at the University of Missouri, puts it just that clearly: "The most useful form of character education encourages children to think for themselves."[5]

The "authoritative" parenting style that relies on warmth and explanation has been shown to be successful in raising ethical children. What could be more compatible with a family culture based on humanistic principles of love and reason?

Questions and Answers

Q: What are humanist ethics?

A: Humanist ethics are founded on two overarching principles: reason and compassion. Parents need to create a list of values that will guide their families' everyday lives and help their children grow into ethical people. For example, we teach our children to take turns because we value fairness (not because "it's a rule"). You can teach values most effectively if you have put them into your own words and decided for yourself which are more important.

Begin with universal values. After intensively researching values prized by societies around the world, the Institute for Global Ethics distilled this list of essential human values:

- Honesty
- Respect
- Responsibility
- Fairness
- Compassion[6]

There are questions you can ask about the list that will help you to add specifically humanist principles. For example: Is respect reserved for those in authority, or given to all members of a family or society? Does "honesty" include intellectual honesty?[7]

These excerpts from the "Core Values" of the Ethical Society of St. Louis Sunday School[8] exemplify humanist thinking:

- Every person is important and unique.
- I can learn from everyone.
- I am part of this earth.
- I learn from the world around me by using senses, mind, and feelings.
- I am a member of the world community.
- I am free to question.
- I am free to choose what I believe.
- I accept responsibility for my choices and actions.

Contrast "I am free to choose what I believe" and "I am free to question" with the idea that heresy is a sin. You might choose to reword some values, or add others, like "humility" or "skepticism and independent thinking." One family might emphasize sustainable living, while another stresses social activism. The result will be an ethical vision tailored to *your* family, framed in widely shared humanist ethics but informed and energized by your own individuality—a set of "family values" that gives that phrase genuine, personal meaning. It will be a vision that can subtly change over the years as you and your children learn and grow together.

An important reminder: Ethics aren't only about how we treat other people, but also about how we treat ourselves. Support your kids' self-respect and help them feel that zest and enjoyment are the best approach to the only life we've got.

Q: I grew up with fairly black-and-white ideas about morality. It's even worse for my friends who grew up in churches where everything was framed in terms of being like Jesus and avoiding Satan's influence. Can you give me a better understanding of how moral development works—something to replace the black-and-white thinking?

A: There certainly is a better answer. You can work with your child's inborn ability to develop into a moral person. Much depends on the stage she has reached in her moral development. One of the most useful moral development frameworks for parents is Lawrence Kohlberg's six-stage model.[9] Fear of punishment is the first stage, followed by hope of reward. Children younger than age 2 are rarely able to apply moral reasoning beyond these incentives.

Most children soon move into the third stage: seeking social approval and avoiding disapproval, especially from their parents. That's why the typical kindergartener is so devastated when Mom's upset about something he did.

The fourth stage is recognition of the value of laws or rules. The tattling second grader and the finger-pointing fourth grader are deep in the stage where rules are followed *because* they are rules. Many adults never get past this level to stage five, the "social contract" level, in which laws or rules are still seen as desirable, but it is understood that they have been created by consensus, and that they may change as the consensus changes.

The sixth level of moral development is reached when a person thinks in terms of universal ethical principles—that is, ethical principles that transcend a single social or cultural framework—and is sometimes even willing to defend such principles at the risk of punishment, disapproval, or even death.

Keep three things in mind when thinking about these stages. First, moral reasoning is developing at the same time as other types of knowledge and reasoning. One study found that until some time between ages 3 and 5, children don't understand that another person can hold beliefs the child knows are untrue.[10] Until they reach that point, children don't fully realize that it is possible for someone to lie to them.

Second, children are simultaneously developing their abilities to perceive the feelings of other people and to care about those feelings. The same 2-year-old who tries to comfort a crying friend may do something that makes that same friend cry 10 minutes later.

Finally, the stages are fluid and open to influence. We want to encourage our children's growth to the next moral stage, but at any stage, a person may act according to different levels of moral reasoning. For example, someone who often acts on principle will choose at other times to act according to what others will think. The rule-follower may still respond to punishments and rewards, and the sophisticated fifth-level teenager may still feel a twinge of guilt when a parent disapproves of her moral choice, even though it's not the potent factor it once was.

Q: What discipline methods are most appropriate to humanist ethics?

A: "Discipline" can mean "a way to get obedience" or "a method of teaching." This distinction is important: Your method of discipline sends powerful messages about how to act. In the rush and routine of daily life, we can forget that *everything* we do teaches values. Saying "Remember to take out the trash," for example, is a reminder to take responsibility and that every family member has an important role to play.

The "five Es" of humanist discipline are the following:

Example. Model behavior you want to encourage. Hearing you say "Thanks" one time is more effective than hearing a dozen reminders to thank somebody else. With young children or new activities, setting an example teaches more than giving orders. Set the table together to show how it's done; later, kids can share tasks or take turns. For example, at breakfast, one kid sets the table, one makes toast, and so on.

Explanation. Explanation teaches your kids to expect reasons for rules, instead of merely obeying authority. In time, they will start offering reasons for their own actions. When there isn't time to explain, promise to explain later; keeping the promise builds trust and underscores the value of having a reason for what one does. Start early: An explanation can be as simple as, "No—hot!"

Encouragement. This is different from praise. *Praise* emphasizes what *you* want from your child and can even discourage the praiseworthy behavior. Encouragement acknowledges *your child's* goals and efforts. Praise is often a global evaluation; encouragement is specific.[11] Contrast, "What a great athlete you are! I am so proud!" with, "Wow, ten laps! All that practicing you've done really shows." Among other problems, the first statement could make your child wonder, "Will she still be proud of me if I have an off day?" The second remark supports the effort that was made, and that won't change.

Empathy. Empathy takes into account your child's feelings *and* thinking, including what can be expected at their age. For example, when my 3-year-old broke a ceramic doll, it was from ignorance, not carelessness. She thought it was metal. When a 10-year-old shouts, "You're mean!" when reminded to do a chore, avoid a war of words by acknowledging his emotions: "Sounds like you're frustrated that this needs to be done when you're almost finished with your drawing."

Engagement. Involve your kids in family decisions, from what to do for fun this weekend to figuring out the consequences for misbehavior. They will learn negotiating and decision-making skills and have more respect for decisions they helped to make.

Q: Those "five Es" are very nice, but sometimes the best approach is good, old-fashioned punishments and rewards . . . isn't it?

A: It's all too common for us to see our highest ideals as luxuries to be indulged in fair weather and abandoned when the going gets tough. Free speech is all very well, goes the reasoning—but not in time of war. The same kind of reasoning says, "Explaining to your child is terrific—unless he gets out of control, at which point only a good thrashing will do."

Nonsense. Unless we are willing to act on our ideals when it's most challenging, they aren't worth pursuing even in the good times. Fortunately, principles are as rugged and workable as our commitment to them.

The "five Es" are practical applications of humanist ideals. Living according to those ideals is your best bet for raising children who will not only do what they are told in the moment, but live by those principles in the long run.

> " The highest ethical duty is often to discard the outmoded ethics of the past. "
>
> —Corliss Lamont, humanist philosopher

Yes, it's an imperfect world. But rewards and punishments are the least effective tools for moral development because they focus on the power of the person who deals them out, like a god controlling people with eternal punishments and rewards. It is better to focus on *experiences* that help children become people who are ethical on their own than to teach them only to behave well by doing what they are told. Kids learn best from experiencing the positive and negative *consequences* of their behavior.

Helping kids learn from consequences of their actions is not a substitute for the "five Es." Again—consequences are a tool, and the "five Es" are their foundation. It's important to explain your goals and engage your children in the process of reaching them. For example, the reason for a curfew is your concern for your child's safety, and the time and conditions of the curfew may be negotiable as your child matures.

Besides being positive and negative, consequences can be *natural, logical,* or *arbitrary* (which isn't always a bad thing). If your child breaks a toy by angrily or carelessly throwing it at the wall, a natural consequence would be delaying or refusing to replace it (especially if something similar has happened before). There's also something to be said for working together to repair the toy.

Sometimes we can't allow "natural consequences" to occur. If your child keeps leaving toys on stairs where someone could trip on them and get hurt, you'll have to step in with preventive action. If she often leaves toys on the stairs, a logical consequence would be taking away any toy you find there and not giving it back until there is evidence that she'll at least try to change.

An arbitrary consequence has no clearly natural or logical relationship to the action that brought it on. If it's a negative consequence, it's likely to seem unfair and not be helpful as discipline. For example, grounding your teen for coming home from a party two hours late is a logical consequence (although there might be some disagreement on how long it should last). But grounding him for getting too involved in a game to set the table on time is illogical overkill. Logical consequences (maybe subject to negotiation) might be adding or substituting another task such as washing the dishes or temporarily taking away the distracting game until you've agreed on a way for him to remember to do chores on time.

Sometimes arbitrary positive consequences are okay. We adults use them ourselves; for example, "I will begin my stop-smoking effort by getting myself a CD for each week I go without cigarettes." Why not teach our kids this method of motivating themselves to do things that are necessary but unpleasant or unrewarding?

Positive consequences can get us into tricky territory. Suppose your child practices hard to learn a new skill, such as batting better or learning a difficult piano piece. Positive natural consequences might include pride in mastering the skill, or pleasure ("flow") in performing more effortlessly (read more about flow in Chapter 5). Logical consequences include such rewards as being chosen for a competitive team, winning a music scholarship, or being asked to play at a friend's party. The last example shows how the reasons an experience is rewarding can be mixed. One doesn't have to play music unusually well to have the fun of helping friends have a good time.

The tricky part comes in when a child feels that your approval, or their friends' acceptance, is conditional on performing well. It feels unavoidably natural to be proud when your child succeeds, but it's just as important to be supportive when kids have made an effort and somehow things don't turn out as well as they had hoped.

Q: How can I help my children develop the widest scope of empathy?

A: First, help your child develop "emotional literacy"—recognizing, expressing, respecting, and responding to his or her own and other people's feelings. With young children, name emotions: theirs, yours, those of characters in stories and of the people around them. ("You look sad." "I'm so happy, I can't stop smiling." "Looks like he's in pain.") Feelings can be mixed, so talk about that, too.

Don't judge emotions. For example, anger is not bad in itself, although it may be uncalled-for at times. As your kids grow older, help them understand that the most obvious emotion may not be the only one a person is feeling. For

Sidewalk Morality

One day in June I watched from our front porch as my 5-year-old daughter Delaney received a moral lesson on a subject that has fascinated philosophers for centuries: ant squishing. Her brother Connor—11 years old and pro-life in the deeply literal sense—found Laney busily stomping her way into ant mythology on the front sidewalk.

"Laney!!" he screamed. "Stop it!"

"What for?" she asked without pausing. "There are lots of others."

He spluttered a bit—then a classic grin spread across his face. He raised his foot and aimed the sole at her. *"Well, there are lots of other little girls, too!"*

She screamed and ran. The ants huzzahed, and Monkey-Who-Pointed-Foot-at-Other-Monkey-and-Saved-Many entered the colony lore.

My boy had applied a great critical thinking technique by using the faulty logic of his opponent to generate a ridiculous counterexample. I wondered from the sidelines if it would stick.

A few days later, as I loaded the last of the boxes for our move, I got my answer. Laney walked with her head hung low, doing the aimless, foot-scraping walk of the bored child in midsummer, then announced her intention to "go squish some ants."

"Hm," I said.

She stopped walking. "What?"

"Well, I dunno. Does that seem like a good thing to do, or no?"

She shrugged.

"Tell you what," I said. "You think about it for a minute and let me know what you decide."

"Okay." She took a little walk around the yard and thought.

I knew that Delaney knew the answer. *Everyone* knows the answer. Like most basic moral questions, *knowing* what's right is not the hard part when your foot is raised above the skittering dots on the sidewalk. The challenge is to do what we already know is right. And the best foundation for that right action is the ability to say *why* something is right.

Not knowing right from wrong is so rare that it is a complete felony defense. You are rightly considered barking mad if you fail to recognize the distinction. And it's so thunderously rare that the defense rarely succeeds. So why do we continue to pretend that our children's moral development is best served by merely dictating lists of rules?

Instead of listing "thou shalt nots," we ought to encourage our kids to discover and articulate what they already *know* is right, then ask them *why* it's right. This, not the passive intake of rules, leads to the development of moral judgment, something that will allow them to think and act morally when we aren't in the room with them.

Delaney came back after 2 minutes. "I'm not gonna squish ants any more," she said.

"Oh. Why did you decide that?"

"Because they should get to have a life, too," she said. "Like me."

That old reciprocity principle. You can't beat it.

—*Dale McGowan, from the blog* The Meming of Life

example, angry behavior might express hurt feelings. Knowing that makes it possible to respond more appropriately.

"Starting small" is okay. While toddlers naturally respond to some emotional cues, a child must be at least 3 before she begins to *understand* that other people's feelings can be different from her own. You can help by explaining how her actions are affecting others: "Joey is crying. He's sad because you took his toy away."

It's okay, too, that kids first learn empathy in small groups, such as their families or playgroups. That's how everyone lived for most of humanity's time on earth. Just as mountain climbers need a base camp to support their explorations, trusted and familiar groups give your child emotional support and security as he or she meets new and different people.

Your child's introduction to diversity starts with interpersonal differences that don't come under the banner of social diversity—like the different size and abilities of younger siblings, differences in taste, or the different skin textures of children and their elderly neighbors.

Then, even if there is social and economic diversity in your kids' schools, and especially if there isn't, there are countless ways you can bring it into their lives. Diversity in your own friendship network, reading stories set in other cultures, and visiting ethnic neighborhoods are just a few examples.

We also need to teach about religious diversity. Even people who are nonreligious need to be able to empathize with religious impulses at least to some degree, if we are going to build a cooperative and coexistent world.

It's important to help your kids find ways to put compassion into action; feeling powerless to help can be so painful that we shut down feelings of empathy. Once again, start with small, intimate acts. Thank your child for bringing you a glass of water when you're sick, or ask, "Could you keep the baby company while I make dinner?" Help an older child find extracurricular activities where he meets different friends than he has at school. Involve your family in volunteer work, or, if you don't have time, encourage your kids to participate in volunteer activities.

Putting empathy into action is a powerful experience: Your kids enrich their lives while learning that they *can* make the world a better place.

> 66 Modern Darwinism makes it abundantly clear that many less ruthless traits, some not always admired by robber barons and Führers—altruism, general intelligence, compassion—may be the key to survival. 99
>
> —Carl Sagan

Q: Sometimes it seems like my kids hang on to their quarrels and grudges endlessly. How can I teach them the value of letting go?

A: It's true: Family life involves conflict, especially when there is more than one child, and you inevitably find yourself in the role of referee for a thousand petty irritations. It's tempting to urge your child to "Forgive and forget," or "Just move on." But don't do it. Moving on without clearing up the original problem leads to running around in circles. This is just as true when there's no clear victim, because each party in a conflict did harm.

Much of the research and writing about these issues uses the word "forgiveness," but there are problems with using such a religiously loaded word. For one thing, it often implies "absolution"—freeing the person who hurt another of the guilt that attaches to that person's action. But, nothing can make a wrong action into a right action. What's needed instead, if possible, is to repair the harm that was done. Also, the idea of "forgiveness" as a virtue unfairly puts all the responsibility on the victim, without offering the wrongdoer a chance to make amends. And finally, using the one word "forgiveness" sometimes confuses two very different processes: "acceptance" and "reconciliation."

Primatologist Frans de Waal has commented, "Forgiveness is not . . . a mysterious and sublime idea that we owe to a few millennia of Judeo-Christianity."[12] True—but the influence of Christianity in our culture has glorified the idea of unconditional forgiveness, no matter what harm was done, putting all the responsibility for healing on the victim.

Acceptance is the decision to let go of corrosive anger or resentment—that is, accepting the reality of the situation. And this is something for which research points to very real emotional and physical benefits.[13]

Acceptance is especially useful when the person who did the harm is unable or unwilling to make amends, and even more so when those in conflict must continue living together—like family members—even if agreement cannot be reached.

Reconciliation is a process in which the victim and the person who hurt him find a way to repair and continue their relationship. The concept of *reconciliation* holds the key to a better approach. Alhough some think of this as a strictly religious concept, de Waal notes that it is a process whose roots go far deeper than religion—even appearing among other species: "The fact that monkeys, apes, and humans all engage in reconciliation behavior means that it is probably over 30 million years old. . . ."[14] If monkeys can reconcile, so can we. Perhaps you can even inject a little humor into the process, noting that at least you're not asking your children to pick off each other's fleas.

There is more than one path to reconciliation, but every path depends on mutual understanding. Alfie Kohn makes a wonderful suggestion that also helps children develop empathy: "[S]ay after a blow up, 'Tell me what just happened, but pretend you are your brother and describe how things might have seemed to him.'"[15] This approach may lead to the discovery that the harm was unintentional—something much easier to forgive. The younger the child, the more likely the harm was unintentional.

Then there are the painful times when a quick, muttered "I'm sorry" just isn't enough to repair a rift. Ideally, your kids will have seen you apologize, so they know how to begin the process. This outline of the "Steps to Seeking Forgiveness" detailed in Appendix 2 is a guide to the reconciliation process that can be used over and over, not only helping your kids get along better, but also giving them skills they can use for a lifetime of relationships.

1. Acknowledge wrong-doing
   - Clarify why a certain behavior was hurtful.
   - Acknowledge to yourself and others that the behavior was a mistake.
   - Express genuine sorrow to all those involved for the mistake you have made.
2. Make amends
   - Act out of a deep sense of honoring yourself and the other party.
   - Find a "stroke" that is equal to your "blow."
   - Make amends in a timely manner.

3. Commit to change
   - Make a clear commitment to change harmful patterns.
   - Act visibly on your commitment.
   - Respect the process of change.

Q: How can I help my child act on principles and not just follow the rules?

A: There is no magic day when your child graduates from only following rules to thinking about them. It was a major accomplishment to learn and follow many sets of rules: rules set by different caregivers, different rules in friends' homes, more rules at school, the rules of games . . . the list goes on. It takes self-control to follow rules and good memory and judgment to know which rules to apply at any time. Build on those skills.

While your child is learning to live with rules, you will be hearing about it. Often a child who doesn't know the rules in a new situation—say, a new school—gets yelled at by the old-timers. That's not all bad; as Arthur Dobrin points out, "[Children's] moral development is spurred by others whose sophistication is slightly more advanced. . . ."[16] As long as the rules are reasonable, and it doesn't sound like other kids are leading yours into trouble, just reassure her that things will get better as she learns the ropes.

> If you put a kid in a pro-social family, in a pro-social culture, with parents who understand how to raise a child effectively, the child comes equipped with the tendency to capitalize on that and develop into a good person.
>
> —Marvin Berkowitz, professor of character education, University of Missouri[17]

Meanwhile, explain the reasons for rules. For example, when you stop for a traffic light, explain that signals help drivers take turns. When your child starts recognizing that some aspects of rules are arbitrary ("But why is the stop light *red*?"), you'll know he's starting to look at rules more thoughtfully.

Bring your child more fully into the process of modifying and making rules. Taking part in rulemaking makes your kid less likely to decide, "If rules come from people, then I can make my own rules."

A first step is to modify rules when possible, in ways that give your child more choices and more responsibility. For example, replace a "clean plate" rule with an "eat healthy foods" rule. Then, if your kid doesn't want to eat her carrots at dinner, say, "Well, the carrots have lots of vitamin A; you could get yourself a slice of cantaloupe or microwave some broccoli." (This approach also gives the child responsibility for the extra work involved.)

A step that some kids can handle by age 10 is to set the rules for a limited situation. They will reach into the toolkit of rules they know, and you can figure out together which will work best. For example, you might ask, "How will we decide what to do for fun on our vacation?" One of your kids might answer, "We could take a vote every day."

Q: How can books and movies contribute to my child's ethical development?

A: Let's begin with something that many of us take for granted—the bedtime story. You already know that reading to your child at any time of day, but especially bedtime, usually creates an island of calm and closeness in your day. But what does that have to do with ethics?

Just this: Nobody is ethical in a vacuum. The support of friends and loved ones can help give us the strength to behave ethically despite pressure or temptation to do wrong. Anything we do that strengthens our bonds with our children makes it more likely that we can continue to support their ethical growth and remain someone they can talk to when they face ethical dilemmas.

When our kids learn to run movies and read to themselves, we can still watch with them and read some of the same books. It's a good way to stay close and to continue conversations about important topics.

Any well-told story offers material for ethical learning, even when it's not preachy. Here's a partial list.

Characters that we can identify or sympathize with give us a chance to learn *compassion* for their problems. For example, reading about the feelings of a character who has been bullied can help your child be more understanding toward a classmate who seems to be "an obvious loser" who "practically asks" to be picked on. A teen reading *Angela's Ashes* (or seeing the movie) might learn compassion toward alcoholics by seeing how the father in the novel drinks in response to hopelessness and prejudice. We can also be *inspired* by the way both real and fictional people respond to life's challenges.[18]

Self-compassion—treating one's own perceived shortcomings with the same kindness and understanding that one would give a friend—isn't always easy to learn or practice. Reading about real or fictional people who have similar problems can make self-compassion easier. Maybe the author's insight into a character offers a reader insight into her own character. Or a parent reading a book with a child might comment, "Does that sound familiar?"

Even when reading about a person with a similar problem (for example, the anxieties that go with attending a new school) doesn't lead to self-compassion, it breaks through the feeling that "I'm the only one." Feeling less isolated reaffirms the sense of connection to other people that underlies ethical behavior.

Reading also stimulates and develops your child's capacity for *moral reasoning*. Some families enjoy the direct approach of books that describe ethical dilemmas the whole family can discuss. Some of those books are recommended in the resource section, but if that's not your style, don't worry about it. Life and literature are full of situations that raise questions worth serious thinking and discussion. For example, there are many movies whose main character is a "charming rascal"; somehow, the director gets us on the side of character(s) trying to get away with committing a clever crime. What do the directors and writers do to get us to like these characters? How do we feel about those manipulations?

By reading books about people in other cultures and socioeconomic groups, we gain *knowledge and understanding* that are crucial to developing the *open-mindedness* we need if we are to develop a peaceful, democratic global culture.

Finally, many freethinkers enjoy giving their children myths and fairy tales to read, reasoning in part that the kids will see the resemblance between those stories and various scriptures.

All true—but let's look at another reason for reading myths and legends. Their common themes are another way of showing us that different human groups have a lot in common. For example, the "trickster" character occurs in many cultures' lore—Loki in Norse mythology, Coyote among Native American cultures, Anansi the spider in many African cultures, and Reynard the Fox in European folklore. Myths also offer a symbolic or allegorical way to talk about real-life problems such as sibling rivalry. Enjoy them, and—for the best medicine against literalist thinking, for imaginative exercise, and just plain fun—encourage your kids to make up their own.

Activities

In addition to specific activities, in this section you'll find ways to generally encourage ethical development and reflection, things to discuss and ways to discuss them, and things to think about and ways to think about them.

If I Made the Rules

All ages

We live in a world abuzz with lists of ethical rules, rights, and responsibilities: Buddhism's "Noble Eightfold Path" of conduct, school honor codes, Franklin Roosevelt's Four Freedoms, our Bill of Rights, the United Nations' Universal Declaration of Human Rights—the lists go on and on (see Appendix 2 for examples). And, of course, these days we hear constant discussion of the Ten Commandments. All of these lists include at least some pretty good rules. There are others that your kids will likely think should not make anyone's top ten list of the most important ethical ideas.

How do those rules come to be? People invent and discuss them, of course, and your kids can have a taste of the experience. Have each family member come up with his or her own list of up to ten rules to make a more perfect world, ones that each person would be willing to live by.

Then compare notes. Where do people agree or disagree, and why? That will stretch everyone's moral reasoning and might even get you to question some assumptions.

> **Bonus 1**: Try cutting your lists down to just five rules. Deciding which rules are more important is another great exercise in moral reasoning. Can you get down to three? One?
>
> **Bonus 2:** Once you've got your rules to live by, enhance the discussion by talking about how you would get people to follow them. Should there be punishments for noncompliance? Rewards? Use Kohlberg's six levels of moral development (in kid terms) to frame it:
>
> Level 1: Fear of punishment
> Level 2: Hope of reward
> Level 3: Desire for social approval
> Level 4: Rules are rules
> Level 5: Rules are good but changeable
> Level 6: Follow universal principles

Should you start at the top, appealing to universal principles, or at the bottom, by threatening rule breakers with punishment? Why?

You Did What Now?

Ages 6+

Materials: index cards

Write a number of one-sentence scenarios on index cards, some embarrassing, some not, some ethical, some not. Examples:

- You put a frog down a bully's pants, and he punched someone else in the nose for it.
- You wrote nasty things about your enemy in the bathroom stall.
- You picked up someone else's trash.
- You started a false rumor that someone's father was in prison.
- You copied your older brother's paper from last year and never got caught.
- You didn't do so well on a test, even though you studied but did not cheat.
- You received a trophy for winning a race when you know you cheated.
- You turned in a friend for shoplifting candy, and now everyone's calling you a snitch.
- Seeing a glow out the window, you jumped out of the tub, ran naked to the neighbors' burning house, and woke them just in time.
- You hurt your ankle and didn't finish the walk-a-thon for homeless kids— but lied to your sponsors so you'd have money to give to the cause.

Now someone takes a turn as a reporter who does an on-the-spot interview based on one of the cards. The script goes something like this: "We're here with Mary who's had a pretty amazing day. Mary, we understand you started a rumor today that Sam's dad was in prison. Why did you do it, and do you think that was the right thing to do?" The interviewee (who didn't know which scenario would be thrown at her) responds on the spot by either justifying the act or saying why she wishes she hadn't done it. The reporter might then follow up ("Would you do it again?" or "Is there anything you'd do differently next time?").

This exercise is a two-for-one game. The interviewee has to practice empathy by imagining the feelings of the person who "did the deed" *and* engage in moral reasoning to explain whatever position she takes.

Invite kids to come up with their own scenarios combining ethical issues and social constraints (right versus wrong *plus* social approval/disapproval, punishment/reward, principles, etc).[19]

Creating a Family Vision

For the parent(s)

With your parenting partner or alone if you are a single parent, create a vision of your family culture. Do this before you start a family, or at any time later on, just to see if you're on the same page.

Each of you take a piece of paper and write down five statements beginning, "In my family, we . . ." Sample endings might be, " . . . have a lot of fun"; " . . . drop everything when somebody says 'Come see this wonderful spider web'"; " . . . create an atmosphere where everyone feels safe."

Show each other what you've written and talk it over. Where is there overlap? Are there any disagreements? Can you merge your lists? You probably don't want more than ten statements because too many are too hard to remember. But, in the future, you can look at your lists to ask, "Does what we are doing reflect our family culture?"

When your kids are older, turn this same activity into a family game that will tell you a lot about how you well you are communicating your values.

Getting Down to the Roots

For the parent(s)

Sooner or later, every parent unconsciously imitates his or her own parents— both the things we liked and the things we disliked. Thinking about this ahead of time can be very helpful down the line. Make a list for each of your parents of three behaviors you would like to emulate and three you would like to avoid: for example, "I loved it when mom/dad was playful," or "I got really scared by mom's/dad's outbursts of anger."

Share this list with your parenting partner(s). Talk about how you would like to handle these issues. For example, if some day you are hypercritical of one of your kids, would you want your co-parent to take you aside later, and say something like, "Did you really want to be so hard on Tom? I was reminded of what you said about how you felt like you could never live up to your parents' standards."

If you are a single parent, check the list now and then to see if there is a comfortable match between your parenting ideals and the reality.

Clarifying Your Family's Ethics

For the parent(s)

A great time to start clarifying your ethics is before your kids are born. Once they're born, and life keeps throwing new challenges at you, you'll continue, and probably never stop. Even when your values don't change, there will be questions about how to apply them in new situations.

Different approaches to defining your values work better for different people. You and your parenting partner(s) might like to begin with the values mentioned in this chapter, or described in the statements listed in the resource section. Or you might start by discussing what you were brought up to value, or what you like and admire about other people. Sometimes you might find that what you like leads you to a deeper discussion. For example, I like people who are unpretentious; if I dig deeper, I realize this is another way of saying I think it's important for people to treat each other as equals.

Try to come up with a list of eight to ten principles that you can agree on. Talk about what they mean in practice.

Especially important for freethinkers: As your children interact with others in their school and your community (and maybe your extended family), how will you help them balance the values of "respecting other people's opinions" and "standing up for your own convictions"?

Encouraging Moral Reasoning at Different Stages

All ages

> *Materials: The Kids' Book of Questions* by Gregory Stock, PhD, or (for older kids) a few issues of the *New York Times Sunday Magazine* (for "The Ethicist" column)

Next time you're headed out for a road trip, pack a copy of the Gregory Stock book, which includes over 250 short, simple questions to discuss. Examples:

- *Would you rather be very poor but have parents who loved you and each other, or be fabulously wealthy but have parents who ignored you and were always fighting with each other?*
- *Adults can do more, but they have more responsibilities. Children can play more, but they get told what to do. Do you think kids or adults have a better deal?*

- *If everyone else in your class would be killed unless you agreed to sacrifice your own life, would you do it? Would it matter if no one would ever know what you had done?*
- *Have you ever gotten yourself into a mess by telling people you could do something you couldn't?*

When your kids take a position, ask them why they think it is right. Give reasons if you have a different opinion.

Bring the ethical dimension into your everyday life as well. When reading fiction or watching movies, talk about the ways characters resolve ethical problems. Do your kids agree with the way they acted? Why? If the character felt he or she had no choice, was that true?

When there are conflicts within your family, or your kids mention problems they're having with friends or at school, bring ethical principles into the discussion of how to resolve them. Introduce the basic language of ethics (fairness, reciprocity, integrity, consistency, etc.) to give them words for their developing concepts.

Keeping Track of Your Family's Values in the Community Setting

Keep informed about "character education" programs at your child's school. Read materials sent home for parents; read materials given to your child; attend parent meetings. Some programs are less effective than others, and some may promote values different from your own. Whether you agree or disagree with what is taught, you will want to talk it over with your child. If you disagree with what is being taught, you may be able to work with others to change the program. If you have the time to volunteer with the parent-teacher association, or on a school site committee, you may be able to encourage use of some of the resources given here or other worthy programs.

Humanistic Discipline: The "5 Es" in Action

For the parent(s)

Example: Set an example of willingness to change by asking your child to help you. For example, if you are trying to lose weight, ask your child to say, "Don't even look!" when you are offered the dessert menu in a restaurant.

Explanation: With very young children: Look for at least one chance a day to explain what you're doing. For example, when your child is finished drawing, say, "Let's put away the crayons now. *We don't want them in the way when we set the table for dinner.*" Or, "*So they won't get lost.*"

For older children: Before introducing new rules, discuss the explanation with your parenting partner. Discuss whether, in this case, it would be appropriate to discuss alternatives with your child.

Encouragement: Together with your parenting partner, read "Five Reasons to Stop Saying 'Good Job!'" by Alfie Kohn (*www.alfiekohn.org/parenting/gj.htm*), or watch the video "How to Praise Children" (*www.greatergood.berkeley.edu/half_full/?p=55*). Think about something each of your children has done that deserves encouragement. Role-play what you will say to your child. Practice encouraging each other, too! It feels good, and you can give each other feedback on whether your words are truly encouraging.

Engagement: Whether you're thinking of discipline as "getting your kid to do what you want her to do," or "teaching your kids life-skills," engaging them in choosing goals and the means of achieving those goals is your best hope for success.

Widening the Circles of Empathy

All ages

A good case can be made that *acceptance and appreciation of difference* is the central value of humanistic ethics. Although this is explored in greater detail in "Finding and Creating Community" chapter 8, here are a few ways for families to accentuate and celebrate difference.

Who's in your boat? In our social relationships, empathy is based on the feeling that we have something in common with others—the awareness that "We're in the same boat." Yet cultural awareness usually classifies us into a few groups such as gender, race, or religion—groups that are often assumed to be in conflict. Sometime, when the issue comes up naturally—your child heard an ethnic slur used at school, for example, or your newspaper reports a bigoted statement made by a politician—play this game:

Have your whole family sit down with pencil and paper, set a timer, and take 5 minutes for each of you to list every group you can think of that you belong to. When the 5 minutes are up, compare lists and make suggestions to each other about how to get a nice, long list—say, thirty items. They can be trivial ("people whose favorite color is purple") or serious ("people with learning disabilities"), voluntary ("favorite sport is hockey") or involuntary ("left-handed"). The game prepares you to talk about how complicated people are, and the many ways in which each of us has something in common with everyone else.[20]

What's in a word? Exploring other languages is fun, and teaches appreciation of cultural diversity, partly because different languages often reflect different ways of thought. If you and/or your parenting partner speak more than one language, speak two languages at home, at least part of the time. Otherwise, get some bilingual dictionaries or use the Internet to learn five ways to say important words and phrases like "please," "thank you," "far away," "silly," or anything else the kids choose (have a "word for the day," a "word for the week," theme words, such as sports terminology or birds' names—whatever your family enjoys).

Out and about. Visit ethnic neighborhoods. Go on holidays like Chinese New Year or Cinco de Mayo, but also at any time of year visit neighborhood cultural centers, grocery stores, and so forth, surrounding yourself with sounds and signs in another language—and maybe bringing home a new food to try. (If you live in a very homogeneous community, save this idea for a vacation.)

Understand the other side. It's always tempting to demonize the opposition, especially when their behavior is obnoxious. But we do need to see their humanity, even if we continue to disagree with their point of view. It's worth watching the movie *Jesus Camp* together to understand the influences that make evangelicals act the way they do—especially if your kids know others who are religiously self-righteous. Watch for the scene in which the kids at the camp are being told that if they ever think "dirty" thoughts, they are "hypocrites," and discuss why the kids are crying.

It's equally important, of course, to point out that the people in *Jesus Camp* don't represent all religious believers, many of whom have values that give them much more in common with the nonreligious than with their more extreme coreligionists. For example, you could visit websites of pro-choice Catholics who speak up against their church's hierarchy, or talk about how segments of many religious denominations support gay rights, and how others refuse to condemn those outside their faiths as "evil."

Using Literature to Talk About Ethics

All ages

Keep your eyes open for opportunities to have conversations with your children about the ethical messages of books and movies. Don't be heavy-handed and bring them up every time, but do it when you feel strongly, and be responsive to your kids' own questions. Ask them what *they* think of statements by the author, or the characters' actions. Here are a couple of examples:

Read the popular children's book *The Little Prince*. In one part of the story, the prince describes his travels to imaginary planets. On one planet, the prince finds a man whose job is to light the village gaslights every night (here's your chance to offer a little history education!). The town is deserted now, but the lamplighter continues his nightly rounds because it is "his duty." The prince admires this attitude. Ask your child, "Do you agree?"

Watch the new movie version of *Charlotte's Web* with your family. In this story, a little girl named Fern makes a pet of a pig who is the runt of the litter, naming him Wilbur. Ultimately, a spider named Charlotte, who lives in the barn with Wilbur, saves his life. Another character in the story is a very self-centered rat named Templeton. Questions you might ask:

- When Fern's father is about to slaughter Wilbur, Fern stops him, protesting, "I promised Wilbur I would protect him." Her father tries to release her from the promise, but she replies, "I promised Wilbur, not you." How about it? Can one person release you from your promise to another person?
- When Wilbur is at the County Fair, Fern barely pays attention to him, instead spending most of her time with a friend from school. Is that disloyal? (The author clearly didn't think so, but it will be interesting to see what your kids think—especially whether the older kids do get what the author was driving at.)
- Templeton the rat runs various errands—sometimes risky ones—for Charlotte and Wilbur, but only when they bribe him. Ask your kids, "Is Templeton a true friend?"
- When Charlotte weaves a web that describes Wilbur as "Some Pig," people call it "a miracle." What does that tell us about miracles?

For more ideas on how to discuss stories with young children, take a look at the website "Teaching Children Philosophy" at *www.teachingchildren philosophy.com*. (At the time of writing, this site was called "Philosophy for

Children: Philosophical Questions from Children's Stories" and was located at *www.mtholyoke.edu/omc/kidsphil/stories.html,* but plans are underway to permanently relocate to the new URL above). There's lots of information for parents, including very specific discussions of the philosophical issues in deservedly popular children's books (not all of them are ethical issues, but all of them are well worth reading). Don't feel you have to use every question from every question set. Adapt to what works for you, and most of all, *have fun!*

Resources

Understanding Ethical Development

Dobrin, Arthur. *Ethical People and How They Get to Be That Way* (in press). This book will be available through the Ethical Humanist Society of Long Island. Check for availability at *www.ehsli.org/pubs/index.php*. Dobrin has taught a wide range of courses including moral education at Hofstra University and led the Ethical Humanist Society of Long Island for over thirty years. *Ethical People* is academic and philosophical in tone, with in-depth treatments of topics including research on children's moral reasoning, empathy, and a chapter on social issues affecting moral development. To get a feel for the scope of this book, see "Forty Things You Can Do to Raise a Moral Child" in the first Appendix of this book.

Faber, Adele, and Elaine Mazlish. *How to Talk So Kids Will Listen & Listen So Kids Will Talk* (New York: Avon Books, 1999) A practical, enjoyable oldie-still-goodie, *How to Talk* teaches communication skills that put parents and kids on the same team, solving problems together. It helps new parents start off right and others change ways that haven't been working. There are plenty of practical exercises and anecdotes; new chapters answer questions from readers. The best chapter may be the one on helping kids step out of old roles.

Greater Good Science Center (at UC Berkeley), "Half Full Blog"

> *http://greatergood.berkeley.edu/half_full/*

"Tools . . . for parents interested in raising happy and emotionally literate kids." A growing list of articles and videos on everything from "how to praise" to "helping kids . . . replace bad habits with good ones." It includes a complete list of references to original research—and translates them into understandable, practical terms.

Institute for Humanist Studies Parenting Resources

> *www.HumanistParenting.org*

Columns by and for humanist parents; reviews of books, DVDs, games, and other products; information on secular ceremonies; analysis of research and claims about parenting and child development; and links to other resources for humanist families.

Kohn, Alfie. *Unconditional Parenting: Moving From Rewards and Punishments to Love and Reason* (New York: Atria Books, 2005). The title says it all. Not a general parenting book, but a thorough, well researched discussion of the disadvantages of both punishments *and* rewards (yes, really!), explaining why they are methods for *controlling* rather than *supporting* children.

Article "Beyond the Golden Rule: A Parent's Guide to Preventing and Responding to Prejudice" at *www.tolerance.org*

Introduction to Parenting Styles

Berkowitz, M.W., and J.H. Grych. "Fostering Goodness: Teaching Parents to Facilitate Children's Moral Development." *Journal of Moral Education*, 27(3) (1998), 371–391. Available online at *http://parenthood.library.wisc.edu/ Berkowitz/Berkowitz.html,* this article includes a table correlating "Child Moral Development Outcomes" with "Selected Parenting Variables"; for example, "induction" is correlated with empathy, conscience, altruism, and moral reasoning.

Crosser, Sandra. "Helping Young Children to Develop Character." *Early Childhood News* (*www.earlychildhoodnews.com/earlychildhood/article_view.aspx? ArticleID=246*). Includes practical tips such as "Listen to children: . . . Physically get down on the child's level. . . . Ask questions . . . ," and advice for setting standards and negotiating solutions.

Exploring Humanist Ethics

American Ethical Union, "Eight Commitments of Ethical Culture"

   http://aeu.org/library/display_article.php?article_id=3

Bennett, Helen. *Humanism, What's That? A Book for Curious Kids* (New York: Prometheus, 2005). For ages 10 and up, this book might be too simple for some 14-year-olds. The circumstances given for a teacher's discussion of humanism with some of her students seem unrealistic, but the students ask questions your kids are likely to hear from their peers, and the teacher's answers are comprehensive and clear. Discuss the book with your kids; don't just hand it to them. It's a reasonable overview, and you can fill in the gaps. Activities and discussion questions mix suggestions that are appropriate for different ages and aren't clearly related to the text.

Pearson, Beth. "The Art of Creating Ethics Man." Originally appearing in *The Herald* of Scotland in January 2006, this outstanding article provides a summary of the latest research in moral development, quite directly opposing the usual perspective of religious adherents. A long excerpt is available at the British Humanist Association website at *www.humanism.org.uk/site/cms/contentViewArticle.asp?article=2134.*

Grayling, A.C. *Meditations for the Humanist: Ethics for a Secular Age* (London: Oxford University Press, 2003). One of the best available titles addressing humanist ethics through naturalistic reflections on human life.

International Humanist and Ethical Union (IHEU). "Statement of Fundamental Principles." *http://iheu.org/amsterdamdeclaration.* A shorter version is at *http://iheu.org/resolutions.*

Wisdom Quotes

www.wisdomquotes.com

Jone Johnson-Lewis, leader of the Northern Virginia Ethical Society has selected eloquent, thought-provoking quotations. Categories include "Humanism," "Ethics," "Compassion."

Books for the Kids

Association for Library Service to Children, "Recommended Book Lists"

www.ala.org/ala/alsc/alscresources/booklists/booklists.htm

Topics include "Holidays," "Growing Up Around the World," " Diversity," and more.

Barker, Dan. *Maybe Right, Maybe Wrong* (Amherst, NY: Prometheus, 1992). A classic and a winner. Ages 6–10.

Dobrin, Arthur. *Love Your Neighbor: Stories of Values and Virtues* (New York: Scholastic, 1999). Kids will want to read this delightfully illustrated book over and over. Stories are rich: In each one, there's more going on than the value in question. For example, different family types are presented, and settings and characters stimulate curiosity ("What is a cuscus?" "Where is Tashkent?"). Each story ends with a thoughtful question, not an obvious "moral." Used in the Ethical Culture curriculum described on p. 61. Pre-K to 6.

Gordon, Sol. *All Families Are Different* (Amherst, NY: Prometheus, 2000). Simple, nonjudgmental descriptions of all kinds of families, emphasizing that what really matters is that "you" (the reader) are loved. Ages 4–8.

Humphrey, Sandra McLeod. *It's Up to You . . . What Do You Do?* (ages 9–12) and *More If You Had to Choose What Would You Do?* (ages 7+) (Amherst, NY: Prometheus, 1999 and 2003). *If You Had to Choose . . .* was reviewed in *Parenting Beyond Belief*, and the stories in *It's Up to You* have much the same strengths and weaknesses. They are conversation starters more than stories. The situations and conflicts they describe are realistic, but characters are not developed. Sometimes, the questions at the end of the stories point to an obvious moral, but you and your child can make up your own questions.

Clegg, Luther B., et al. "How to Choose the Best Multicultural Books" in *Scholastic Books Parents' Resources, http://content.scholastic.com/browse/article .jsp?id=3757.* Article includes reviews of fifty children's books—ten each for five ethnic groups.

Cohen, Randy. *The Good, the Bad, and the Difference: How to Tell Right from Wrong in Everyday Situations* (New York: Doubleday, 2002). Reprints of the *New York Times Magazine* column "The Ethicist." Chapters include "Family Life" and "School Life," with replies to readers' criticisms. Don't miss "I Demand a Recant," describing how Cohen changed his mind after getting more information, demonstrating how people may justifiably change their minds. Witty answers to questions so down-to-earth that my grocer posted a column in the produce section. Ages 14 and up.

Helping Parents Find Books on Ethics for Kids

Council on Interracial Books for Children. "10 Quick Ways to Analyze Children's Books," *www.birchlane.davis.ca.us/library/10quick.htm.*

Linville, Darla. "Queer & Questioning Teens." *www.nypl.org/branch/features/ index2.cfm?PFID=160.* Reviews of twelve novels and story collections with gay teen characters.

Roberts, Lisen C., and Heather T. Hill. "Children's Books That Break Gender Role Stereotypes" (National Association for the Education of Young Children, 2003) *www.journal.naeyc.org/btj/200303/Books4Children.pdf*

Ethical Education Curricula

Lassen, Veronica, and Debbie Grieb. "Heart Talk for Kids" curriculum. "Our community has tried the 'Heart Talk' curriculum," says Jone Johnson-Lewis, Leader of the Northern Virginia Ethical Society. "It's based on the principles of Non-Violent Communication and is wonderfully humanistic. The teachers tell me it's one of the best they've worked with, for detailed instructions that help them feel confident about teaching. They only needed to make a couple of minor adaptations. Parents are using words like 'transformed' about how it's impacted their families." The curriculum has different modules for different age groups.

The curriculum is designed for use in established moral education programs. You could recommend it to your group's educator or use it in a parents' group that has been functioning for at least two years.

Outline, ordering information, sample lesson at *www.uucards.org/ lassen0807.php.*

Religious Education Committee of the American Ethical Union. "Love Your Neighbor: An Exploration of Values"—preschool through elementary age. Free download from American Ethical Union at *http://64.118.87.15/~aeuorg/ library/articles/Love_Your_Neighbor_exploration.pdf.* Each lesson is based on a story from Arthur Dobrin's *Love Your Neighbor* (reviewed with other books on moral reasoning), with lots of optional activities and ideas that parents can use a small groups or even one child. What's great about this curriculum is that it shows how to bring stories to life or your children, integrating with other experiences and leading to reflection.

Forgiveness

Spring, Janis A. *How Can I Forgive You? The Courage to Forgive, the Freedom Not to* (New York: HarperCollins, 2004). The examples and discussions in this book emphasize adult relationships and experiences, but it goes deeply into the principles and practices outlined in the "Steps to Seeking Forgiveness" in the Appendix. Also, if you have unresolved problems with your parents, this book might help you cope with pain that could otherwise affect your relationships with your own children.

Greater Good magazine. Symposium on forgiveness, including an article on how to apologize. *http://peacecenter.berkeley.edu/greatergood/archive/2004fallwinter/*

Experiencing and Appreciating Diversity
Nondiscriminatory Extracurricular Programs for Kids

> 4-H clubs serve 6.5 million urban and rural youth nationwide, with programs in science, engineering and technology, healthy living, and citizenship. 4-H groups are sponsored by extension programs at public universities and cannot discriminate on the basis of religion. Find a nearby club at *www.FourHCouncil.edu/find4H.aspx.*

> Camp Fire USA now serves both boys and girls. Camp Fire is "inclusive, open to every person in the communities we serve, welcoming children, youth and adults regardless of race, religion, or other aspect of diversity. [Our] programs are designed . . . to reduce . . . stereotypes and to foster positive intercultural relationships." Use the "Council Locator" at *www.campfire.org* to find a group near you.

> The National Camp Association (NCA) provides a free summer camp referral service online, offering personalized guidance and referrals for parents selecting a residential "sleepaway." All camps recommended by NCA "are accredited in accordance with government regulations and have received a positive evaluation from NCA and from parents." NCA does not accredit camps that have discriminatory policies. *www.summercamp.org*

> The Sierra Club Inner City Outings program provides low-income, inner-city youth with trips to the wilderness. "Is moving towards its long-term commitment to give every child in America an opportunity to have an outdoor experience." So far this program has developed activities in only a few states. *www.sierraclub.org/ico*

Programs for Ethical Education and Action
Facing History and Ourselves

> *www.facinghistory.org/campus/reslib.nsf*

This nonprofit offers teacher education, curriculum resource development, traveling exhibits (with study guides), community conversations, and other programs to promote tolerance and civic engagement by teaching about historical events such as the Holocaust and desegregation. Visit this site to find out how you can bring its programs to your children's schools or your community.

Tell your middle- and high-school-age kids about the "Be the Change" website with stories of students around the world who have found ways to make a difference. *www.facinghistory.org/Campus/bethechange.nsf/home?OpenForm*

Tolerance.org

www.tolerance.org

This award-winning website is a project of the Southern Poverty Law Center. With pages for parents, teachers, teens, and kids, this site is brimming with resources for promoting tolerance, fighting bigotry, and celebrating diversity. Look for the map to locate social justice groups in your community (*www .tolerance.org/maps/social_justice/index.html*). *Beyond the Golden Rule: A Parent's Guide to Preventing and Responding to Prejudice* is a 31-page handbook with age-specific advice, downloadable by clicking the book-cover icon at *www .tolerance.org/parents/index.jsp*.

Uno Hon, Ochen Idees[21]

Perry, Susan K. *Playing Smart: The Family Guide to Enriching, Offbeat Learning Activities* (Minneapolis: Free Spirit Publishing, 2001). Chapter 12, "Cultural Diversity: It's All Relative" is jam-packed with fascinating activities and information, including body language in different cultures and "Global Game-Playing." Order online at *www.BunnyApe.com*.

Notes

1. Darling, Nancy. "Parenting Style and Its Correlates." Clearinghouse on Elementary and Early Childhood Education EDO-PS-99-3, March 1999. Accessed May 2, 2008, from *www.athealth.com/Practitioner/ceduc/ parentingstyles.html*

2. Grusec, J.E., and J. J. Goodnow, "Impact of Parental Discipline on the Child's Internalization of Values: A Reconceptualization of Current Points of View," *Developmental Psychology, 30* (1994). Cited in Dobrin, Arthur, *Ethical People and How They Get to Be That Way* (in press), chapter 5.

3. Oliner, pp. 181–182.

4. Quoted in Pearson, Beth, "The Art of Creating Ethics Man," *The Herald* (Scotland), January 23, 2006.

5. Pearson, ibid.

6. Quoted by permission from Kidder, Rushworth M., *Moral Courage* (Institute for Global Ethics. All rights reserved.). This list first appears on page 10.

7. At one point in the movie *Jesus Camp*, a child of fundamentalist parents says that Galileo was right to renounce his scientific findings for religious reasons.

8. Quoted by permission. The complete list is at *www.ethicalstl.org/ sunschool.shtml* and in the first Appendix. Accessed May 2, 2008.

9. While there are concerns that Kohlberg's research is limited by its methodology and by its emphasis on reasoning about justice, it is undeniably useful in understanding the many levels and facets of moral understanding. For further exploration of these stages and their implications, see Dobrin, Arthur, *Ethical People and How They Got That Way* (in press), Chapter 3.

10. Callaghan, T., P. Rochat, A. Lillard, M.L. Claux, H. Odden, S. Itakura, S. Tapanya, and S. Singh, "Synchrony in the Onset of Mental State Reasoning: Evidence from 5 Cultures," *Psychological Science*. (At time of writing this article is still in press, and available online at *www.faculty.virginia.edu/ early-social-cognition-lab/reprints/reprints.html*. Accessed May 11, 2008.) Children in numerous cultures, both schooled and unschooled, were studied.

11. Kohn, pp. 34–36; Faber and Mazlish, pp. 174–176 (complete citations in Resources).

12. De Waal, Frans, *Peacemaking Among Primates* (Boston: Harvard University Press, 1990), p. 270.

13. Spring, Janice Abrahms, *How Can I Forgive You?* (New York: Harper-Collins, 2005), pp. 51–117.

14. De Waal, p. 270.

15. Kohn, Alfie, *Unconditional Parenting* (New York: Atria Books, 2005), p. 204.

16. Dobrin, Chapter 3.

17. Pearson, Beth, "The Art of Creating Ethics Man," *The Herald* (Scotland), January 23, 2006. Accessed February 15, 2008, from *www.humanism.org.uk/ site/cms/contentViewArticle.asp?article=2134*

18. When I attended a lecture by Paul Rusesabagina, the person on whose story the movie *Hotel Rwanda* is based, an audience member asked him how he

found the courage to protect and provide for the people he helped—sometimes at gunpoint. He replied that he was just being himself, a hotel manager, whose job was to take care of his guests. (Not surprisingly, his autobiography is titled *An Ordinary Man*. Proceeds of the book's sales are donated to a foundation that helps orphans and survivors of the Rwandan genocide.)

19. Adapted from the Camp Quest ethics curriculum. Used by permission.

20. This suggestion is inspired by Sen, Amartya, *Identity and Violence: The Illusion of Destiny* (New York: W. W. Norton, 2007). The book is really an extended essay; it's 240 pages but they're small pages. Written by a humanist and Nobel-winning economist, it *might* be worth reading with some high-school-age children. An argument against a worldview that divides people into "boxes" defined by religion, it also includes some very interesting personal anecdotes and discussions of cultural history. Some people might find it too repetitive, so you might prefer to try finding it at the library.

21. That's Spanish for "one," Japanese for "book," Russian for "many," and French for "ideas."

CHAPTER 3

Secular Family, Religious World

Jan Devor

The religious landscape of the United States is changing rapidly. As recently as 1990, nine out of ten U.S. residents claimed either Protestant or Catholic affiliation, while the nonreligious stood at 8 percent and non-Christian religions at 3 percent. Just a single generation later, a far richer diversity of beliefs is now the norm in our society. Three in four U.S. residents identify as Christians, one in ten identify with another religion, and one out of six are nonreligious.

Although the percentage of the nonreligious continues to rise, it is also clear that religion, in its many forms, will continue to be with us. Nonreligious people and their children meet and interact with people of many different faiths in schools, in the workplace, in politics, in sports, and socially. The Pluralism Project at Harvard University points out that "in the past forty years, immigration has dramatically changed the religious landscape of the United States."[1] The Pluralism Project's home page scrolls through an amazing variety of images of different religions practiced in the United States, representing Hindu, Buddhist, Christian, Sikh,

What Americans Believe

Believe in God	86%
Believe in heaven	81%
Believe in the Devil	70%
Believe in hell	69%
Bible is literally word of God	31%
Bible inspired by God	47%
God guided human evolution	38%
Evolution occurred without God	13%
Literal belief in biblical creation story	61%
Literal belief in biblical Flood and Ark[2]	60%
The principles of astrology are true[3]	25%

and Muslim beliefs among others. An estimated 2 million Muslims are currently in the United States,[5] as well as 700 Hindu temples.[6]

Christian belief is simultaneously more fervent and less "literate" in the United States than elsewhere in the developed world. In his book *Religious Literacy, What Every American Should Know and Doesn't,* Stephen Prothero notes that "many theological doctrines that Europeans now dismiss as fables—heaven and hell, and the devil—are enthusiastically affirmed by the vast majority of Americans. Out of every ten adults in the United States, more than nine believe in God, more than eight say that religion is important to them personally, and more than seven report praying daily."[7]

Children will see people who dress differently because of their religion, who seek alternative space for daily prayers in schools, who gather around the flagpole to pray, and who can't go to Friday night football games because it is the Sabbath. As a result of these and other interactions, even kids raised in a nonreligious home will have plenty of religious questions. They will observe other children going to church and wonder why they aren't going, ask what a church (or temple or mosque) is and why people go. Nonreligious parents will hear questions like "Who is God?" when their children are still in preschool.

There will also be questions specifically related to religious disbelief. The policies of organizations that preclude nonreligious people from membership, such as the Boy Scouts of America, will have to be explained to children who see their friends joining. Children raised in nonreligious homes will be asked about what they believe and may receive invitations to attend church, Bible study, or religious events with their friends.

As children watch the news, they will quickly come to understand that much of the turmoil in the world is motivated by religious beliefs. It will fall to nonreligious parents to offer information, facts, and their own thoughts to help children make sense of the religious influence, for better and worse, on the world.

More than ever before, families are now experiencing their own "pluralism projects" as family members date or marry people of various religious backgrounds. The old guideline restricting courtship and marriage to members of

Religious identification of U.S. adults[4]

	1990	(est.) 2001	2008
Christian	88%	77%	70%
Nonreligious	8%	14%	18%
Other religions	4%	9%	12%

" Whatever conclusions we reach about the reality of God, the history of this idea must tell us something important about the human mind and the nature of our aspiration. "

—Karen Armstrong,
A History of God

one's own faith tradition is less and less common. The result is both interreligious partnerships and partnerships between nonreligious and religious people. The heart chooses as it will! So how do you work through the issues raised by such partnerships? What are the family implications of religiously diverse in-laws? How does a nonreligious person live with a faithfully religious partner? What happens when children come along? This chapter is intended to help sort through these very questions.

> 66 **The "universal spirit" effect**
> When asked in a 2007 Gallup poll whether they believe in God, 86 percent of Americans said "yes." But if "I believe in a universal spirit" was included as an option, belief in God dropped to 78 percent, with 14 percent choosing "universal spirit." 99

By being a nonreligious parent in the United States, you have chosen the road less traveled. With this position comes the responsibility to educate your children about both religion and your non-religious stance. It is never enough to tell our children, "We don't believe," and leave it at that. Such a head-in-the-sand approach will put your child at a cultural and social disadvantage.

Europe and the United States are diametrically opposed in not one but two religious respects: belief *in* and knowledge *of* religion. The United States is both the most religiously enthusiastic and the least religiously literate country in the developed world. We believe with great fervor but know very little about the tenets, history, and elements of our own belief systems, let alone those of our neighbors. Europeans, on the other hand, show very low levels of religious belief[8] but, thanks to formal religious education in the schools, tend to have a very deep knowledge *of* religion.

Because U.S. schools shy away from teaching about religion, religious education falls to the parents—*all* parents. Religious parents can take advantage of whatever religious education is offered at church but have the detriment of a single, limiting point of view. Nonreligious parents reverse the polarity—the responsibility for the religious education of their children is primarily theirs, but unhindered by an organized doctrinal system, we have a greater opportunity to bring multiple perspectives to bear. And we *must*. Children who are ignorant of the elements of religion will be easy targets for religious zealotry and will be hobbled in their own free decision making. Ignorance is impotence. Knowledge is power.

Nonreligious parents must be ready to interact with their children around a host of religious topics. They need to know the laws governing the separation of church and state to make sure that boundaries in schools are not being crossed. Children must be prepared to interact productively with religious classmates, teammates, neighbors, and extended family members. Nonreligious parents will also want to be sure that their children know about the range and history of nontheistic thinking, from atheism to agnosticism to humanism to general freethought.

This chapter will help nonreligious parents sort through common questions and concerns related to the interface between nonreligious families and the religious world around us. We'll offer answers to some of the most common questions followed by activities to reframe many commonly religious practices into nonreligious activities and celebrate many of life's passages in nonreligious ways. The chapter concludes with resources for improving religious literacy, places to find alternative nonreligious clubs, and organizations that can help to sort through common church/state issues.

Questions and Answers

Q: Why is it important for my children to be religiously literate?

A: There are four main reasons religious literacy—knowledge *of* religion, as opposed to belief *in* it—is crucial:

1. **To understand the world.** Ours is a religiously inflected world. An overwhelming portion of the news—including medical, political, legal, military, and educational issues—include a large religious component. Add to this the fact that 90 percent of our fellow human beings express themselves and their understanding of the world through religion, and it becomes clear that ignorance of religion cuts our children off from understanding what is happening in the world around them—and why.

2. **To be empowered.** In the U.S. presidential election of 2004, candidate Howard Dean identified Job as his favorite book of the New Testament. That Job is actually in the Old Testament was a matter of small concern to many of us. But to an enormous swath of the religious electorate, Dean had revealed an unconscionable ignorance about the central narrative of their lives. For those people, Dean was instantly discounted, irrelevant. Because we want our children's voices heard in the many issues with a religious component, it is vital for them to demonstrate knowledge of that component.

3. **To make a truly informed opinion.** Nonreligious parents who claim their children are free to think for themselves about religion but never expose their children to religion or religious ideas are undermining their own stated values and shortchanging their kids. For kids to make a truly informed judgment about religion, they must have access to it.

■ ■ ■ ■ ■

I'd Like to Buy a Consonant

Went with Delaney to the "Dads 'n' Donuts" event at her school the other day. A fine selection. We finished eating and socializing in the gym a bit early, so we sauntered back to her kindergarten classroom. A couple of dads were already there, being toured by the hand around the classroom by their progeny. Laney grabbed my hand and we joined the conga line.

"This is where alllll of the books are," Laney said. "And that's the whiteboard. Here's the globe, and the puppets . . . and this," she gestured proudly, "is my desk!"

I barely heard the last two, since I was still riveted on the whiteboard, in the middle of which was the headline "THIS WEEK!!"—and under it, a glorious, radiant cross.

And what a cross it was! Every color of the rainbow! I'd have burst into a chorus of *Crown Him with Many Crowns* if not for eleven or twelve things.

It was only four weeks since we'd made the move to Atlanta, and here I stood in my daughter's public school classroom, gazing at church and state, locked in passionate embrace.

I was completely frozen and trying to stay that way. Time stopped, looked at me funny, then continued on its way. I knew that if I came to, I'd leap onto a chair and point and squeal "CROSS! CRAWWWWWWSSSSS!!" I'd have no choice: The point-and-shriek is mandated for all encounters with crosses in the bylaws of the Atheist-Vampire Accords of 1294.

A little girl entered my periphery, guiding her father by the hand. "And this," she said, pointing to the cross, "is what we're learning about this week!"

She paused for dramatic effect, then announced, with pedantic precision, "Lowercase t!"

—*Dale McGowan, from the blog* The Meming of Life

■ ■ ■ ■ ■

4. **To avoid the "teen epiphany."** Struggles with identity, confidence, and countless other issues are part and parcel of the teen years. Sometimes these struggles can add up to a genuine personal crisis, at which point well-meaning religious peers often pose a single question: "Don't you know about Jesus?" Jesus is presented as the answer to all problems, even those that seem insurmountable. A child with little or no exposure to religion can experience a kind of emotional hijacking in moments of personal crisis. The resulting conversion is more often than not to evangelical fundamentalism. A little knowledge about religion allows the teen to say, "Yes, I know about Jesus"—and to know that reliable answers to personal problems are better found elsewhere.

Q: It seems to me that there are different degrees of literacy. What should kids know to be religiously literate?

A: First, keep in mind that it is *religious* literacy we're after, not just Christian literacy. Comparative religion of many traditions is the difference between broad knowledge and indoctrination to a single point of view.

Here are some of the things your kids should eventually know:

- The basic stories and characters in the Bible (see below).
- The basic tenets of the five major religions (Judaism, Buddhism, Islam, Christianity, and Hinduism) and where in the world they are mainly practiced.
- Which religions believe in higher deities and which do not.
- The religious backgrounds of your extended families and what your relatives believe and why you do or don't believe as they do.

All of this should be presented as information, not as raves for or against various worldviews. Your children have the right to sort through the facts for themselves, but it is your responsibility to make sure that they have access to material on religion.

Because Christianity constitutes the dominant religious expression in our culture, some additional detail in that tradition will serve your children well. At minimum they should eventually know the following stories:

- The creation story with Adam and Eve.
- Noah and the Ark.
- Moses and the Ten Commandments.
- The exodus of the Jews from Egypt.

- John the Baptist.
- The life and death of Jesus.

Your children should know the difference between the Old and New Testaments. They should know that Jesus was raised a Jew and that it was the Roman government under a man named Pilate who sentenced Jesus to death.

Q: How can I help my children to be religiously literate without exposing them to indoctrination?

A: We think of indoctrination as the default, but indoctrination is actually harder to achieve than literacy and openness. Indoctrination is hard work. It requires cutting off information from other points of view and denying the right to question and to doubt. Including many cultures and traditions in your religious literacy plan and specifically inviting questioning and doubt is the antithesis of indoctrination. Do that and you're well on your way to a truly honest exploration.

Like other types of literacy, religious literacy comes in small bundles over time. It's not about sitting down with your children and reading the Bible—a plan that never works terribly well in any case. Instead, try these literacy boosters:

1. **Talk, talk, talk.** As Lucy Calkins notes in *Raising Lifelong Learners,* all literacy begins with oral language.[9] Toss tidbits of religious knowledge into your everyday conversations. If you drive by a mosque and your 4-year-old points out the pretty gold dome, take the opportunity to fill in some blanks: "Isn't that pretty? It's a kind of church called a mosque. People who go there pray five times every day, and they all face a city far away when they do it." No need to get into the Five Pillars of Islam. A few months later, you see a woman on the street wearing a *hijab* and connect it to previous knowledge: "Remember the mosque, the church with that gold dome? That's what some people wear who go to that church."

   As children mature, include more complex information—including good, bad, and ugly. No discussion of Martin Luther King, Jr., is complete without noting that he was a Baptist minister and that his religion was important to him. Likewise, no discussion of the American Revolution is complete without noting that the majority of the founders were religious skeptics of one stripe or another. Talk about the religious components of events in the news, from the stem cell debate to global warming to terrorism to nonviolence advocacy.

2. **Read myths of many traditions.** Myths make terrific bedtime stories. Start with creation myths from around the world, then move into the many rich mythic traditions—Greek, Roman, Norse, Native American, Pacific Islander, African, Asian, and more. And don't forget the Judeo-Christian stories. Placing them side by side with other traditions removes the pedestal and underlines what they have in common.

3. **Attend church on occasion with trusted relatives.** It is essential that children see the inside of a church—not necessarily every Sunday, but many times. Keeping them entirely separated from the experience leaves them open to the claim that something magical happens therein, a potent claim indeed during moments of emotional vulnerability. If you'd prefer not to go yourself, put them in the hands of churchgoing relatives who can be trusted to respect your position and to refrain from proselytizing.

   If your children are invited by friends, say yes—and go along. The conversations afterward can be some of the most productive in your entire religious education plan.

4. **Movies.** One of the most potent and effective means of achieving religious education painlessly is through movies with religious elements. For the youngest children this might be *Prince of Egypt, Little Buddha, Kirikou and the Sorceress,* and *Fiddler on the Roof.* By middle school, it's *Jason and the Argonauts, Gandhi, Bruce Almighty, Evan Almighty,* and *Kundun.* High schoolers can see and enjoy such meaty fare as *The Last Temptation of Christ, Seven Years in Tibet, Romero, Schindler's List, Jesus Camp,* and *Inherit the Wind.* A more extensive list of suggested films can be found in the Appendix, but this abbreviated list alone brings a child into contact with eight different religious systems and both the positive and negative influences of religion in history.

   Special gem: Whatever you do, don't forget *Jesus Christ Superstar.* Nonreligious parents may roll their eyes at the thought of seeing this movie, forgetting how subversive and thought-provoking this retelling of the last days of Christ is. There are no miracles; the story ends with the crucifixion, not the resurrection; and Judas is the hero, urging Jesus not to forget about the poor as the ministry becomes something of a personality cult. Put it in your Netflix queue. You'll thank me!

Q: My sister-in-law babysits my 6-year-old daughter at her home once a week, and I do the same for her son once a week. I am grateful for the help, but my daughter has begun coming home full of Bible stories and religious ideas. It turns out they watch religious videos every time. I feel as if my sister-in-law is crossing a boundary, even if her intentions are good. What can I do to protect my daughter from indoctrination without being disrespectful?

A: First, I would make sure that my sister-in-law is aware of my beliefs about religion. This might seem a scary prospect, but it's a necessary step and almost always goes better than we think it will. She may be showing the videos without realizing that you are not comfortable with these activities. If she asserts the right to show and talk about whatever she wants to, you have a choice: Find other daycare arrangements or begin the discussion with your child about the variety of beliefs and her right to make her own decisions. Depending on your child, it might not be a bad thing after all—an opportunity to practice early engagement with a variety of ideas.

Q: How can I help my kids respond to pressure from religious peers—from "You're going to hell" to "You need to accept Jesus"?

A: You don't want their first exposure to such ideas to be from peers. It's important that your kids hear about hell from you first. Inoculate them from fear by dismissing the idea, not just as wrong, but also as the profoundly silly idea it is. "Would God really send good people to hell just because they didn't believe in him?"

Second, give them specific language by modeling at home. Responses should be short and delivered calmly and with confidence. "I don't believe that." "I believe that Jesus was just a good person." "It's okay for people to believe different things." "I can change my mind a thousand times if I want." "A good God wouldn't punish people for honest doubts."

It's also important to moderate your own reaction. We parents tend to worry about these things much more than the kids do.

Q: My extended family all lives in the area. Each week we have Sunday dinner at one of our houses. An extended religious grace is said before every meal, and my kids' eyes always go to me to see what I'm doing during grace. I don't want to appear hypocritical, but I also want to model respect for the benign traditions of others. What is the best way to deal with this—and what should I suggest to the kids?

A: Whatever you do, decide *ahead of time* what is appropriate when you go to other people's homes who pray before eating. Talk about this with your children so they are not at a loss as to what to do and so they can be involved in deciding what's best. *Do you think we should bow our heads? Say Amen? Sit quietly?* Be very specific so that your children feel comfortable. No need to all respond alike: Allow them to find their personal comfort level. Talk about the precise issues you just raised (personal integrity versus respect for others).

Most nonreligious parents choose to bow their heads as a sign of respect for a benign tradition. Many choose to forgo the "amen" at the end, since the word literally means "I agree." There is no single best approach, and the working out of the issues is great practice for kids.

Q: What about when the family comes to our completely secular home? I've begun to feel the need to express my preference that we do something different when dinner's in our space. What are my options?

A: You are right: In your home you should do what seems appropriate to you, just as they do in theirs. Otherwise, you risk demeaning your own values and views by appearing to be ashamed of them. If this means not going along with the family's extended prayer at mealtimes, then I would suggest you create alternate ways to begin the meals in your home—a toast, applause for the cook, a ritual where everyone says what they value about the gathering, a moment of silent reflection, or a secular blessing that is appropriate for your family. Announce with enthusiasm that you have created this especially for your family gatherings in your home.

It's best to make the announcement *before* someone else has offered or invited a prayer. Ask for a moment of silence immediately when people are at the table and then launch into what you have prepared. Do this with the pleasant confidence that you are doing something good, then just continue on with the festivities. If negative comments are made, frame your answer in terms of fairness: You can have your way at your home, I will do it my way in my home, and all should be fine!

Nonreligious parents across the country report, to their surprise, that the reaction is better than they had expected and often downright positive—including such surprised responses as, "My goodness—that was so *beautiful!*" The unspoken additional thought is, *"And it didn't even mention Jesus!"*

If a relative continues to insist that a group prayer be said, you might protest that you simply have too much respect for the words of Jesus to allow it: "When you pray, do not be like the hypocrites, for they love to pray standing in the synagogues and on the street corner to be seen by men. . . . When you pray, go into your room, close the door and pray to your Father in secret" (Matthew 6:5–6).

That often ends the debate—and constitutes a fine display of religious literacy on your part!

Many secular families adopt everyday mealtime rituals that serve the same emotional purpose as grace—slowing down, reflecting, acknowledging—without the religious overtones. See the Activities section at the end of this chapter for some ideas.

Q: Wednesday night is "church night" in our town, and our son is constantly being invited by his friends to the local church youth group. He is told that it "rocks" with lots of cool music, and the leader is "awesome!" This comes up in the summer too, because the camp "all" the kids go to is religiously based. What should I do? Do I let him go to these activities?

A: Start by remembering your goal—not to protect your child from all religious experience and information, but to protect them from an emotional hijacking that interferes with their own reasoned decision making. Much depends on the maturity and developmental level of your child. Is he developmentally ready to make decisions on his own, to sort out thoughts and feelings without succumbing to peer pressure? Would your relationship with your child permit an open discussion afterwards?

It's also important to learn what you can about the program in question. Can your child ask questions and voice disbelief? Is there a stated attempt to "win souls for Christ"? Regardless of the answers, children 12 and under should generally be accompanied by a parent. Any program that prohibits this—and there are many—is specifically seeking to proselytize the child and should be declined.

Teenagers, on the other hand, will often see a request to accompany as an indication that the parent does not trust the child, even if it is the program or event that is really in question. In general, it is far wiser to let your child go and then talk about the experience than to present the youth group as "forbidden fruit." If you have developed both religious literacy and critical thinking skills over the years, your teenager should be entirely capable of processing the experience and even gaining a great deal from it.

You can also find interesting and FUN secular or religiously low-key alternatives to religious camps and youth groups. Camp Quest, the first residential summer camp for the children of nonreligious parents, now has six locations in North America and a new program beginning in the U.K. The Unitarian Universalist denomination has nonsectarian family camps and youth group programs for teens, and countless local youth organizations are available that include no religious component whatsoever. (For more on secular community alternatives, see Chapter 8, "Finding and Creating Community.)

Q: My 8-year-old daughter has told us that she wants to go to church like the rest of her friends. Now what?

A: Ahh, the power of peer pressure. We can write this off as parents, but children wanting to go to church and be like their friends is powerful and must be addressed directly. There are several options:

1. Give children something to say that you do on Sunday as a family (even as simple as going to the park or having a big Sunday breakfast together).

2. Seek out a religiously liberal church like Unitarian Universalism, Humanistic Judaism, or Ethical Cultural Society, all of whom can provide the community your child is seeking without indoctrinating them with dogma.

3. Help them recognize and articulate the endless benefits of *not* going to church on Sunday.

4. Talk about the ways in which meaning and reflection are woven into your everyday lives—and that they do not require a special place and time.

As noted above, you can also allow children to attend church with their friends, assuming you are comfortable with the program in question and/or attend with them. This alone will often put the fascination to rest.

Q: My preschooler told me that she believes in God. How should I respond to her?

A: A preschooler who does *not* experiment with a variety of beliefs would be very unusual. Depending on the age and maturity of the child, a simple, "That's interesting" might suffice, or you might ask why—the time-tested beginning of many fabulous conversations.

Don't feel the need to jump-start skepticism or debunk claims too vigorously at this point. It's more important that children at this age develop a love of questioning and hypothesizing than be shepherded toward "the right answers." Let them take positions, change positions, try on different hats. It's good practice.

Children will come back to you when they are ready and ask what you think, at which point you can explain your beliefs. Avoid saying, "Our family doesn't believe in God." Families don't believe; individuals do. Instead you might say, "I believe such and such, but a lot of people believe differently, and that's okay."

It is also good to give children permission to change their minds. Remind children that they have permission to change their beliefs a thousand times if they wish as new evidence and experience present themselves. They should keep thinking about religious questions, gather information as they grow up, and keep an open mind. You will always be interested in what they are thinking! It's the parent's job to keep an open mind as their children verbalize various beliefs or disbeliefs. Don't be upset as children try out various thoughts. A complete and varied exploration of ideas will have the firmest foundation.

Q: What's wrong with simply raising my children as atheists? Why must I pretend that I think religion might also have valid answers?

A: Two different questions. Let's dispense with the second one first.

There is *never* a need for you to pretend about what you think. Quite the contrary: It is impossible to parent from a place of genuine integrity if you pretend to have convictions you don't really have—or worse yet, pretend to have none at all. You will and should have an *influence* on your child's own developing worldview, but influence and indoctrination are two different things. Only the former is good.

I came to my own conclusions about the big questions as a result of long reflection, introspection, study, and discourse. I'm proud to have worked my way toward it. It's that effort that makes my worldview a deep and valued part of who I am. I not only know what I believe—I know *why* I believe it, because I was present and active every step of the way. I'll bet it's the same for you. So do we really want to deprive our kids of the journey that makes that final choice so meaningful?

Now there are times when a parent *must* substitute his or her judgment for the judgment of the child. You have to decide whether a bag of chips is really a wise replacement for dinner. You have to set and enforce boundaries, define household responsibilities, and insist on honesty and fair play. As kids get older, you'll want to involve them more and more in these decisions, but until their developing judgment is up to the task, a parent must make certain decisions *for* the child.

But is selecting a belief system one of them? If it was necessary for children to declare a personal worldview at the age of 5, parents would indeed have to choose it for them. And that's the way it's been done for millennia, of course:

A child is simply informed that she is a Christian, or a Hindu, etc. Richard Dawkins's reaction to a photo caption in *The Guardian* several years ago, in which three children in a Nativity play were referred to as "A Sikh child, a Muslim child, and a Christian child," illustrates this perfectly. "No one bats an eye," he noted in a recent speech. "But just imagine if the caption had read 'a Monetarist child, a Keynesian child, and a Marxist child.' Ridiculous! Yet not one bit less ridiculous than the other."[10]

By the time she is old enough to begin searching for her own place in the world, it's difficult for a labeled child to think objectively about the declaration she's worn like a robe for as long as she can remember. If she decides to take it off, it becomes an emotionally charged act of defiance, a rejection of something given to her. And in some cases, the natural urge to separate from her parents can lead the teenager to throw it off *because* her parents gave it to her.

If there is one highest value in freethought, it must surely be the freedom to think for oneself—and something as personal and all-defining as a worldview is most meaningful and enduring when it is freely chosen.

Teach your child tolerance, critical thinking, empathy, and a love of the truth, then trust him to decide what those values add up to. They will not, I'll wager, add up to a person who speaks in tongues and believes that Jesus appears in tortillas and hates homosexuals. They may add up to one of the more benign religious expressions—a liberal Anglican, for example, or a Congregationalist, Unitarian, or Quaker. Or they may add up to secular humanism. Regardless, you owe it to your child to preserve the space around her to make her own choice without having to deal with someone else's idea of the right choice—even if that someone else is her loving parent.

Q: How can I help my children think critically about religion without indoctrinating them to *my* point of view?

A: Children should indeed be invited to think critically about religion. Make it clear that the factual claims of religion and science alike are hypotheses and that hypotheses stand or fall on their ability to withstand scrutiny. This isn't indoctrination—it simply removes religion from the protected category it has traditionally demanded.

Beyond that, here are three ingredients for an indoctrination-free home:

1. **Make a serious effort at evenhandedness.** In addition to causing undoubted harm, religion has at times had a positive influence on people and events. Just as a child of Christian parents is unlikely to hear much

about the ill effects of religion, a child of nonreligious parents will often grow up in an environment skewed hard in the opposite direction. It requires a conscious effort on the part of a nonreligious parent to keep the playing field as level as honesty permits—to balance dinnertable mutterings about televangelists and praying presidents with an occasional reference to Martin Luther King, Jr., Mahatma Gandhi, Elizabeth Fry, Gautama Buddha, and Corrie ten Boom, all of whom were energized by, and made positive use of, religion and religious ideas.

Why make the effort? Because *genuine critical thinking calls for finding and hearing the best advocates of both sides of an issue.* If critical thinking is a sincere value for you as a parent, giving equal opportunity to the best of religion is a no-brainer.

2. **Provide unfiltered access to religious ideas.** Do you have a religious friend or relatives, or two, or twelve? Find one you trust (i.e., one who will forgo the threats of hell) and arrange a time for the kids to ask him or her questions about beliefs. If the kids ask to see what church is all about, take 'em! In short, build up their critical thinking skills, then trust them to use them. Follow up with a chat about your own convictions, then invite them to think for themselves.

3. **Specifically invite them to doubt and to question *your* conclusions.** I give myself permission to express my convictions in no uncertain terms. But I specifically invite my kids to question my ideas, to think all they want about them, to disagree with them, and to change their minds a thousand times as they consider them. I have told them that I would rather have them think for themselves and disagree with me than share my opinions only because I hold them.

The introduction of doubt is not an insignificant accomplishment. It has the power to achieve precisely what you are seeking. This is why doubt is such a serious sin in orthodox religious traditions—and why we must champion it as the highest intellectual virtue. Parents who honestly make these efforts will influence their children without indoctrinating them. More importantly, they will earn their children's respect and gratitude in the long run for having allowed their minds to breathe freely and without fear as they grew.

Q: I am a secular humanist who recently married a devout Lutheran. We plan to have a family soon. How do we create a cohesive family unit with these differing faith issues? Do we need to be on the same page about religion as we do about discipline? Are there techniques for sorting out this question?

A: In many areas of parenting—discipline, for example—it is essential for parents to be on the same page. But it is entirely possible to raise children in a family with a variety of religious perspectives. What it does require is that parents set up ground rules to live by. Rule Number 1: No proselytizing! The fine art of active listening and communication has to be perfected. Use of "I" statements is an integral part of this communication ("I believe that there is a heaven") as is the invitation to seek other points of view ("but your father believes differently").

A religious education plan must be agreed upon. Partners may want to seek out professional help to bring out all of the areas that need to be talked about surrounding this issue. (See Pete Wernick's essay in *Parenting Beyond Belief* to get an insight into Pete and his wife's journey as they raised their son in a religiously diverse family.)

> ❝ I have known many good people who did not believe in God. But I have never known a human being who was good who did not believe in people. ❞
>
> —John Lovejoy Elliott (1868–1942), Ethical Culture leader in New York

Q: I have decided that I want to take our young children to church. Going to church was a positive experience for me growing up, but I have not gone as an adult. My husband is an atheist and can't stand the idea of his children going to church. Should I take them over his objections?

A: Goodness no. NEVER take your child(ren) to a religious organization over your partner's objections. Such an act would constitute a serious breach of trust and respect. If it became a point of contention with your husband, going to church would not be a positive experience for the children no matter how wonderful the experience itself might be.

At the same time, it wouldn't be fair to you for his position to become the default. Instead, try to talk it through together. What exactly is it that he hopes to avoid, and what is it you hope to achieve? Discuss the specifics of the program your child would be exposed to instead of simply talking about "going to church" in the abstract. It should be possible to find a denomination or program that satisfies you both—or at least represents a bearable compromise. If no compromise appears possible, seek professional counseling. It is not necessary for parents to have the same belief system, but it is mandatory that they agree on *how* to disagree and what the ground rules are for dealing with religion and the children.

Q: My son is on a basketball team, and I was shocked when one of the captains asked that he be allowed to lead a team prayer before the game. The coach has agreed to it. How do I handle this?

A: Assuming your son is old enough to begin taking positions of this kind—generally age 12 and up—it is best if you facilitate your child's own decision making rather than substitute your own. Knowing in advance that this will happen can allow you to work though some scenarios with your child. Some kids won't care, preferring to simply kneel and remain silent. Faced with this situation, my own son just stood outside of the kneeling circle politely and did not participate. Others might choose a more active approach.

You might want to look at the religious diversity of the members of the team. If there are other players besides your son who are not participating, you might want to point out to the coach that the prayer is not comfortable for several members of the team. He might be sensitive enough to talk with the captain. In some cases, your son might be willing to take a stand even if he is the only one affected. If so, don't miss the opportunity to praise his willingness to stand on principle, then help him to approach it reasonably and well.

As for the legality of this activity, it depends on where and how the praying is initiated. Private institutions can do as they wish in this area. Public teams cannot have a coach or teacher lead or suggest a prayer, but the team members are permitted to institute the practice independently.

Q: My daughter is constantly being asked to pray around the flagpole at her school with her friends. How can I help her say no and still be in that social group?

A: A single request politely declined would be fine. But if your daughter has politely refused to pray around the flagpole and is still being asked, this can amount to harassment, depending on the way it is asked and the ardor of the group. If her friends are persisting because they mean well and genuinely seek her companionship, they might simply need to be thanked for their good intentions and informed that her decision not to join them is final.

If she feels comfortable with the group of friends, she could engage the question of why she will not be joining them. If the invitation is mean-spirited, I would suggest that she not try to fit in with this group but find another set of friends. Joining a sports team, singing group, journalism group, or any afterschool program can help with switching groups. Talking with the school counselor may generate some ideas about how to handle this as well as different groups to join. It will also give the administration some information about how students are feeling about this activity.

Q: My son wants to become a Boy Scout like all of his friends. We think that the Boy Scouts are homophobic, theistic elitists and certainly don't want our son joining. What do we say to our son, and are there alternatives to the Boy Scouts?

A: Although it's a good rule to involve our children in ethical decisions that impact them, some important decisions are fraught with issues too advanced or complex for children to understand or grapple with until they are older. Weighing the moral costs of membership in a group with abhorrent social positions is one situation in which parents must make the decision for very young children, and whether to join the Boy Scouts is one of the most common. We were faced with this decision in our own family when our son asked to join the Boy Scouts in early elementary school. At the time, we simply said that we disagreed with a number of positions that the Boy Scouts of America take as a group and thus he wouldn't be joining. In the later elementary years, we talked to our son about the specific policies of the Boy Scouts that we believed were ethically wrong, such as excluding potential members and leaders on the basis of belief or sexual orientation.

Fortunately there are now some alternatives to the Boy Scouts. Research Spiral Scouts or Earth Scouts online (see the Resources section for URLs), or create a program yourself after the model of the British Acorn Scouting Program.[11]

Q: Our first child is on the way, and I'm wondering if I should explain to my very religious mother that we will be parenting without religion—or should I just deal with it as issues come up?

A: You are going to have to address the issue of not raising your child in a specific religious faith sooner rather than later with your mother. The question of baptism will come up almost immediately, and you will have to lay your cards on the table at that point anyway.

Q: Okay, I'll take the initiative with Mom. What's the best approach?

A: Make a date specifically for this purpose. Sit down in person if at all possible—and under *no* circumstances do this by email!

Most family conflict is not about disagreement, but about feeling dishonored and unheard. Approach with the intention to hear and honor each others' concerns, *knowing that you may not actually come to agreement*. Listen first, then restate your mother's concerns in your own words to let her know she has been understood. Avoid blame, avoid "but" statements ("I know you think church is important, but . . ."), and find common ground.[12]

For example, assure your mother that, although you are not raising your child in a specific religious tradition, you will not be excluding religious thought from the child's life—that you will, in fact, be pursuing a broad religious education, then allowing your child to decide for him- or herself what to believe when the child is old enough to do so.

Most important of all, encourage her help in this endeavor. Let her know that she will be invited to share her beliefs and traditions with the child, so long as she respects the child's right to question, doubt, and decide for herself. Knowing that she can share her faith and that you intend to raise the child with many of the values and ethics that you have been taught will go a long way in relieving tension and preserving relationships.

Q: My kids ask why people believe all these different things about religion and who is right and who is wrong. What should I tell them?

A: Depending on the developmental level of your child, there are different answers to these questions. When children are little, they might just be asking what you believe about religion. When they are in upper elementary and concerned with right and wrong and fairness, a utilitarian answer might be appropriate: "You can decide for yourself. Some would say that the religion that is right is the one that makes you the most tolerant, respectful, and good person." As they get older, you can go into religious claims that are demonstrably false (historical claims in the Bible, for example), those which are demonstrably true, and other claims which are completely nonempirical and will always be in question. But at every stage, in every way possible, underline the fact that she has the right to decide for herself.

Q: We have decided not to circumcise our newborn son, and my Jewish parents are really upset. How do I handle this?

A: The decision to not circumcise your child is often difficult for Jewish grandparents to accept. You should enter into the discussion with your parents so that they have a chance to air their opinions and you yours. It is likely that you will have to agree to disagree, but you will have some heavy hitters on your side: The Council on Scientific Affairs, the American Medical Association, and dozens of similar organizations around the world have issued statements calling the practice "not recommended" because of associated risks.[13] The United

States is the only remaining developed country in which the practice of circumcision is still somewhat common. Even so, many American HMOs no longer cover it.

Q: We have raised our children without religion but lately I have heard them being disrespectful to people expressing religious beliefs. What should I say to them?

A: You should tell them that because your family respects people of different races and abilities and aren't rude to them, they also have to extend the same courtesy to people of various religious faiths. It's a matter of being a good person yourself. You can also make a distinction between respect for people and respect for ideas. Although ideas must earn respect, people are inherently deserving of respect.

Another way you might approach this is (if you'll excuse the phrase) by inviting he who is without sin to cast the first stone. A friend of mine once described a moment of arrogance from his preteen son: "I just don't understand how people can believe stupid things that make no sense," said the boy.

My friend thought for a moment, then said, "Uh huh. Say, could you go get me a soda from the basement?"

"I . . . but . . ." his son stammered. "I can't go into the basement by myself."

"Why not?"

"I . . . I just can't!"

"Oh," my friend said gently. "And does *that* make sense?"

The point was made: We *all* have irrational beliefs and fears. It's part of being human. My friend then shared some of his own irrational quirks with his son. There's nothing wrong with reasoned criticism, but before we throw too many stones, we have to acknowledge that no matter how thoroughly we think we've attended to our own rationality, we all live in glass houses. And that's not entirely bad. If nothing else, it can keep us humble.

I would also ask the parents to take a good hard look at what they are verbalizing about people of religious faith. Children often imitate parental behavior, and lessons about how to treat others start at home.

> " I feel no need for any other faith than my faith in the kindness of human beings. I am so absorbed in the wonder of earth and the life upon it that I cannot think of heaven and angels. "
>
> —Pearl S. Buck, human rights activist and Nobel Laureate for Literature

Activities

Reflections

All ages

Reframe the idea of prayer to match your nonreligious stance, perhaps using the term *promise* ("Be sure to say your promises before bed"). Unitarian Universalist Kathleen Carpenter offers these secular graces:

- *Earth, we thank you for this food, for the rest and home and all things good, for wind and rain and sun above, but most of all for those we love.*
- *In the light of love and the warmth of this family, we gather to seek, to sustain, and to share.*

You might also consider joining hands around the table to enjoy about a half minute of silence together. Ask the kids (and adults) to take that time to go inside themselves and think about whatever they wish—something about the day just passed, a hope for the next day, good thoughts for someone who is sick, or nothing at all. And make it clear that they're welcome to pray if they'd like to.

But here's the key: It's a *personal*, private moment. Don't include a practice of sharing thoughts afterwards, or it quickly devolves into a spitting contest for who was thinking the most lofty thought ("You know what *I* was thinking about? *I* was thinking about *homeless children.*") Kids will try this at first. Just nod and change the subject. Eventually, they figure out that it really is a private moment, which changes the nature of it.

When you have guests, simply tell them (before anyone can launch into prayer) that we begin our evening meal with a moment of silent reflection, during which they may pray, meditate, or simply sit quietly as they wish.

Book Talk

All ages

After reading some of the books in the resource section as a family or with your child, talk about what you think of the stories. What do you believe? How were these stories passed on? Play telephone (a.k.a. "Chinese whispers") and point out how things get mixed up traveling from one person to the next. What human principles are the stories talking about? Could we agree with those without having a belief in God?

Writing Your Own Chapter

Age 6+

Read *What I Believe, Kids Talk About Faith* by Debbie and Tom Birdseye. Have members of your family write short chapters about what they believe and what guides their choices in life.

Be of Service

Age varies

The secular and religious worlds can and often do unite around the idea of service to the world we live in. Find places in your community that allow families to do good works. Make lunches at a homeless shelter. Build together at a Habitat for Humanity site. March for peace. Package toiletries for runaway youth. Make Birthday Boxes for young kids in shelters, or help pack and distribute food at a food pantry/food shelf.

Make a Bedtime Ritual

All ages

Create a bedtime poem that your family can enjoy. Ours was "All tucked in, roasty, toasty, give me a kiss goodnight. Sweet dreams 'til morning comes. I love you. Goodnight." Kids love the security of the repetition of a bedtime blessing, but it needn't be God-focused.

Look into Current Events

Ages 7–18

When your child has an assignment to report on a current event, go online and find stories about current church/state issues or the Boy Scouts' exclusionary policies. Read and talk about them with your family. By way of contrast, research Spiral Scouts and talk about their basic principles (*www.SpiralScouts.org*).

Frontline programs offer a rich assortment of shows touching on religious issues. See *www.pbs.org/wgbh/pages/frontline/shows/religion*.

For high school youth, investigate the Pennsylvania court case in which the Dover public schools were sued by a group of parents who were fighting to have intelligent design labeled a religious belief and thus taken out of the classroom. A wonderful documentary on *Nova* titled "Judgment Day: Intelligent Design on Trial" offers a behind-the-scenes look at what may be the most important trial in the history of public school science education in the United States. Watch the whole program online at *www.pbs.org/wgbh/nova/id/program.html.*

Be Informed and Informative with Your School District

Parents

Make an appointment with your school's principal, chair of the Board of Education in your district, or the district's superintendent *before* there is a problem to talk about the district's policy on separation of church and state.

Create a Religiously Mixed Partnership Discussion Group

Parents

Form a group of friends who are in mixed marriages/partnerships of religious and nonreligious perspectives. Arrange to meet once a month to talk over issues. Form a Meetup for the topic in your city at *www.Meetup.com*, Craigslist it, or simply put up a notice in the local supermarket and library.

Word Association for Mixed Marriages

Parents

Take this list of words and talk about their meaning to you and your partner. See if you and your partner can agree on (1) which words both of you could use with your children, (2) which are too loaded to use, and (3) which you could create your own family meaning for. Sample words: *altar, amen, awe, baptize, bible, blessing, benediction, born again, Christ, communion, church, confession, covenant, crucifixion, devil, divine, enlightenment, evil, faith, God, gospel, grace, heaven, hell, holy, Holy Spirit, Holy Ghost, Jehovah, Jesus, Lord, miracle, mystery, original sin, pray, prayer, predestination, priest, prophecy, prophet, redemption, resurrection, revelation, sacrament, sacred, salvation, saved, savior, sin, son of God, spirit, spiritual, spirituality, temple, testament.*

Look into Unitarian Universalism

All ages

Consider taking part in a Unitarian Universalist Church where all belief traditions are honored and respected, and your family can start its own traditions. This denomination is creedless and allows for people to come together in community for social action and for thoughts on how to live an ethical life. The church is based on seven Purposes and Principles, which are the following:

- The inherent worth and dignity of every person.
- Justice, equity, and compassion in human relations.
- Acceptance of one another and encouragement to spiritual growth in our congregations.
- A free and responsible search for truth and meaning.
- The right of conscience and the use of the democratic process within our congregations and in society at large.
- The goal of world community with peace, liberty, and justice.
- Respect for the interdependent web of all existence of which we are a part.

Role-Play 1: Engaging Sensitive Issues with Religious Relatives

Parents

Before engaging such topics as baptism, not going to church/temple/mosque, and other sensitive issues across religious lines in your extended family, role-play with your partner what you are going to say. Which approaches seem likely to increase tension, and which decrease it? Write down the best answers and practice them. You will feel much more comfortable when the questions come along if you have thought the answers through ahead of time.

Role-Play 2: Anticipate Sensitive Questions from the Kids

Parents

The greatest and most important questions come from our kids without warning. Role-play answering the questions that your children will surely ask:

- Who is God?
- Why don't we go to church/temple/mosque?
- Are we going to hell because we don't go to church? (Don't feel the need to say, "Well, some people believe we are." The doctrine of hell exists solely to paralyze thought. Dismiss it out of hand as a silly, human-made idea that a good God would never allow.)
- Why don't you believe in God?
- What do you believe in?

Write and practice the best answers to these questions. Role-playing can also draw out differences between parenting partners, which can lead to productive discussions between the two of you!

Role-Play 3: Help Kids Prepare for Questions and Comments They Will Hear

Age 7+

Kids are also certain to hear certain questions and comments about religious belief: *Do you believe in God? Why don't you go to church? You have to believe or you'll go to hell! You can't be good without God, and many others.* Ask your kids what they could say if they hear one of the above or something similar.

Revisit Your Own Religious Past

Parents

Visit the church/temple/mosque of your childhood religious tradition. Talk to your children about what you liked about going there and what you disliked. You can do this during the week or by attending a service.

Engage in Religious Anthropology

Age 7+

Take your children to various services in town and talk about the religion and their religious practices. Push the boundaries by visiting a Sikh gurdwara, a Mormon church, a Hindu temple. Think of it as cultural anthropology, exposing your kids to human diversity.

As you drive around town, talk to the kids about what others believe as you pass their places of worship—and why you don't believe those same things. Car time is the perfect captive time for conversation!

The Religious Diversity Film Festival

All ages

Watch movies together on occasion that include themes from various religious traditions. We're not talking about heavy-handed films that treat religion with kid gloves, but the many entertaining and enlightening films that dig into the real essence of religion and culture—both positive and negative. As your children give their opinions about the religious ideas given in the movie, you can begin a dialogue.

Some suggestions for movies exploring religious themes:

- *Heaven Can Wait* (PG): Comedy about a football player who dies and claims it is a mistake. Ages 7+.
- *Oh, God!* (PG): Comedy with George Burns playing God. A supermarket manager claims he talks with God. Ages 7+.
- *Little Buddha* (PG): Tibetan monks believe that an American boy is the next reincarnation of the Buddha. Good introduction to Buddhism for elementary children. Ages 7+.
- *Jesus Christ Superstar* (G): A subversive musical takes on the story of Jesus: no miracles or resurrection depicted, and Judas is the hero! Ages 7+.
- *Fiddler on the Roof* (G): The musical story of a family of Russian Jews, their life, trials, and traditions. All ages.
- *The Ten Commandments* (G): Somewhat dated but classic movie on the creation of the Ten Commandments. Many parents question the rating due to the scene in which infants are slain by the fog-like Angel of Death. Ages 11+.
- *Bruce Almighty* (PG-13): Bruce Almighty becomes disillusioned with God and struggles with what is divine. Ages 11+.
- *Romero* (PG-13): The life of an activist priest. Ages 11+.
- *Gandhi* (PG): The life and times of a great leader. Ages 11+ (primarily due to length).
- *Jesus Camp* (PG-13): A disturbing look at how an evangelical group indoctrinates young children at a summer camp. Ages 12+.
- *Schindler's List* (R): The efforts of one man to save a group of Jews during the Holocaust. For older youth and young adults. Ages 14+.

(See Appendix I for a more extensive list of films to encourage religious literacy.)

Resources

Religious Literacy

Boritzer, Ethan. *What Is God?* (Ontario: Firefly Books, 1990). Broadens the definition of God and underlines our interconnected to all things.

Bennett, Helen. *Humanism, What's That? A Book for Curious Kids* (Amherst, NY: Prometheus Books, 2005). For older elementary children who want to understand the basics of Humanism.

Gunney, Lynn Tuttle. *Meet Jesus: The Life and Lessons of a Beloved Teacher* (Boston: Skinner Publishing, 2007). This book will give the elementary child a basic, naturalistic view of Jesus and the parables.

Gellman, Marc. *Does God Have a Big Toe?* (New York: HarperCollins, 1989). Tells the Bible stories in a humorous fashion. A sure-fire hit with the kids.

Hastings, Selina. *The Children's Illustrated Bible* (New York: DK Publishing, 1994). Tells the stories of the Old and New Testaments with excellent illustrations.

Birdseye, Debbie Holsclaw, and Tom Birdseye. *What I Believe: Kids Talk About Faith* (New York: Holiday House, 1996). This book presents six different kids from six different religious backgrounds to tell the story of what they believe.

Osborne, Mary Pope. *One World Many Religions: The Way We Worship* (New York: Random House, 1996). Excellent world map and time line. A fair look at all religions.

Prothero, Stephen. *Religious Literacy: What Every American Needs to Know—and Doesn't* (New York: HarperCollins, 2007). Chapter 6 gives clear definitions for religious terms. Best for parents to get a clear understanding of concepts to put into kid language.

McGowan, Dale, et al. *Parenting Beyond Belief* (New York: AMACOM, 2007). The Glossary in PBB is an excellent source of definitions for religious terms.

OABITAR (Objectivity, Accuracy, and Balance in Teaching About Religion)

www.teachingaboutreligion.org

OABITAR provides excellent information and guidelines for teaching about religion in the public schools. There are lesson plans available and guidelines for teaching about religion versus religious teaching. It also defines the important distinction between teaching about religious holidays, which is permissible, and *celebrating* religious holidays, which is not. A helpful site for parents and lay people as well as teachers.

Unitarian Universalism

www.uua.org

Unitarian Universalism (UU) is a creedless, socially progressive denomination consisting primarily of self-identified humanists. UU fellowships have youth programs that can fill the need for a group experience for teens. They have a year-long sexuality program called Our Whole Lives, a Coming of Age Program, and youth groups that focus on social justice work. It is lonely to be out there in the midst of the religious majority, and teens like to travel in groups.

The Unitarian Universalist Social Justice Committee has a program called Just Works that provides opportunities for young people 16 and older to go on social justice trips all over the United States to help those in need. For more details, email *justworks@uusc.com*.

Separation of Church and State

Freedom from Religion Foundation. Accessed July 10, 2008, from *www.ffrf.org*

Americans United for the Separation of Church and State. Accessed May 4, 2008, from *www.au.org*

ACLU Students' Rights resource. Accessed May 4, 2008, from *www.aclu.org/studentsrights/index.html*

Notes

1. The Pluralism Project at Harvard University: *www.pluralism.org*.
2. ABC News poll, February 2004.
3. Based on polls by the Gallup organization, 2005–2007.
4. American Religious Identification Survey, Graduate Center of the City University of New York. Accessed March 11, 2008, from *www.gc.cuny.edu/faculty/research_briefs/aris/aris_index.htm*. 2008 projected.
5. American Religious Identification Survey (ARIS), Graduate Center, City University of New York.

6. Op. cit.

7. It should be noted that as many as 10 percent of those affirming belief in God nonetheless refer to themselves as "nonreligious."

8. The most recent European Values Study measured the percentage of self-identified religious believers in European countries, including Germany (47%), United Kingdom (38%), France (34%), Norway (32%), and Sweden (23%). Yet all of these populations rank far higher than the United States in all measures of religious literacy.

9. Calkins, Lucy. *Raising Lifelong Learners* (New York: Da Capo, 1998). Mentioned as well in Chapter 1 Resources, this is a brilliant and well-written book for parents wishing to raise curious, inquisitive kids. Not to be missed.

10. Address to Atheist Alliance International, September 29, 2007.

11. It should be noted here that the Girl Scouts organization is quite different from Boy Scouts, having gone out of its way to implement nondiscriminatory practices. For more on Girl Scouts, Boy Scouts, and alternative organizations, see Chapter 8, "Finding and Creating Community."

12. These techniques are derived from the excellent book *Nonviolent Communication* (Jacksonville, FL: PuddleDancer Press, 2003) by Marshall Rosenberg, PhD.

13. Report 10 of the Council on Scientific Affairs (I-99). Accessed February 15, 2008, from *www.ama-assn.org/ama/pub/category/13585.html*

CHAPTER 4

The Physical Self

Amanda Metskas

Many parents, whether religious or nonreligious, are uncomfortable talking with their kids about body issues, including sexuality. Although the questions that secular parents have about sexuality may not differ from those of religious parents, the answers that secular parents seek, informed as they are by different principles, are often different.

Because secular parents forgo the easy answers that some religious parents rely on—"Wait until marriage because that's what God wants"—the question of what to tell kids about sex becomes more complex.

Being nonreligious obviously doesn't mean rejecting moral values in general or sexual morality in particular—but lacking handy catchphrases, it can be more difficult to articulate the values that do inform our decision making. Some nonreligious parents, having been raised in a religious sexual ethic, reject that ethic along with its religious clothing. Others who have rejected religious belief still retain some or all of the moral messages about sexual behavior that they were taught as children.

Beyond Sin Talk

> *Life in Lubbock, Texas, taught me two things: One is that God loves you and you're going to burn in hell. The other is that sex is the most awful, filthy thing on Earth, and you should save it for someone you love.*
>
> —Butch Hancock, country singer/songwriter

It's not surprising that so many of us have psychological obstacles to the topic of sex. Perhaps our parents never talked with us about it, or perhaps they sent the message that sex was dirty and shameful. It can be hard to get beyond the ways in which we were raised so we can approach the topic more straightfor-wardly with our own kids.

Step one in shaking loose those unhelpful messages is to frame sex in nat-uralistic terms. Far from being "the most filthy, awful thing on Earth," sex is an essential fact of our existence. Every one of your direct ancestors had sex— and thank Zeus for that, or this book would have one less reader. That reli-gion could turn the central requirement of life on Earth into something shameful is a good candidate for the single most perverse and twisted of our inheritances from religious thought. Countless generations of boys have been driven into despairing shame as the naturally irresistible urge to masturbate was portrayed as "self-abuse" or "onanism." Church opposition to sensible con-traception and family planning has kept millions in destitute poverty, while the enforced celibacy of priests led to the abuse of children—those least likely to tell. The point of this list is not just to criticize religion but to point out that whether it comes from their religious background or from our cultural Puri-tanism, even nonreligious parents bring many of these distorted and misin-formed notions of sexuality into their own lives and their own parenting.

These messages have now found their way into national policy. Over $176 million has been poured into the promotion of abstinence-only sex educa-tion, despite studies indicating that a majority of kids taking a virginity pledge fail to keep the pledge, are more likely to have unprotected sex than non-pledgers when they do have sex, and are equally likely to contract STDs.[1]

Rather than pursuing vague notions of sin and satanic temptation, non-religious parents can ground their sexual values in a reason-based considera-tion of consequences. Sex should be abstained from when the risk of adverse consequences is great. And teen pregnancy is, by almost any measure, an ad-verse consequence, leading to higher school dropout rates, lower income po-tential, and severely reduced assets and increased risks for the child.[2] Fortunately, teen pregnancy is on the decline. According the Guttmacher In-stitute's 2006 report, teen pregnancy rates are down 36 percent from 1990 to the lowest level in thirty years. Fourteen percent of this decrease is attributed to teens waiting longer to have sex; the other 86 percent is the result of im-proved contraceptive use.[3]

Percentage decline in teen pregnancy between 1990 and 2002: 36%

Percentage of decline due to delaying sex or having sex less often: 14%

Percentage of decline due to increased use of contraceptives: 86%[4]

Total federal funding of abstinence-only sex education programs in 2006: $176 million

Federal programs promoting comprehensive sex ed, including contraceptive use: 0

Average age of first sex for students in abstinence-only programs: 14.9 years

Average age for students *not* in abstinence-only programs: 14.9 years[5]

Percentage of U.S. teens receiving abstinence-only sex education in 1995: 9%

Percentage receiving abstinence-only sex education in 2002: 21–24%[6]

U.S. sex education teachers teaching abstinence-only in 1988: 1 in 50

U.S. sex education teachers teaching abstinence-only in 1999: 1 in 4[7]

Proportion of U.S. sex ed teachers who believe students should be taught about contraception: 9 in 10

Proportion prohibited by law from doing so: 1 in 4[8]

In a nutshell: "To date, no abstinence program of the type eligible for funding under the federal government's $176 million abstinence-only-until-marriage program has been found in a methodologically rigorous study to positively impact teen sexual behavior. Therefore, there is no evidence base to support continued investments of public funds in abstinence-only-until-marriage programs. A substantial majority of the comprehensive sex education programs reviewed—which receive no dedicated federal funding—are effective. The positive outcomes included delaying the initiation of sex, reducing the frequency of sex, reducing the number of sexual partners and increasing condom or contraceptive use."

—from "Emerging Answers 2007," a study by the National Campaign to Prevent Teen and Unplanned Pregnancy

In addition to being insufficiently prepared for parenthood, a 15-year-old is almost always insufficiently prepared for the emotional and social complexities of sexual relationships. It is these concerns about real-world consequences, rather than some strange distrust of bodily pleasure, that should guide the sexual education of our children—an opinion shared by most professional health and sexuality educators.

In addition to issues of sexuality, parents must help kids navigate more general issues surrounding body image, health, gender identity, sexual orientation, and drug use. This chapter provides questions and answers, activities, and resources for talking with kids about the many topics related to the physical self. While each of these topics could be (and is) addressed in whole books, this chapter is intended as an introduction to these issues that can point secular parents to some of the many other resources out there that will be more consistent with their secular values and approach to parenting.

Not every topic that could be addressed here will be. Questions about how to answer your kid's questions about where babies come from, how to talk to your kids about the changes their bodies are experiencing during puberty, and how to recognize the signs of an eating disorder and get treatment, for example, are not included, in part because so many excellent resources are now easily available for these topics. Our focus is on those issues over which religious and secular parenting approaches might differ.

There is neither need nor justification for a separate set of ethics related to sexuality or a separate set of principles to guide decision making about sex. The principles are the same as for other areas of life, centering on responsibility, consequences, honesty, and consistency. These and other humanistic virtues can help us guide our children toward a healthy and happy understanding of the physical self and their obligations to it.

Questions and Answers

Q: What are the basic humanist principles related to the body?

A: When I was growing up, my dad always explained that in our house there is no compromise on rules about safety or health, but that everything else is negotiable. He also pointed out that our bodies are natural and good, not something about which we should feel uncomfortable or ashamed. He may not have realized it at the time, but I think he hit on the two main humanist principles relating to the body:

1. Health and safety come first.
2. Our bodies are good and natural.

Humanists celebrate sexuality and the natural pleasures of the body, but that doesn't mean that anything goes. For humanists, responsible behavior comes down to an understanding of consequences both for yourself and others.

That's where these principles come in. It's important to flesh them out a little bit more.

Health and safety come first. Clearly, everything we do in life involves some degree of risk, and this principle isn't meant to imply that you should try to remove every element of risk from your child's life. First of all, that's not possible. Second of all, your child will likely rebel against this when he gets the chance, and he won't have learned what he needs to about managing risks responsibly.

The principle of putting health and safety first means that we need to *rationally* assess the risks posed by activities and use *reasonable* means to reduce those risks when possible. Reasonable people will differ in these assessments to some degree, but, as an example, you wouldn't use this principle to ban your child from bicycling because she might hurt herself, but you would use it to require that she wears a helmet when biking.

Because secular parenting is based on reason-giving, even though you don't want to compromise on issues of safety and health, you still want to talk with your kids about *why* something is required because of safety and health. You can also have a discussion about how serious the risks are and how reasonable the step is that removes or reduces the risk. Since reasonable people can disagree about these things, even though there is no compromise when it comes to safety and health, you might still end up changing your mind if your child demonstrates that something isn't as great a risk as you think, or if he finds some other method for protecting safety and health while engaging in an activity he wants to do.

Our bodies are good and natural. Not everything natural is good—illness, for example, is natural—which is why this principle mentions that our bodies are both good *and* natural. We believe that people are physical beings, evolved animals, not spirits housed within some physical shell. The physical form we have *is* us, in a very important way. We don't believe that human beings are "born sinful and need to be saved." Neither are we born perfect. Human beings are born *natural*. We have hormones, emotions, and thoughts that are results of natural processes and make us who we are. These include strengths and weaknesses that make up our human nature.

Sex is a natural part of being physical beings and is pleasurable and healthy (if you're doing it right). Physical pleasures are not to be looked down upon as somehow debasing or bad. They are an important part of what it means to be a human being. In fact—and this is a crucial realization—they are a necessary part. Sex is pleasurable for evolutionary reasons. It is what causes the species to continue. This is part of the complete understanding of sexuality we should impart to our kids. It's evolution, not Satan, that brings on these urges, and when the situation is right, participating in sexual pleasures is part of participating in humanness. And if it wasn't fun, we'd have a lot fewer human beings running around, or more likely none at all.

Q: How will the values about sexuality that I am trying to impart to my child differ from his or her religious peers?

A: As a secular parent, you might be worried that what you are teaching your kids about sexuality will be very different from what other parents in your area are teaching their kids. Because this issue is so emotionally charged for parents, you might be concerned that parents of your children's friends may view your parenting practices or your child's behavior as immoral or as a bad influence on their children.

The degree to which your values in this area differ from the values of religious parents will vary quite a bit depending on the religious parents. Although more fundamentalist forms of Christianity get considerable media attention and have come to dominate the popular conception of what religious people are like in the United States, there is in fact a great deal of diversity among religious parents in their views of sexuality. You are not unlikely to find many religious parents with values and views in this area that are very similar to yours.

Even conservative Christian parenting resources, like those produced by Focus on the Family, may present some advice you agree with. Focus on the Family advises teaching children that their bodies are a special gift from God—they teach that the body is good, but rather than being natural, it is sacred. Rather than denouncing sexuality as sinful, which tended to be the tactic of conservative religious groups in the past, they advise sending a message that "purity" is to be valued, and the joys of sexuality are something that should be saved for one's spouse.[9] Despite these possible points of disagreement, the shift from the religious messages that many of us were taught, that sex was dirty and shameful, to a more sex-positive message has even permeated these resources to some degree. On issues related to safety and health, conservative religious parents share our values of wanting children to have safe and healthy experiences and a positive view of their sexuality. Clearly, these general agreements will often lead to different conclusions on issues like comprehensive sex education and acceptance of gay, lesbian, bisexual, and transgender (GLBT) sexuality.

Many moderate religious groups are noticing the changes in our society, including earlier puberty and later marriage, and recognizing the need for a sexual ethics beyond the simplistic command to "wait until marriage."[10]

One outstanding example of religious people and groups advocating for healthy and ethical attitudes related to sexuality is the Religious Institute on Sexual Morality, Justice, and Healing (*www.religiousinstitute.org*). Rev. Debra Haffner, the director of the institute, served for twelve years as the CEO of the Sexuality Information and Education Council of the United States (SIECUS), a prime advocate for comprehensive science-based sex education. She holds a Masters in Public Health, and after her tenure at SIECUS, pursued a Master of Divinity degree, became a Unitarian Universalist minister, and founded the Religious Institute.

Haffner has written several books and articles on sexual development and adolescent sexuality, including *Beyond the Big Talk: Every Parent's Guide to Raising Sexually Healthy Teens—From Middle School to High School and Beyond*. She recommends getting together with the parents of your child's close friends and trying to come up with rules that are similar for things like dating, supervision at parties, makeup and suggestive clothing, and other issues that you will be facing as your kids begin puberty and enter middle school. You may be surprised at how much agreement you can reach with parents who have different religious views than you have about these practical matters. This can have several benefits for you as a parent—first of all, if your child tells you "Aww Mom, Katie's mom lets her do _____," you'll know whether it's true. If you've managed to come up with similar standards, odds

> **'Waiting for marriage' now nearly twice as long as in 1960**
> The average age of first marriage is increasing even as the onset of puberty drops. In 1960, the two events were separated by an average of eight to nine years (depending on gender and other factors). In 2008, the separation averages sixteen years.[11]

are your child won't be able to make this argument as often, and when the rules differ, you'll have a much easier time explaining why Katie's family allows something that you don't allow. Additionally, you'll have an opportunity to explain your rules and values to your fellow parents, so they will be more likely to understand where your family is coming from when their child comes home and claims that your kid is allowed to do something that their kid isn't.

Q: What are the humanist principles that relate to sex and relationships?

A: The two humanist principles related to the body apply here, but there are also a few other humanist principles that come into play here because sex and relationships involve other people.

The principles that safety and health come first and that our bodies are good and natural cover a lot of ground related to sex and relationships. Make sure your kids know that these are your principles, and give them some examples of how they apply. The obvious one is that they need to use appropriate protection for both sexually transmitted diseases and pregnancy prevention. In addition, it's very important that kids know that sexuality comes along with strong emotions that are to some extent driven by hormones. Make sure to let them know that part of having safety and health come first includes taking care of one's emotional health. Sexuality can create strong emotional attachments to partners, and people should make sure that there is mutual trust, respect, and honesty in a relationship that involves sexual behavior.

Because our bodies are natural and good, sexuality should be pleasurable. Let your kids know that, and let them know that means that no one should do things with his or her body with which he or she is uncomfortable. People have the right to control what happens to their bodies and the right to change their minds. This last point is so important. Make sure your kids understand that just because they kissed someone or allowed someone to put a hand down their pants doesn't mean they are obligated to go further. Sexuality is a way that people share intimacy with each other, and it should feel wonderful. If it doesn't feel good, that's a good reason not to do it.

In *Parenting Beyond Belief*, Dale McGowan identified seven secular virtues. Although it is not exhaustive, it's a pretty good list to turn to for thinking about ethical sexuality and relationships. Although sexuality is an area fraught with hangups and mixed messages in our society, the same ethical principles that apply to the rest of our lives apply here as well. Here is Dale's list, with some added explanation of how these principles might play out in talking with your kids about sexuality and relationships:

Humility. Have the humility to recognize that you don't have all the answers about sexuality and relationships. This applies both to parents and kids. Let your kids know that you don't know everything about this, and that it's okay for them to admit that they don't know everything. That's why it's important for you to talk to each other and that when you don't know the answers, you can find out.

Empathy. This is a key value in relationships and sexuality. Help your kids to understand that they deserve a partner who tries to understand how they feel and respects them and that they need to treat their partner with the same consideration. You can model this by showing empathy in your relationship with your partner and in your parenting and by encouraging your kids to show empathy to family members, friends, and others in their lives.

Courage. This virtue helps to resist pressure from others and to do what you think is right. In sex and relationships, let your kids know that they should have the courage to stand up for the limits they set about sexuality. No one should do more than he or she wants to do sexually because of pressure from a partner or peers. You might also want to talk about having the courage to stand up for others who are picked on or discriminated against because they are GLBT or otherwise differ in their sexuality or their gender identity.

Honesty. Let kids know that honesty is something that they deserve in a relationship and something that their partner deserves from them. Because sexuality is something that can have serious consequences for safety and health, it is very important that partners are honest with each other about their past experiences and whether they are being monogamous with each other or are seeing other people. Being honest about feelings for the other person, and expectations from the relationship, is important so that someone can make decisions about his sexual behavior that are based on an honest understanding of how seriously he and his partner take the relationship. Let your kids know that it is never okay to lie to a partner to entice him or her to have sex. Let them know that if a partner lies to them, they should consider whether they are being treated with the respect they deserve and whether the relationship is based on enough trust to involve sexual behavior.

Openness. Openness doesn't mean that anything goes. It does mean that there is a range in which people's ideas and behaviors will differ, and that's okay. Help your children understand where the limits are (safety and health, respect for themselves and their partner), but recognize that your child may make decisions that are different from what you would ideally want for sexual and relationship behavior. As long as your child is staying within those limits, the important thing is to keep the lines of communication open—express your differences but respect her decision-making abilities. Similarly, help your child understand that she may be making different decisions about relationships and sexuality than her peers. This doesn't necessarily mean that one is right and one is wrong, and children can accept their peers' choices (if they are safe and healthy) without having to do the same thing. Let them know that their friends and partners should extend the same acceptance and respect to them.

Generosity. People in healthy relationships are generous with each other. They don't take cheap shots at each other and put each other down. People in healthy relationships care about their partners and take their needs and feelings seriously. The relationship that you model with your partner shows this generosity in relationships to your kids. You can also comment favorably on your child's behavior when you see him or her treating a boyfriend or girlfriend in a generous and caring way. Similarly, say something complimentary about your child's partner when he or she does something generous for your child. Let your child know that this generosity needs to be a two-way street in relationships, and that neither partner should be the one who is always giving in or making sacrifices for the other.

Gratitude. Gratitude is the proper response to generosity in relationships. When your partner does something kind, gratitude is found in an acknowledgment of his generosity. That is another virtue that you can model for your kids through your own relationships.

In a sense these virtues are all reflections of the golden rule (treat others as you would like to be treated) and the silver rule (don't treat others as you would not like to be treated). The bottom line is that they should be treated well in relationships and that in turn they should treat their partners well.

A good shorthand list of things that must be present for an ethical sexual relationship was developed by SIECUS: Relationships should be consensual, nonexploitative, honest, mutually pleasurable, and protected against disease and unintended pregnancy.[12]

Q: How can I help my kids understand the risks associated with premature sexual activity without giving the impression that there is anything wrong or "dirty" about sexuality itself?

A: Part of making sure you send messages about sexuality that don't treat it as wrong or dirty involves checking in with yourself and understanding your own ideas and hangups about sexuality. How did your parents talk with you about sex? Did they talk to you about it at all? Did they treat sex as something dirty or shameful?

Often kids get the impression that sex is dirty when it is something that their parents are afraid to talk about or treat as a topic that is off limits. Kids also get that impression when parents overreact to something they see or hear. It can be very easy as a parent to speak before you think when you see or hear your kids saying or doing things that shock you. Take a breath and approach them as calmly as you can. If you can't talk about what is happening with them calmly in the moment, let them know that you want to talk with them later about what you saw them doing on the computer or heard them talking about with their friend.

Justin Richardson and Mark A. Schuster's book *Everything You Never Wanted Your Kids to Know About Sex (but Were Afraid They'd Ask)* reports similar techniques correlated with kids delaying having sex as those discussed by Debra Haffner. The first is a general parenting style known as "authoritative parenting." Authoritative parents combine two important features: They set high standards for their kids' behavior and are emotionally supportive of their kids, listening to what they have to say. This is distinct from "*authoritarian* parents*,*" who set high standards but don't listen and emotionally support their kids—they simply make the rules and expect their kids to obey. It is also distinct from permissive parents who are emotionally supportive and listen to their kids, but who don't set high standards for their kids' behavior—who try to be friends with their kids and don't set up the kind of limits that parents must set.

Authoritative parenting is very consistent with the kind of parenting approach outlined in *Parenting Beyond Belief* and throughout this book. Let your kids know that you have high expectations of them, and you set rules, but use reason giving as a way to explain and potentially modify those rules. Help your kids understand why your family has certain rules, and if they convince you that the rules should be modified, change them.

Families in which kids are more likely to delay having sex are those in which the parents are involved in their kids' lives. This takes two forms. One is having open communication with your kids. Contrary to popular belief, talking with your kids about sex doesn't make them go out and have it sooner. To the contrary, children in families that talked about sexuality are statistically *more* likely to wait.

When you discuss sexuality with younger kids, make sure you are giving them facts about their bodies, what their body parts are called, how things work. As kids get older, talk about feelings in addition to facts. Make sure you give them the information they need, but also discuss your family's values and ethics and how they might feel as they deal with sexual decision making and relationships. It's best to talk with kids about stages they are about to enter before they get there so they know what to expect.

When you talk with kids about the risks involved in sexual activity—STDs and unplanned pregnancy—approach the issues factually and avoid taking a tone of moral panic. If you try to scare kids away from having sex by overstating the risks, they are likely to ignore what you've said and *underestimate* the risks. If, instead, you give them accurate information about the risks and potential consequences, you will increase your credibility, and they are more likely to listen.

The second way that parents can delay their kids' sexual activity is through monitoring. Monitoring means knowing where your children are and checking in on them. For example, if your teen is going to party, make sure the parents are going to be home. This might mean calling the parents directly. If your child is having a party at your house, bring snacks over to the room in which the party is being held periodically. Monitoring can be a little tricky. Adolescents are growing up and asserting their independence. They need more privacy and independence than younger children, but that doesn't mean that they are ready to make adult decisions on their own. Monitor too closely and adolescents may rebel and engage in more risky behaviors than they would have with a longer leash. This might be part of the reason that teenage boys with fundamentalist mothers are more likely to have had sex than their peers.[13]

Strike a balance, giving your adolescent more privacy and freedom while continuing to set and enforce rules. You might even talk directly about this tension with your teen. Let her know that you trust her, and you know that as she grows up she needs more freedom, but that you also need to have certain rules so that you know she is safe.

Being an involved parent who sets standards but also provides love and emotional support is the best way to help your kids wait to have sex until they are ready for it. Keep the lines of communication open. Pass on your family's values about sexuality and make sure to listen when your kids talk to you about their thinking about sexual decision making. When the time comes, they will need to make these decisions for themselves without you there to tell them what to do. Help them talk through their thinking about sex and relationships so that they can make their own healthy choices. That makes it more likely that their first experience will be a positive one that allows them to experience sex for the wonderful, pleasurable, intimate experience that it should be.

Q: Our high school is promoting an abstinence-only sex ed curriculum based mostly on the Christian right in our town. I feel very strongly that other birth control options should be taught. My daughter, however, tells me that she will be "humiliated" if I approach the school on this issue. What should I do?

A: The first thing on your mind should be making sure that your daughter is getting accurate and effective sex education. Since you know that isn't happening in her school, you need to make sure that it is happening in other settings, at home and/or in connection with a non-school-sponsored sex education program.

The next question is whether you should approach the school about the problems with its sex education program. First of all, I recommend reading Stu Tanquist's essay in *Parenting Beyond Belief* called "Choosing Your Battles." Stu outlines a list of things to consider when deciding whether to challenge inappropriate religious intrusion into the public schools. Think about the impact your actions will have on your child—after all, she is the one who has to live in that school environment, not you. Find out from your daughter what she expects to happen if you approach the school and how she believes she will be humiliated. Use that information to see if you and your daughter can come up with a way to approach the school about the problem that she doesn't think will humiliate her.

She may be concerned that you raising this issue will make people at school think she is sexually active or a "slut." She may be concerned about looking like she is calling in a parent to fight her battles for her. She may be concerned that the teacher will single her out in class if you approach the school about the curriculum. All of these are valid concerns, and depending on which concerns your daughter has, you have a few things to think about. First, it's important to let your daughter know you respect her concerns and that you won't take action on this issue without consulting her and keeping her informed. Second, you need to weigh the costs and benefits of taking action.

Try to figure out if there is a way you can achieve the benefits without the negative impacts for your daughter. You might want to approach an organization like Planned Parenthood or SIECUS about the problem so it can contact the school about your concerns anonymously and your family won't be singled out.

Maybe after you and your daughter have a good talk about the issue, she will change her mind and be supportive of your intervention. Maybe she would prefer to take on the issue herself with some friends from the class. But be prepared for the possibility that she just isn't comfortable with your getting involved in this. If, after a good discussion of the issue, she is still not comfortable, it might be best to back off.

Take home point one: No matter what is going on in their school, make sure your children are getting accurate and effective sex education at home and from other sources.

Take home point two: Don't let fighting a battle in the community damage your relationship with your child. If you decide to take the issue on, keep your child in the loop, take her concerns seriously, and try to work together to come up with a way to approach the issue. Think creatively to find a solution that you can both live with.

Q: It seems that all of my daughter's friends are getting "promise rings" from their fundamentalist Christian dads. We are certainly not going to do that, but it makes my daughter look like the slut in the crowd. How can I help her with this issue?

A: This provides an excellent opportunity to talk with your daughter about your family's values related to sexuality. Make sure she understands that just because your family has no specific rule to abstain until marriage, it doesn't mean that you don't have values. Help her to think through issues like health and safety, respecting yourself and your partner, and waiting until you are ready instead of giving into pressure. Once you've talked through these things, it might help your daughter to role-play a conversation with her friends about her values. If she is comfortable explaining what her values are, then she will be able to respond to anyone who insinuates that she is a slut because she doesn't have a promise ring.

It's also possible that your daughter may be feeling left out of this ritual that all of her friends seem to have with their families. You may want to come up your own way of recognizing your daughter's transition to adolescence. Perhaps you might even incorporate a special piece of jewelry into this occasion. That way when her friends are showing off their promise rings, your daughter will have her own symbol to point to of how much her parents care about her, trust her, and recognize that she is growing up.

Q: How can I guide my child into standing up for what she wants to do and not to be pressured into having sex when she isn't ready?

A: Arming your child with correct information is a necessary part of helping him or her avoid being pressured. There's no shortage of myths that peers or partners may use to try to pressure someone into sex. They may claim that "everyone" is doing it. Statistics indicate otherwise: About half of high school students reported having had sexual intercourse in a 1999 study—which means, of course, that roughly half are not.[14] That large percentage can let your kids know that they are in good company if they choose to wait.

Partners may use myths like "blue balls"—the claim that men who have become sexually aroused will suffer agonizing pain if sex is not forthcoming—to make their partner go all the way. Letting your kids know that there is no such thing is a great start to helping them overcome this kind of pressure. You can also point out that their partner has the option of masturbation to relieve sexual tension.

In addition to correct information, kids need a sense of self-worth and the courage to do what they believe is right. They also need to understand what a healthy sexual relationship involves—consent rather than coercion or exploitation. Talking through possible scenarios is one way to help your kids develop sexual decision-making skills.

Additionally, encourage kids to talk openly with their partners about sexual decision making. Both boys and girls need to know how to say no and mean it, and both boys and girls need to understand that they need to listen and stop when a partner says no. In dating relationships, when things go further than one partner would like, sometimes it is because the partners weren't communicating clearly about what was okay and what was too far. A good guideline for encouraging your kids to talk with their partners about sex is that if they aren't comfortable talking with their partner about it, then they shouldn't be doing it with their partner.

Q: My son is about to turn 12, the age when boys often begin experimenting with masturbation. I remember having a lot of feelings of guilt and shame during this time. How can I talk to my son about this?

A: Congratulations on recognizing the need to do this. In the absence of communication on the issue, boys are virtually guaranteed to feel tremendous and unnecessary shame and guilt. A few words can do wonders. Simply let him know

- What masturbation is.
- That it's a normal thing nearly everyone does at some point.
- That it's a natural indication that the body is becoming ready for sexual activity and reproduction.
- That all of the stories about grave consequences are complete nonsense.
- That although it is not shameful, it is private.

Invite his questions and answer them straightforwardly.

Q: Are his religious peers likely to get different messages about masturbation from their parents?

A: Yes, and it's best to let him know that. Regardless of their families' religious orientations, your son's peers are most likely to hear nothing at all from their parents about masturbation. But if they *are* religious, they may hear that it is sinful or perverse. The majority of traditional religions explicitly condemn masturbation, often in weirdly over-the-top terms.

The Catholic catechism calls masturbation "an intrinsically and gravely disordered action."[15] One popular nineteenth-century Jewish theologian called it "a graver sin than any other in the Torah."[16] Mormonism teaches that "masturbation is a sinful habit that robs one of the Spirit," while Shi'a Islam forbids it completely, quoting sect founder (and son-in-law of Muhammad) Imam Ali as saying "one who masturbates commits a sin equal to killing me eighty times."[17] *¡Ay caramba!*

But at least one influential religious conservative has voiced support for a more accepting, naturalistic parenting approach to masturbation—and has been excoriated for it by his fellows. The following passage refers to a conversation he had as a boy with his minister father:

> We were riding in the car, and my dad said, "Jim, when I was a boy, I worried so much about masturbation. It really became a scary thing for me because I thought God was condemning me for what I couldn't help. So I'm telling you now that I hope you don't feel the need to engage in this act when you reach the teen years, but if you do, you shouldn't be too con-

cerned about it. I don't believe it has much to do with your relationship with God." What a compassionate thing my father did for me that night in the car.[18]

Aside from "I hope you don't feel the need" and the reference to God, this is a message nonreligious parents can relate to. And it comes from none other than James Dobson.

He still tangles it with silliness, suggesting that boys in the act think not of any girls they know but only of their "eventual wives." Christian author Herbert J. Miles goes one better, suggesting that boys pray first, thanking God for the gift of sexuality, then think only of him during orgasm (which certainly gives "Oh, God!" a whole new meaning).[19] But let's give credit to both of them for getting the basic message right and thereby reducing the number of children growing up with unnecessary self-loathing and sexual repression.

At least we've progressed since pilgrim days when the Puritan colony of New Haven, Connecticut, specified the death penalty for "blasphemers, homosexuals and masturbators"![20]

Q: My 16-year-old and I are able to talk openly about sexuality. I've always stressed that sex is natural and enjoyable if you do it safely, make sure you and your partner are respectful of each other, and wait until you are ready to handle the responsibilities it brings. My teenager has been in a relationship for several months and came to me and said that she and her partner have talked about sex, and they think they are ready. How can I raise the concerns I have while keeping the open communication that we have built? Even though I trust my daughter and think she makes good choices, it's hard for me to be comfortable with her taking this step.

A: Although there is no single correct answer to this question, families must take the same basic issues into consideration. And as with all naturalistic parenting, consequences are key:

Legal consequences. The legal age of consent for sexual intercourse varies by state in the United States but is generally between 16 and 18 (Tennessee and Pennsylvania recognize consent as young as age 13 in some cases). The age difference between partners is often relevant in determining questions of legality (e.g., whether sexual contact constitutes statutory rape). If your child is under 18, a close look at the laws in your state should precede any discussion.

Personal consequences. A healthy sexual relationship must be fully consensual, regardless of age. Make sure your child knows that sex must never be used to try to "earn" someone else's love and that neither partner should be pressured in any way. A good rule: If you aren't sure whether you are ready, you aren't—and any partner who pressures or threatens is not worth being with.

There are countless bad reasons for having sex: because friends are already doing so, because she thinks she "should have" by now, because a partner is pressuring her, or because a person is worried about the consequences of saying no.

Invite your child to consider other options for expressing love and relieving the natural sexual tension that comes with adolescence.

Physical consequences. No matter what precautions are taken, heterosexual intercourse should always be seen as an act that can lead to pregnancy. If that consequence would be unthinkable, intercourse should also be unthinkable. Make sure your child knows that the stories of "sure-fire ways" to avoid pregnancy (coitus interruptus, certain positions, first sex, etc.) are myths.

Make sure that she and her partner have a good plan in place for preventing pregnancy and disease. This is an important thing to talk about even though you are encouraging her to hold off, because you won't be there when the moment arrives where she makes the decision. You can frame this discussion in terms like "If you decide to go ahead, what is your plan for protection?" You may want to offer to make an appointment for your daughter with a gynecologist (most likely not the same doctor her mother sees) to talk about birth control and disease prevention options. Sometimes teens are more comfortable talking with a medical professional rather than a parent about specific options, and a gynecologist will have information that you may not. You can make it clear that since she's considering sex, it is a good time to see the gynecologist, regardless of whether she decides to have sex with her partner, and that seeing the gynecologist doesn't in any way mean that she has to take that step.

If you have confidence in your child's decision making and maturity, this guidance should be sufficient to make sure she is taking all factors into account and making a decision with the head as well as the heart.

Q: My daughter wants to join the GLBT Allies Club, but she is being called a lesbian by some of the conservative religious kids at school. What can I say to help her with this situation?

A: Remind your daughter that the reason she is interested in joining the club is that she knows that there is nothing wrong with being gay or lesbian. Ask her why she is concerned that these kids are calling her a lesbian. Is she offended? Is she worried that the rumor will keep boys from asking her out? Is it something else?

Compliment her on her courage and the empathy that made her interested in joining the club. Ask what her friends think about those who join the club. Ask whose opinions she most respects and what *those* people think of the club. Let her know that you are proud of her for standing on the right side of one of the foremost civil rights issues of our day and that you would completely support her joining the club.

This is also an excellent opportunity to underline the value of dissent discussed in Chapter 1. As much as anything, gay rights is about standing up for the right of others to be different as long as that difference does no harm.

It is also possible that your daughter is questioning her sexual orientation and that being called a lesbian is hitting a nerve because she isn't sure. This is a good time to let her know that you support her and love her regardless of her sexual orientation. A way to do that subtly would be to talk about how silly it is that they are calling her a lesbian as though that is something to be ashamed of, because there is nothing wrong with being a lesbian. Let her know that she can really throw them off by saying, "So what if I was?" Whatever her sexual orientation, she knows that being a lesbian is nothing to be ashamed of and can tell that to her classmates who don't seem to get it.

Q: I think my child might be gay. How do I let him know that it's okay with me, without putting him on the defensive about the issue or making an unwarranted assumption?

A: As a nonreligious parent, you have a real advantage here over many religious parents because you haven't raised your child in a setting that disapproves of homosexuality (or of difference in general). Even so, your child may still assume that you would disapprove of his being gay. One thing you should do is examine your own assumptions about gays and lesbians and educate yourself. Even nonreligious people are sometimes uncomfortable with homosexuality and may have some stereotypes to overcome. A good place to start looking for resources is Parents, Families, and Friends of Lesbians and Gays (PFLAG), an organization with local support groups and an excellent website (*www.pflag.org*). Click on "Family and Friends" to learn about the process of having a loved one come out and to find answers to your questions.

One thing that all parents can do, regardless of whether they think their child may be gay, is to send messages in the home that are inclusive and accepting of gay people. The attitudes you model toward gays and lesbians are important, regardless of whether your child is gay, because they help form the attitudes that your child will have toward people who are gay. Modeling an attitude that is accepting toward gays and lesbians also helps establish an environment in which your child will feel comfortable coming out to you when he is ready if he identifies as gay.

One way to establish a welcoming environment is to try to use more gender-neutral language about your child's future relationship partners. Instead of asking your son, "Do you have a girlfriend?" you can ask, "Are you dating anyone?" Instead of telling your daughter that you hope she finds a good man, you can say, "I hope you find a partner who really appreciates you." If the language you use doesn't presume that your child is heterosexual, it sends a signal that it wouldn't be a problem for you if he or she isn't.

If you have friends or family members who are gay or lesbian, the relationship with them that you model for your child is important. Your welcoming acceptance and normal interaction with these friends and family members shows your child that your relationship with him or her wouldn't be hurt if you learned that he or she is gay or lesbian. These friends or family members can also serve as people you might be able to turn to for advice and whom your child can talk to about his or her sexual orientation. Ask them about how and when they came out to their parents and what their parents did that made that easier or harder.

You may get to a point where you want to address the issue more directly with your child. Try to find a natural opening into the conversation. If it feels forced or out of the blue, it is harder to have a good talk. Maybe your child will tell you about a friend who is gay and is afraid to tell his parents. Maybe you will watch a movie or a TV show where a character is struggling with coming out. You can use that as an opportunity to send a message without making any assumptions about your child. You might be able to say something like "I hope if you had something important like that going on in your life, you would know that I would listen to you and accept you, no matter what it was." At that point your child may change the subject; if so, let the conversation move on. Just because your child doesn't take the opportunity to tell you right then and there doesn't mean that he didn't receive your message.

Justin Richardson and Mark A. Schuster's book *Everything You Never Wanted Your Kids to Know About Sex (but Were Afraid They'd Ask)*, which is reviewed in the Resources section, includes an excellent chapter about GLBT teens.

Q: What humanist ideas can help my kids resist the lure of drugs and other practices that threaten their health?

A: Both *Parenting Beyond Belief* and *Raising Freethinkers* advocate reason-giving as a central tenet of good parenting. Rather than saying, "Drugs are bad—m'kay, don't use drugs," like Mr. Mackey in South Park, we want to follow up with information about *how* drugs can be harmful to your health and safety.

As with all complex topics, the drug conversation shouldn't come out of the blue sky. From the earliest years, children should be made aware of how amazing their brains and bodies are. This leads naturally to a desire to treat them well and keep them working properly by putting good things in (healthy foods, plenty of fluids, etc.) and avoiding the bad (junk foods, poisons, etc). This in turn forms a sensible foundation for later discussion about drugs and other risky behaviors. The humanist principles from the beginning of this chapter apply very well to issues of drugs and alcohol.

For the sake of credibility and effectiveness, it's important to be well-informed yourself when you engage drug and alcohol questions. Generic warnings and scare tactics are less effective than specific, concrete information. Kids get information and ideas about drugs from many sources. Trying to scare them with horror stories that don't jibe with what they see happening around them will lead them to disregard what you say about drugs. If, instead, you approach them with real information about the risks and consequences of drug use and empower them with tools they need to resist unhealthy behaviors, kids are much more likely to make good decisions.

I highly recommend the book *Just Say Know: Talking with Kids About Drugs and Alcohol* by Cynthia Kuhn, Scott Swartzwelder, and Wilkie Wilson. The authors are scientists and parents and discuss the topic in a way that is approachable and informational. They don't take a tone of moral panic, preferring to suggest techniques that arm the kids with the information they need to make good decisions.

Q: My husband and I allow our kids a sip of our wine or beer at the dinner table. My Baptist sister-in-law, visiting from out of town, saw us do this and hit the roof. She warned that we were setting our kids up for a life of alcoholism and an early death. This seems ridiculous to me, but is there anything hard and fast I can offer to counter it?

A: Research indicates that your sister has it precisely backwards. As with so many other things (religion, sexuality, death, etc.), children are more likely to develop dysfunctional and unhealthy habits and concepts if alcohol is made into forbidden fruit and a magical rite of passage into adulthood.

"The best evidence shows that teaching kids to drink responsibly is better than shutting them off entirely from it," says Dr. Paul Steinberg, former director of counseling at Georgetown University. "You want to introduce your kids to it, and get across the point that this is to be enjoyed but not abused."[21]

In his landmark 1983 study *The Natural History of Alcoholism,* Harvard psychiatrist Dr. George E. Vaillant found that people who grew up in families where alcohol was forbidden at the table but consumed elsewhere were seven times more likely to be alcoholics that those who came from families where wine was served with meals but drunkenness was not tolerated.

Vaillant also looked at cross-cultural data, finding a much higher frequency of alcohol abuse in cultures that prohibit drinking among children but condone adult drunkenness (such as Ireland) and a relatively low occurrence of alcohol abuse in countries that allow children to occasionally sample wine or beer but frown on adult drunkenness (such as Italy). Moderate exposure coupled with mature adult modeling is the key.

Vaillant concluded that teens should be allowed to enjoy wine with family meals. "The way you teach responsibility," he noted recently, "is to let parents teach appropriate use."[22]

This is another area in which you want to be informed about the laws in your state. In most states it is legal for parents to serve alcohol to their children, but not to others under the age of 21. Also, many states have a "not a drop" law that sets a legal limit of zero for the blood alcohol level of drivers under the age of 21, which you want to be aware of if your teenager has activities involving driving later in the evening.

Q: My son's friend is fighting depression. His family is "trusting in God" to pull him through. This is very hard for my son and us to watch. How should teens intervene (if at all) when they see a friend that is suffering and not getting help because of the family's religious beliefs?

A: It's not uncommon for religious families to receive very questionable advice regarding depression. One prominent Christian psychologist asks those with family members suffering from depression to consider whether "[the] depression stem[s] from unconfessed sin, or guilt over past sins," to seek rest "as prescribed in the New Testament in Hebrews 4," and to try to "see the blessing in this difficulty" before he finally notes that medication may be needed.[23]

If the family of your son's friend is mired in this head-in-the-sand approach, it is crucial that your son intervene. The keys to helping those suffering from depression are (1) taking the person's depression seriously, (2) listening to the person's feelings and concerns, and (3) getting the person to seek out help from a (secular) medical professional.

Many depressed people do not know that depression is a recognizable and treatable disease. Your son's biggest contribution might simply be sharing this information, insisting his friend see a physician or mental health professional, and going with him. Reports are common of depressed teens declining to seek treatment until a friend offers to go along. Your son's willingness to intervene could very well save his friend's life.

Activities

Role-Play Responses

Ages 12+

Role-play situations in which your children have a choice to be passive or active in the presence of homophobic language. Ask what they might say in the lunchroom with a group of kids when one person says, "Pete is such a fag!" or on the bus when someone says, "That sweater is so gay."

Born Again!

Ages 3–6

> *Materials:* sheet, 25-watt red light bulb, 6' length of yarn, drum

Children with a sibling on the way are often interested in the birth process. Create a reenactment with the child under a sheet (womb), a piece of yarn (umbilical cord) tied to the child's belt, and a single red low-wattage bulb in an otherwise darkened room. Simulate the mother's heartbeat with a small drum pulsing a beat. Press down (gently!) on the child with your hands to simulate contractions, at which point the heartbeat begins to increase in tempo. As the child emerges from the sheet, flip on the lights. Child squeals with delight. Be prepared to do it again . . . and again . . . and again.

Body Myth or Body Fact?

Ages 12+

> *Materials:* blank index cards (other variations can include dice or a game board of your creation)

Write a body/sex myth or body/sex fact on each of 30–40 index cards. On the opposite side of each card, identify as MYTH or FACT. Examples:

- Sex education results in kids having sex earlier. (MYTH)
- The U.S. average for first intercourse for girls is 17. (FACT)
- Most teenagers are sexually active. (MYTH)
- You can't get pregnant the first time you have sex. (MYTH)
- Condoms keep you from feeling anything during sex. (MYTH)
- If you masturbate, you can go blind. (MYTH)
- 98 percent of boys masturbate (FACT)

(Sources of myths and facts include the PBS website for IN THE MIX at *www.pbs.org/inthemix/educators/lessons/sex1/myths.html* and the LiveScience Sex Quiz at *www.livescience.com/php/trivia/?quiz=sex*)

Divide the family or group into two teams. Read a myth or fact about sexuality and have the teams compete for the right answer.

The Vagina Monologues

Ages 15+

Consider seeing a production of *The Vagina Monologues* with your high schooler. Many college campuses put on productions of this play around Valentine's Day (or V-Day) to support organizations opposing violence against women. Read up on the controversies surrounding the play and make your own decision regarding suitability. **Other possibilities:** Rent a film dealing with issues of sexual identity and societal pressures. Consider *Before Night Falls* (2000), *Philadelphia* (1993), or *Brokeback Mountain* (2005).

Movie and a Chat

Ages 15+

Go to an R-rated movie with your teen in exchange for a half-hour chat over pizza afterwards. (Based on a recommendation by Debra Haffner.)

Create a Reference Library for Sexuality and Body Issues

Ages 13+

Create a small library of books dealing with various issues related to sexuality, body image, development, and gender identity. Locate it in a private area of the house and invite your teen to make use of it.

Resources
Sexuality Information
Sexuality Information and Education Council of the United States (SIECUS)

www.siecus.org

A first-rate advocate for comprehensive science-based sex education.

Religious Institute on Sexual Morality, Justice, and Healing

www.religiousinstitute.org

An outstanding counterpoint to conservative religious dogma regarding sexuality.

Planned Parenthood

www.plannedparenthood.org

Excellent source of information and resources related to reproductive health.

Parents, Friends, and Family of Lesbians and Gays (PFLAG)

www.pflag.org

A national nonprofit organization with over 200,000 members. "PFLAG promotes the health and well-being of gay, lesbian, bisexual and transgender persons, their families and friends through: support, to cope with an adverse society; education, to enlighten an ill-informed public; and advocacy, to end discrimination and to secure equal civil rights."

Also see: www.anyoneandeveryone.com. An outstanding information and advocacy site for parents of gay and lesbian persons.

COLAGE (Children of Lesbians and Gays Everywhere)

www.colage.org

"A national movement of children, youth, and adults with one or more lesbian, gay, bisexual, transgender, and/or queer parents."

Dr. Marty Klein—Straight talk on sex, love, and intimacy

www.sexed.org

Richardson, Justin, and Mark Schuster. *Everything You Never Wanted Your Kids to Know About Sex (but Were Afraid They'd Ask): The Secrets to Surviving Your*

Child's Sexual Development from Birth to the Teens (New York: Crown Publishers, 2003). A top-flight resource. Rather than treating sexuality as something that suddenly pops up at puberty, the authors cover sexual development from birth onwards. Recommendations are based on actual data, and the authors are careful to let the reader know when they are offering an opinion and data is limited or inconclusive. They treat sexual development as natural and pleasurable and provide information about STDs and unplanned pregnancy in a way that is informative without taking a tone of moral panic. Last, they recognize that different parents will have different values related to sexuality that they want to pass on to their kids, and they direct their advice to helping you pass on the messages that you want to pass on in a healthy way.

The presentation is accessible, containing threaded real and hypothetical parenting situations throughout the book. Includes an excellent chapter on children's sexual orientation.

Haffner, Debra. *Beyond the Big Talk: Every Parent's Guide to Raising Sexually Healthy Teens—From Middle School to High School and Beyond* (New York: Newmarket Press, 2001). Haffner draws on her expertise gained through twelve years as the CEO of SIECUS, the Sexuality Information and Education Council of the United States, as well as her personal experience raising children. Her daughter, aged 15 at the time of publication, wrote the Foreword for this book. Her focus on "teachable moments" rather than one "big talk" is really sensible. The book is accessible and provides helpful tools for parents to assess what their values are related to sexuality in addition to providing insights on how to pass those values on to children and help them develop good sexual decision-making skills. This book is the followup to her previous work, *From Diapers to Dating*, and it focuses on middle school up through college, while the previous book focuses on the early years.

Krasny Brown, Laura, and Marc Brown. *What's the Big Secret? Talking About Sex with Girls and Boys* (New York: Little, Brown Young Readers, 2000). Terrific first look at the issues surrounding sexuality. Ages 4–8.

VIDEO: *Abstinence Comes to Albuquerque* (2006). The compelling story of a faith-based organization using federal funds to bring abstinence-only sex education into public schools in Albuquerque. Available in full on Google Video (*http://video.google.com*). 27 minutes. A must-see.

The Unitarian Universalist Church has produced a sexuality curriculum for various age groups called Our Whole Lives. There are grades K–1, 4–6, 7–9, high school, and adult programs. The programs build on one another and by the time the youth are in the junior high the program is a series of one-hour year-long programs that covers

a. Examining Values

b. Sexuality and Body Awareness

c. Gender and Diversity

d. Sexual Orientation and Gender Identity

e. Relationships

f. Lovemaking

g. Preparing for Parenthood

h. Responsible Sexual Behavior

i. Sexually Transmitted Diseases

j. Abuse of Sexuality

All programs are taught by trained lay leaders, and parental permission is required.

General Health and Body Issues

Kuhn, Cynthia, Scott Swartzwelder, and Wilkie Wilson. *Just Say Know: Talking with Kids About Drugs and Alcohol* (New York: W.W. Norton, 2002). A scientific yet very accessible guide to talking with kids about drugs. It avoids taking a tone of moral panic and focuses instead on giving kids accurate information about the effects of drugs so that kids will listen rather than tune out. The authors provide a good general overview of how brains work and how drugs affect them, as well as a brief overview of the legal issues involved. The last several chapters cover specific types of drugs including their effects, statistics about use rates, and what the main talking points are about each type for your conversation with your kids. The authors include caffeine, over-the-counter and prescription medicines, in addition to alcohol, tobacco, and illegal drugs. The chapter about marijuana is especially good because it provides compelling reasons for avoiding it, without resorting to exaggerations. The book is a short yet comprehensive reference that is well focused on providing the necessary information for your conversations with your kids while avoiding getting bogged down in more technical detail than is necessary.

Mayle, Peter. *Where Did I Come From?* (Fort Lee, NJ: Lyle Stuart, 2000). A factual, kid-accessible account of where babies come from. Animated anatomical illustrations help explain the process. Ages 4–8.

Schaefer, Valorie Lee. *The Care and Keeping of You: The Body Book for Girls* (Middleton, WI: American Girl, 1998). An unbeatable, readable, approachable, and accurate resource for girls age 10+.

Harris, Robie, and Michael Emberley. *It's So Amazing! A Book About Eggs, Sperm, Birth, Babies, and Families* (Cambridge, MA: Candlewick, 2004, ages 7–12) and *It's Perfectly Normal: Changing Bodies, Growing Up, Sex, and Sexual Health* (Cambridge, MA: Candlewick, 2004, ages 9–12). The titles say it all. Naturalistic, wonder-filled approaches to the topics surrounding reproduction, puberty, and sex.

Celebrating Difference

Gillespie, Peggy, and Gigi Kaeser. *Love Makes a Family: Portraits of Lesbian, Gay, Bisexual, and Transgender Parents and Their Families* (Amherst, MA: University of Massachusetts Press, 1999). Age 14+.

Mills, Andy, Becky Osborn, and Erica Neitz. *Shapesville* (Carlsbad, CA: Gurze Books, 2003). An early introduction to a healthy attitude regarding body image and diversity. Shapesville is a town in which friends of different shapes, sizes, colors, and skills discuss their differences and celebrate what makes each one unique. Ages 2–5.

Huegel, Kelly. *GLBTQ: The Survival Guide for Queer and Questioning Teens* (Minneapolis: Free Spirit Publishing, 2003). A one-of-a-kind resource for teens who are gay, questioning their sexuality, or simply want to know more about the issues. Age 12+.

Videos

Let's Get Real (2004). Documentary short examines causes of taunting and bullying, including racial differences, sexual orientation, religious differences, sexual harassment, and others. Includes perspective of the bullies themselves to learn why they behave as they do. Available at *www.womedia.org*. Ages 12+.

The Point! (original 1971, remake 1986, re-released in 2004). A fabulous, off-beat TV special with psychedelic roots and a huge following. Original narrated by Dustin Hoffman, remake narrated by Ringo Starr, based on the song by Harry Nilsson. Oblio, a boy who lives in the Land of Point, becomes "pointless" and is rejected by those around him. Should he try to conform, or be himself? Available on Netflix, YouTube, and elsewhere. Ages 4–10.

That's a Family (2000). Created by The Respect for All Project and available through *www.womedia.org, That's a Family* is a remarkable and entertaining film exploring the variety of forms a loving family can take. Ages 5–10.

It's Elementary (2008). "The first film of its kind to address anti-gay prejudice by providing adults with practical lessons on how to talk with kids about gay people. . . . *It's Elementary* shows that children are eager and able to wrestle with stereotypes and absorb new facts about what it means to be gay or lesbian." Created by The Respect for All Project and available through *www .womedia.org.*

Finding Additional Resources

As a person who engages in critical thinking, you probably already have the skills you need to evaluate the resources on the parenting shelf at the library or bookstore, or the curriculum being used by your school district's sex education program. A few quick things to look at when evaluating books or curricula—what publishing house or organization released this information, what year was it published, and what are the qualifications of the authors. Just because an organization has a reputable-sounding name doesn't mean it is promoting accurate information. One example: An organization called "The Medical Institute for Sexual Health" is actually an abstinence-only advocacy organization that releases information and statistics that exclusively support its agenda, despite scientific evidence to the contrary.[24] The publication date is especially important if you are looking for technical information, like contraceptive options, since updated information and new options become available as research progresses.

Notes

1. "Abstinence Education Faces An Uncertain Future," *New York Times,* July 18, 2007; Bearman, Peter, and Hannah Brückner, "Promising the Future: Virginity Pledges and First Intercourse," *American Journal of Sociology, 106* (4), (January 2001), 859–912.

2. The National Campaign to Prevent Teen Pregnancy, "Not Just Another Single Issue: Teen Pregnancy Prevention's Link to Other Critical Social Issues" (February 2002). Accessed March 22, 2008, from *www.teenpregnancy .org/resources/data/pdf/notjust.pdf*

3. The Guttmacher Institute, "U.S. Teenage Pregnancy Statistics: National and State Trends and Trends by Race and Ethnicity" (September 2006). Available at *www.guttmacher.org/pubs/2006/09/12/USTPstats.pdf*

4. Abma, J.C., et al., "Teenagers in the United States: Sexual Activity, Contraceptive Use, and Childbearing, 2002," *Vital and Health Statistics*, 2004, Series 23, No. 24; Santelli, J.S., et al., "Explaining Recent Declines in Adolescent Pregnancy in the United States: The Contribution of Abstinence and Improved Contraceptive Use," *American Journal of Public Health* (2007) *97*(1), 1–7.

5. Study commissioned by U.S. Congress and conducted by Mathematica Policy Research, Inc. See *www.mathematica-mpr.com/welfare/abstinence.asp*

6. Darroch, J.E., J.J. Frost, and S. Singh, "Teenage Sexual and Reproductive Behavior in Developed Countries: Can More Progress Be Made?" *Occasional Report* (New York: The Alan Guttmacher Institute, 2001), No. 3.

7. Darroch, J.E., et al., "Changing Emphases in Sexuality Education in U.S. Public Secondary Schools, 1988–1999," *Family Planning Perspectives* (2000) *32*(5), 204–211, 265.

8. Ibid.

9. Reisser, Paul C., *Focus on the Family Parents' Guide to Teen Health: Raising Physically & Emotionally Healthy Teens* (Wheaton, IL: Tyndale House Publishers, 1997).

10. Martens Miller, Patricia, *Sex Is Not a Four-Letter Word! Talking Sex with Your Children Made Easier* (New York: Crossroad, 1994), p. 66–68.

11. Quoted at *www.contemporaryfamilies.org/subtemplate.php?t=pressReleases &ext=marryolder*, based on studies by Evelyn Lehrer at the University of Illinois, Chicago.

12. Haffner, pp. 113–114.

13. Haffner, p. 27.

14. Richardson and Schuster, p. 288.

15. Accessed March 5, 2008, from *www.vatican.va/archive/catechism/p3s2c2a6.htm#II*

16. Ganzfried, Rabbi Shlomo in the *Kitzur Shulchan Aruch* (1870).

17. Quoted in Rizvi, Sayyid Muhammad, "Marriage and Morals in Islam" (Ontario, Canada: Islamic Education & Information Centre, 1990).

18. He then begs forgiveness from those Christians who find his relatively reasonable attitude "inflammatory." The full text is at *www.focusonyourchild.com/develop/art1/A0000553.html*

19. Miles, Herbert, *Sexual Understanding Before Marriage* (Grand Rapids, MI: Zondervan, 2000).

20. James, Lawrence, *The Rise and Fall of the British Empire* (London: St. Martin's Griffin, 1997).

21. Quoted in Asimov, Eric, "Can Sips at Home Prevent Binges?" *New York Times*, March 26, 2008.

22. Ibid.

23. Hawkins, Dr. David B. "How Can I Help My Depressed Spouse?" Accessed April 23, 2008, from *www.crosswalk.com/marriage/1407328*

24. *www.siecus.org/policy/PUpdates/arch00/arch000004.html*

CHAPTER 5

Ingredients of a Life Worth Living

Molleen Matsumura

Okay. We humanists agree that there is no karmic law, no Grand Plan, and no Grand Planner to make the world make sense for us. Instead of discovering "The Meaning of Life," we're faced with the job of creating meaningful lives for ourselves. We also agree that happiness is to be found here and now, not in some imaginary hereafter.

But, how do we prepare our kids to do the same for themselves? This question may seem even more challenging for those of us who have set aside the religious views of our parents (especially if they were dogmatic), or who are determined not to "brainwash" our kids. None of us is satisfied with automatic answers, and we know we can't wave a magic wand over our kids and order them to "be happy."

It helps to remember that anyone of parenting age—or, for that matter, grandparenting age—is still living an unfinished story, whose meaning changes with new experiences. And that's the key. We don't have to do the impossible and give our kids all the answers to life's questions. Instead, we can join them in the adventure of meaningful living and help them develop the emotional and intellectual skills that make for a full life.

Just as humanists recognize that there is no one true meaning of life, the same is true for definitions of happiness. There are different sources of happiness; for any one person, some types of happiness are more meaningful and more attainable than others. But we can draw upon accumulated human wisdom for ideas that will resonate with our own and our children's experiences.

Even a casual search through quotations about happiness will reveal some common themes. People define happiness as:

> There is not one big cosmic meaning for all, there is only the meaning we each give to our life, an individual meaning, an individual plot, like an individual novel, a book for each person.
>
> —Anais Nin, novelist

Pleasure: "Then I commended mirth, because a man hath no better thing under the sun, than to eat, and to drink, and to be merry. . . ."[1]

Rewarding work: "The happiness that is genuinely satisfying is accompanied by the fullest exercise of our faculties and the fullest realization of the world in which we live."[2] "Happiness . . . lies in the joy of achievement and the thrill of creative effort."[3]

Love and connection: "There is only one happiness in life, to love and be loved."[4]

Altruism, or dedication to something larger than oneself: "The way to be happy is to try and make somebody else so."[5] "Many people have a wrong idea of what constitutes true happiness. It is not attained through self-gratification, but through fidelity to a worthy purpose."[6]

These same themes emerge from research in the field of positive psychology, which has developed a tremendous amount of information on what makes people feel that life is worthwhile.[7] This chapter will include some core ideas you can apply right away, followed up by resources you can use to build on your own experiences. And, since there is more information than can be covered in one book, let alone one chapter, it will emphasize issues that particularly concern humanist parents.

One idea I will borrow from researchers is that it is useful to understand and cultivate many different components of a satisfying life.

Questions and Answers

Q: Aren't some people naturally more cheerful than others? What can a parent be expected to do about natural temperament?

A: Yes, there is evidence that some people are born more cheerful or optimistic. This isn't surprising, considering that body chemistry affects our moods. But . . . well, there are two big "buts":

First, it isn't easy to take into account all the factors affecting a person's mood. For example, if one of your kids tends to get whiny just before dinnertime, that doesn't necessarily mean he is your grouchiest child. It could be that this child's moods are more affected by hunger. Another example would be a child who is more easily frustrated by certain kinds of tasks, presenting her parents with the challenges of recognizing that what looks like bad temper is really frustration, then figuring out what it is that frustrates her and how to help her cope.

Second, having a less cheerful temperament doesn't automatically condemn people to unhappy lives. They can learn to maximize their capacity for enjoyment and find other sources of life satisfaction that are based on their particular strengths, and their parents can help them learn how to do so. For example, a child who is always curious and asks lots of questions may find fulfillment as a scientist or explorer. The caring, generous child may grow into a passionate advocate for social justice.

> " Meaning is not what you start with, but what you end up with. "
>
> —Peter Elbow, writer

Q: The search for meaning is often depicted as some grand experience—six months in a cave, climbing a mountain, crossing a desert in your bare feet. How can simpler, more ordinary pleasures contribute to a meaningful life?

A: On a December day twenty-odd years ago, my 3-year-old and I made a gumdrop wreath. Chatting and laughing as we used toothpicks to attach the gumdrops to a circular base, we tasted each color.

When we were almost done, she sighed and said dreamily, "Life is good!"

This simple pleasure was more complicated than it seems at first glance. We had fun fitting different-sized gumdrops onto the base like pieces of a puzzle, and there was a warm undercurrent of affection as we worked together.

But the sensory pleasure was certainly important, and that wasn't entirely simple, either: Quickly gobbling ten gum drops of any one flavor wouldn't have been nearly as much fun as stretching out the experience, slowly nibbling at and comparing the different flavors. Without planning to, I gave my daughter an important lesson in savoring a simple pleasure. It was an example of the proverbial advice to linger and smell the roses.

Q: We hear a lot of complaints (some of them valid) about too much hedonism and materialism in everyday life, but there is also a strong puritanical streak in our culture that distrusts pleasure. Just think about the phrase "sinfully delicious." How can I protect my kids from picking up this same puritanical streak?

A: One way or another, we've all heard these messages. Let's look at some examples:

"Avoid pleasure to prevent overindulgence." Please give me some bathwater—I have a baby to throw away! We can teach our kids moderation. For example, "Are you sure you want a second slice of cake? Last time it gave you a tummyache."

"Pleasure-seeking is selfish and self-centered." It can be; but if pleasure-seeking isn't interfering with any obligations, then it's not selfish. Also, pleasure is often more fun when it involves sharing or cooperation. Think of waterskiing—somebody has to be at the wheel while somebody's on the skis.

Every time you say something like, "I can't wait till everybody else gets home so they can hear this music," you are modeling the fun of sharing pleasure. On the other hand, you will want to help your children understand that we don't all enjoy the same things. Often, there is some reciprocity involved: "I won't drag you into my game of Scrabble, and you won't pester me to go for a walk right now."

"Because pleasure doesn't last, we shouldn't bother with it." This line of thought, embedded deep in the Protestant ethic and other ascetic religious traditions, contrasts "bad," transient, earthly pleasures with "good," supposedly eternal pleasures. It is closely related to a question often asked of the nonreligious: "If you think you will someday cease to exist, why even bother getting up in the morning?"

Yes, life itself is transient, and the humanist response is to treasure life all the more for that very reason. In valuing life, we value what makes life good. The fragility of a spiderweb sparkling with morning dew doesn't make it any less beautiful.

If we understand that sensory pleasures are only one part of a good life, it's enough that pleasure is good as long as it lasts. And, we can help our children learn to recognize which activities give them most pleasure, as well as helping them be open to enjoying new experiences.

Pleasures are the sugars in the feast of life. They are enjoyable in themselves, and often handy as a quick energy source, but we also need more substantial sources of satisfaction. "Flow" is an emotional experience that more strongly sustains the feeling that life is meaningful.

Q: What is "flow," and how does it contribute to a worthwhile life?

A: Flow is a state of being we've all experienced, although many of us don't necessarily have a name for it, or know what has been learned about it in scientific studies. By identifying positive emotions in categories more specific than "happiness" and investigating which of these emotions people experience during various activities, researchers have characterized the type of experience called "flow." Some familiar examples from daily life will make it easier to grasp a description of what "flow" is:

- A musician rehearsing just before a concert.
- A toddler focused on learning to walk.
- A novelist who is "on a roll."
- A hobbyist concentrating on putting together a jigsaw puzzle.
- Friends lost in intense conversation.

Flow is not as simple as "being happy." It is about being present in the moment, thinking neither of past nor future, attending fully to the activity at

Taking Time to Savor Life

According to the Institute on Character, of the twenty-four strengths that they have measured among thousands of people, five are most important to life satisfaction: gratitude, optimism, zest, curiosity, and the ability to love and be loved.

What's notable about "gratitude" is that you don't have to be grateful *to* anyone or anything in particular; what's needed is the ability to *appreciate* or savor the little gems that stud everyday life.

I wasn't thinking about this on the rainy winter day about twenty years ago when I was climbing the steps home and saw a millipede, the first I'd ever seen. I'd never heard of the twenty-four strengths. I just knew that here was something beautiful and amazing. I ran up another thirty steps, burst into the front door, and told my family, "There is something you've got to see!"

We trooped back down the stairs to admire the lovely insect. I placed a leaf in front of it and it crawled on, then I gently lifted the leaf so we could study the finely segmented body.

Our new friend fell off the leaf onto its back—fortunately, it didn't fall too far and was unhurt. We watched in admiration as, moving a few pairs of legs at a time, the millipede gracefully spiraled back onto its belly and resumed its journey across the step. Then we went indoors and made dinner.

Finding the millipede was just one of many wonderful moments for our family. The best thing about them is that we never said anything about appreciating life—we were just prepared to all come running when someone said, "You've got to see this."

Some years later, my daughter was writing a college admissions essay. Of the list of possible topics, she chose to describe what she would tell a friend about dinner at our house. I've memorized the beginning of the essay:

"It's seven o'clock; do you know where your dinner is?

"I hear my mother's chair creak reluctantly as she gets up from her desk in reaction to my merry shout . . . ." [Of course I was not teaching procrastination, I had been in flow and was teaching the importance of interrupting the flow experience for a good enough reason—such as feeding my child.]

My daughter's essay then went on to describe other barriers to dinner actually reaching the table—like her telling me, "You've got to come and see this gorgeous sunset," or her father calling out, "Look! A perfect spider web!"

The essay ends with a happy description of wide-ranging dinner conversations, and my daughter obviously has not starved to death. But she has learned the other reason that it is important not to structure all our time. Flexibility not only increases our chances to achieve flow—it also gives us time to savor the little experiences that add up to major joy.

—*Molleen Matsumura*

■ ■ ■ ■

hand. Someone who is simply happy may be very relaxed, while flow involves concentration.

During flow, a person is completely focused on the chosen activity, so he's not distracted by background activities like traffic noise or rain falling on him as he walks. He often loses track of time. When you look up from an absorbing project or a long conversation and wonder, "Where did the time go?" you've just been in flow.

Like happiness, flow is an experience that people seek for its own sake. A flow experience starts with an activity that a person considers worthwhile; it may not be very long-lasting or completely voluntary, it may even be something she feels obligated to do, but it is *not* being done only because there's nothing better to do. A flow experience, in other words, is something we do because we value it, not just to "kill time."

Finding flow also involves finding just the right balance between an activity that is not so easy it's boring, but not so hard that it's frustrating. When you've found the balance, and an activity is challenging enough to call into play all of one's relevant skills—and maybe also bring about some improvement or learning—the flow experience is most likely to occur.[8]

Q: I see what you mean by "flow"—but how does this relate to parenting?

A: Since flow experiences are some of the most meaningful we can have, parents can help their children have a deeper experience of life by helping them find and engage in flow. And one of the most common enemies of flow is something over which parents have a good deal of control—*schedules.*

> 66 Flow with whatever may happen and let your mind be free. Stay centered by accepting whatever you are doing. This is the ultimate. 99
>
> —Chuang Tzu, Chinese philosopher (389–286 BC)`

Just when an activity is getting really interesting and the flow experience begins to take hold, it's time to set the table, leave for preschool, go to gymnastics. Your own time pressures can make it difficult to see that your child isn't necessarily just being stubborn when she doesn't want to be interrupted. It can also be challenging to set aside appropriate and adequate times for extended concentration to be possible.

Not all activities that offer the flow experience are meaningful and enriching. Take computer games. You can see why some are so attractive: They offer clear goals, immediate feedback, and a choice of skill levels so the game stays "just hard enough." But the skills involved are often useless outside the world of the game. There's nothing wrong with that by itself, of course. The same could be said of many other recreational activities. The key is to not allow these less enriching activities to overwhelm and push out the deeper, more meaningful opportunities for flow.

Helping your child have flow experiences that are both inherently satisfying and enhancing other aspects of life will depend on identifying his or her particular abilities. Practice is a good thing, but practicing hard at a particular activity, such as playing the piano or playing basketball, will be more worthwhile to some kids than others. It takes careful observation to know whether a child really needs to try a little harder or needs to try something different.

Q: How can we give our kids meaningful encouragement in ways that promotes their growth, identity, and learning?

A: Once when I was young and inexperienced (that's my excuse), I watched a toddler practice walking. When he had walked some distance without grabbing any furniture, I clapped and cheered. More walking—more cheering. After a while, he looked back over his shoulder, smiling and waiting for me to cheer . . . and toppled backwards. That incident is a perfect illustration of how *not* to encourage your child's learning and growth.

> " Our obligation is to give meaning to life and in doing so to overcome the passive, indifferent life. "
>
> —Elie Wiesel,
> Nobel Peace Laureate

Kids are born ready to learn. A toddler is driven to learn to walk. No coaxing or cheering is needed—just some furniture to grab or an adult hand to hang onto. After a fall, a baby may cry or need some comforting—then begin again. The next day, no baby asks, "But what if I fall?" He just keeps practicing until he's learned to walk, then takes on another challenge—maybe stair-climbing.

The learning process sounds much like a recipe for flow in that it takes concentration and stretches one's previous limits. When a learner has chosen her goal, or at least understands its value, learning may indeed lead to flow and be loved for its own sake—as well as helping kids acquire skills they value. Yet unfortunately, older children often seem less enthusiastic about learning.

Some aspects of that problem are outside our control—but not outside our influence. Some of our children's friends may dampen their enthusiasm for learning. We can try to support friendships with children who share excitement about learning, although sometimes we have to stand back and let kids solve this problem themselves as they mature.

Also, we can help our kids make the best of school and extracurricular experiences, which, frankly, are sometimes disappointing. For example, we can explain to kids the value of studying topics whose importance is not obvious to them or help them get along with a perfectionist teacher or coach.

Luckily, the most important thing we can do *is* within our control: We can nurture what has come to be known as a "growth mindset." Researchers and parenting advisors contrast "growth mindsets" with "fixed mindsets." If you have a fixed mindset, you think of your abilities as unchanging and may be unwilling to try new learning experiences. With a growth mindset, you believe you can increase your abilities with effort and are willing to risk setbacks as part of learning.

Some experiments studying mindsets involved giving different types of praise to two groups of children who had succeeded in the same task. Some children were told, "You must be very smart," while another group was told, "You must have tried very hard." The second group was significantly more willing than the first to try a new task that they were told would be more challenging and that they might learn something while trying to solve it.[9]

What such research has shown is that well-meaning comments that describe kids in fixed terms, such as, "You're smart," or, "You're a natural athlete," can actually have negative results: A child may fear that if he fails, he won't be valued as "a smart kid"; or she may feel something like, "I impressed them *this* time, but what happens when they find out I'm not really much of an athlete?"

In a family atmosphere that supports learning, parents praise the willingness to make necessary efforts. They recognize achievements while making clear that their affection is not contingent on success. They try new activities with their children as well as sharing familiar pleasures and talk frankly about what they have learned from their own mistakes.

Q: One aspect of parenting that continues to amaze and challenge me is how different my children are from each other. How can I recognize and encourage their individual strengths?

A: A friend of mine was being visited by her son for a few days, during which he offered to help her shop for a new car. By the end of the visit, she was still undecided about even what make of car she wanted. He was impatient, feeling that they had spent plenty of time on a relatively easy decision. She thought she needed more information before making a major purchase. "I think he was irritated with me," she commented.

What's interesting about this story is that both these people are health professionals. The mother began her career as a rehabilitation nurse and now is a project manager developing health education programs. Her first job required much patience and sensitivity to tiny signs of progress. For the current job she needs to amass enough accurate information to justify launching a project, and she has to think through everything that might come up during its implementation. Her son is an emergency room physician—he has to collect the right information quickly, often without enough time to collect all the information he would like to have before making life-and-death decisions. Their tension over how to reach a decision grew from different personal strengths that serve each of them well. They are both fortunate to have found circumstances where they can take advantage of their respective strengths—circumstances that are likely to lead to an increased daily experience of flow.

The understanding of character strengths and how to nurture them is an active field of research. A "character strength" is a personal attitude or pattern of behavior that helps get through life in a constructive, satisfying way. Many researchers in this area focus on twenty-four strengths that are quite varied; for example, the VIA [Values in Action] Classification of Character Strengths and Virtues includes persistence, kindness, gratitude, and humor.[10]

These strengths are not unchanging characteristics; while each person will tend to be stronger in certain areas, we can increase a strength if we choose to make the effort. And, we may change over time: One study found that, on average, adolescents and adults show different strengths.[11]

It is important for parents using these ideas to understand that

> . . . The . . . [VIA] understanding of character goes beyond "having it" or not. These scholars found character to be "plural with individual differences that are stable and general, but also . . . capable of change." Individuals are found to exhibit particular, unique constellations of character strengths which can be identified and nurtured. . . . Unlike the more common one-size-fits-all conceptualizations of "good character" (e.g., all children should possess a set of six character traits), VIA asserts that each person has their own profile of positive characteristics. . . ."[12]

While it can't be said that that one strength is "better" than another, there are studies suggesting that some strengths are more strongly correlated with life satisfaction.[13,14]

Understanding their children's strengths can help parents in a number of ways:

- By giving us a different lens on children's behavior. For example, a child who seems to be dawdling on the way to school, or while on an errand with you, might be slowing down to notice the silvery trails that snails leave on leaves, exhibiting *curiosity* by wondering how they got there, or *appreciation* by simply admiring their beauty.

- By helping us encourage our children to use their strengths, which is both intrinsically enjoyable and a source of positive outcomes. (For example, doing science experiments with your child encourages curiosity and critical thinking *and* broadens her knowledge of the natural world.)
- By helping us see when apparent "faults" are actually strengths that need to be moderated or re-channeled. For example, "stubbornness" can be persistence that needs to be re-channeled into finding a different way to reach a goal.
- By giving us a way to help our children think about interpersonal differences.
- By giving families a way to deepen their bonds while engaging in activities that increase various strengths. (I encourage looking for ways for the *entire family* to engage in such activities; you avoid the risk of seeming to disapprove of your child when pointing out areas that could be strengthened. When the whole family works together, the message is that we *all* have room to grow.)

Q: As my children move into their teen years, I find myself worrying about the growing influence of their peers. How can I best understand this transition?

A: We are social animals. Thousands of pages have been written about what that means for all aspects of our lives. And much of what we know—for example, how important it is that children be securely attached to their caregivers—is true for all families, regardless of their beliefs. Rather than repeat universally relevant information, I want to talk about something that is especially significant for humanist parents.

Parents hope that their children will choose appropriate friends who are a positive influence. At the same time, here in the United States at least, when kids reach their early teens, parents become especially worried about "peer pressure." Parents also worry about the "cliquishness" of teenage social groups. The special twist for freethinking parents is that we are probably more concerned than average about independent thinking and the ability to "go against the crowd."

Concerns about conformity look different when you think about what adult friendships are like. Even those of us who enjoy meeting and learning from people who are different from ourselves have a special place in our lives for friends who are similar to us. For example, atheists frequently express their desire to meet "like-minded" people. In the best friendships, not only do we feel more comfortable around like-minded people, we know we can count on them to give advice (when needed) that's in accordance with our values, to challenge us to live up to our standards, to understand our moods without detailed explanations. We also understand that there are different levels of friendship. For example, your golf buddy may or may not be someone you'd talk with about emotional problems.

It's not so different for our teens. They want the same things, just more intensely.[15] Our teens are learning how to choose truly compatible friends, how to maintain friendships, how to recognize the obligations and limits of loyalty. Acquiring these skills is an important part of their transition to adulthood. It's also important to their growing independence from their parents. We won't be around forever to provide advice and emotional support. Our kids need to learn which other people to reach out to, and how.

One of my happiest moments during my daughter's adolescence was when she was talking to me about a difficult relationship. By then she had patiently trained me to ask, "Do you want my advice or my sympathy?" I was listening sympathetically when she said, "I know what I'll do! I'll ask Adi. She always has good advice." Adi was one of her oldest friends, and I could honestly reply, "Good idea!" Adi's advice was excellent, and my daughter's ability to ask the right person for advice, and then to follow that advice, gave me confidence in her future happiness.

This is not to say that we shouldn't be concerned about how hurtful teens can be when they exclude or tease their peers. At best it's the clumsiness that comes with learning new skills; at worst it is intolerance and bullying that calls for adult intervention. It's essential that we give our children respect and unconditional affection so that they will refuse to settle for less from their friends.

It's also important to take seriously the ups and downs of our children's friendships; remember how powerful those experiences were for you when you were a teen and be as supportive as you can. In particular, be sensitive and cautious when your child is deciding whether the way someone has treated him or her means that the friendship should be ended or that the friend should be confronted. Those kinds of decisions are important preparation for adult life. (Yes, that's assuming they want your opinion. Often they prefer to stumble through on their own).

Finally, be careful when deciding to discipline a teen by "grounding" him or her. Think of it this way: We no longer think it's appropriate to send a misbehaving child to bed without dinner, because he needs that nutrition for his growth. In the same way, most teens need the emotional sustenance of their friendships. If a group of friends have seriously misbehaved together (for example, by playing a stupid prank or drinking and driving), then their time together should be supervised, and maybe limited. But if a generally well-behaved kid makes a more normal and minor mistake like skipping some chores, that's not grounds for grounding.

Q: I have very mixed feelings about fantasy. It seems to me that we humans tend to cling to imaginary things instead of seeking the beauty in reality. On the other hand, my reading as a kid was all about dragons and elves; I loved it and never confused it with the real world. As a humanistic parent, what place should I expect fantasy and imagination to have in my kids' world?

A: They belong somewhere very close to the center of that world.

In his introduction to *The Log from the Sea of Cortez*, John Steinbeck wrote, "The impulse that drives a man to poetry will send another man into the tide pools and force him to report what he finds there." If anybody could say that with confidence, it would be a novelist on a scientific expedition. This remark was a profound comment on human nature: Both art *and* science spring from human tendencies to seek patterns in the world around us and to wonder, "What if . . . ?"

Steinbeck's deceptively simple comment has a powerful message for humanist parents. It is just as important to encourage our children's imagination and artistry as it is to encourage their reasoning abilities and love for science.

Humanist parents surely *do* encourage imagination and artistry as much as other parents. But in our public discussions, these concerns are overshadowed by worries about the influences of superstition and dogmatism in our culture. This creates the false impression that there has to be a choice. In fact, we really do have more options than either maintaining supernatural illusions or adopting a cold, gritty realism that sometimes consists of nothing more than resignation to the worst in life.

A key to giving our children more choices is to abandon guilt by association. Drums and trumpets have urged soldiers into battle, but rather than abandon music because it has been used in war, we can use it for love songs and joyous celebrations. Imagination—the ability to conceptualize events and experiences that don't exist—has been pressed into the service of oppressive political and religious institutions and often abused. But instead of abandoning imagination, we can reclaim it as a resource for individuals.

It's easy to make high-minded statements about the blessings that imagination offers as the source of art, literature, and practical inventions. They'd be true, but if that's all we say, we imply that we have to justify the use of imagination. A more distinctively humanistic approach is to celebrate and nurture at least two uses of fantasy: fantasy as a tool children use in coming to terms with the world, and fantasy as a source of pleasure.

One of the greatest joys of childhood is fantasy, and children's fantasies are endlessly varied. It's fun to watch this play, and parents should feel free to join in. Humanist parents with religious spouses may be frightened when their children come home from Sunday school repeating myths; feminist parents may worry that old-fashioned fairy tales will make their daughters feel worthless and their sons disrespectful. But if we learn to understand how children use fantasy, it can be a gentle and powerful means of communication.

I once spent a full half-hour watching two little girls play Snow White. I might not have recognized the story if they hadn't mentioned it aloud, because they re-enacted only one scene, over and over—Snow White's resurrection. They ignored all sorts of details that worry adults: The wicked stepmother was nothing like their loving mommies, and the prince was nothing like the muddy little boys they played with. But, like many 4-year-olds, they had learned about death, and their play revealed a feeling shared by many adults—the wish that death could somehow be undone.

Later, grieving a death in the family, my daughter and I acted out the story of Buddha and the mustard seed; another time, we made up our own story about reincarnation. Another family might choose to read stories about different views of the afterlife: Valhalla is a different place from the Christian heaven. Another might choose to tell the story of Demeter and Persephone, and a child hearing it would make his or her own comparison, some day, between that tale and the one about Abraham and Isaac. Telling and inventing stories both encourages children to use their own imaginations and communicates that fantasy is a worthwhile activity. At the same time, myths and allegories are put into perspective; a child who has played with, then outgrown, imaginary friends and read about the fantastic spirits of other cultures will be less vulnerable to the latest craze for angels or aliens.

A child who has looked for animal shapes in clouds and in pieces of popcorn is prepared to understand how people imagine that they see a Madonna in the burned spots on a tortilla—and may be inspired to produce some highly imaginative art.

Wishing is another type of fantasy that influences reality. Children who pretend to be each other's siblings often develop lifelong friendships.

As adults, we continue to daydream. Sometimes daydreams are the only pleasure we have, and, as long as we aren't distracted from acting to improve our situations, daydreaming is an act of psychological resilience. Yet daydreaming that isn't institutionalized (like political fervor and faith-healing) is commonly put down as childish. After all, daydreaming is fun in itself, and the things we dream of are sex, power, wealth, and love—worthy human pleasures derided by the most oppressive religious traditions.

Fantasy also nurtures the capacity to hope. Hope is radically different from faith. To hope is not to assume that things will be better, but to be sustained by the sense that they *can* be better and to act accordingly. With hope, we recognize those moments that call on us not merely to adapt to circumstances, but to seek, recognize, and seize the opportunity for change.

Seeking the opportunity means beginning with an act of imagination that can only be fulfilled through determination and rational striving, integrating all our human potentials.

So don't wait for your child to ask. Have a wonderful time seeing what happens when you begin by saying, "Let's pretend."

Activities

Creating a meaningful life is a lifelong pursuit—and not one that translates easily into individual activities for a rainy afternoon. On the other hand, there are countless general ways in which we can promote creative engagement with meaning in our families. This section provides a few ideas and suggestions for making meaningful activities an integral part of your family's life.

Simple Pleasures

All ages

The most meaningful and engaging activities are often the simplest: flying kites, a walk in the woods, a trip to the aquarium. The greatest obstacle to a life of simple pleasures is the ruthless schedule. Free up time from routine activities. Schedule some unplanned time every week. Turn work into play and waiting time into game time with word games, observation games, storytelling. **Great resource for waiting games:** Chapter 1 of Susan Perry's *Playing Smart: The Family Guide to Enriching, Offbeat Learning Activities for Ages 4–14.*

Engage your kids in activities that use *all* the senses—the traditional senses of touch, taste, smell, sight, and sound and the kinesthetic (position of your body in space—what makes it fun to go swimming or just run around). Enjoy both passively *and* actively—for example, both listening to music and singing. **Great resource for sensory play:** Chapter 3 of *Playing Smart.*

Mix familiarity and novelty, choosing times when your kids are energetic and alert to try new activities. Make it a family tradition to try at least one new sensation a week—miniature golf, karaoke, an exotic fruit you haven't tried before. Build on your child's likes and dislikes. For example, a "picky eater" could have fun with blind tastings. Can your kid *really* taste the differences between different colored M&Ms? How about the difference between puréed carrots and squash? Singing together might lead to helping a verbally adept child make up funny words to familiar tunes, or giving musical toys and instruments to a kid who's more interested in the melody might encourage new music.

Encouraging Flow Experiences

All ages

Give your child the vocabulary to understand and recognize flow experiences and their value. For example, there are times either one of you should be able to say to the other, "Can we talk later? I'm concentrating." And, you can model enjoyment of challenges with comments like, "That was fun! I really had to try hard to figure out how to balance on a unicycle." **Great resource for encouraging flow:** Pages 1–4 of *Playing Smart*.

Encouraging Positive Attitudes Toward Growth and Learning

For parents

View parenting videos at the "Half Full" website (*http://peacecenter.berkeley .edu/tools.html*), including "Effort, Not Achievement," "Embracing Kids' Failure," and "Fostering Growth Mindsets." Discuss these ideas with parenting partners. Reach a consensus on when a mistake should be considered an opportunity to grow and when it means a child needs help.

When you make mistakes, model honesty and lifelong learning. Find the humor or the lesson in the situation. For example, "Whoops! I left the sugar out of the lemonade. How silly can you get? You think I should try it with limes next time?" Or, after assembling furniture from a kit, "No wonder the chair is lopsided. I didn't follow the instructions on page 6. Next time, I'll look over the instructions *before* I start a project."

The Signature Strengths Questionnaire

Ages 10–18

Preteens and teens enjoy taking questionnaires designed to tell them more about themselves. Encourage them to take the "Authentic Happiness" website's "Signature Strengths" questionnaire. It could be fun for you to talk about these tests with your kids, or even take them together and compare notes, but be aware that many teens may prefer to talk about it with their peers—it goes with the territory of being a teen. Either way, taking the tests opens the door for reflection.

Talk about what insight into your personalities and relationships is offered by the Strengths questionnaire results: for example, "No wonder you are always asking me questions! Curiosity is one of your key strengths."

As a family, choose a character strength that you will all work on for a month. For example, use the exercises in the "Caring" chapter of *What Do You Stand For?* Or, increase your appreciation of the good things in life by setting aside time each day for each family member to talk about "three good things that happened to me." (This exercise is based on research findings that people who keep a "gratitude diary" increase their happiness and appreciation of life.) **Another excellent questionnaire:** Barbara Lewis's *What Do You Stand For? A Kid's Guide to Building Character* (page 7).

Thinking About Friendship

Young children

Help your kids develop "emotional intelligence" about themselves and others. Comment on the evident feelings of people around you and characters in stories. "Joey is crying; he must be feeling sad." "Why do you think Maria is laughing?" Comment on your child's feelings and encourage him or her to express them. Help with simple terms for complex feelings; for example, when my 3-year-old was obviously feeling ambivalent, I talked about her seeming to have "mixed-up feelings." Also, keep communications clear by commenting on the feelings underlying a statement or an action. For example, if your child says, "I hate you!" answer, "Wow! You are really mad at me, aren't you?"

Talk with your child about who she likes or doesn't like to play with, and why. When she doesn't want to play with another child, it may be a problem you can help resolve. But some kids really are incompatible, and their choices need to be respected as much as possible. Sometimes kids play in different ways with different friends, and it isn't until they're older that they can figure out how to bring these friends together (for example, your child may feel uncomfortable bringing together a friend who goes in for rough-and-tumble play and a friend who likes to act out stories). All these issues affect your child's developing sense of identity.

Middle school

This is the time when many parents worry that their kids are too driven by pressure to conform. Often that's true, but it's more complicated than that. Kids are also choosing friends as a part of figuring out who they are or would like to be and as part of the process of becoming more independent from their families. Knowing your child's particular strengths enables you to help him choose friends who are also curious/kind/in love with learning. On the other hand, if she's interested in people who are very different, it takes sensitive attention to figure out whether she's exploring new possibilities in a way you want to support, or indeed yielding to unhealthy social pressures.

Late middle school and high school

Help your teen choose extracurricular activities that involve his personal strength—science camp for the curious critical thinker, for example, or appropriate volunteer work for an especially kind, generous kid.

Encouraging Fantasy and Creativity

All ages

Enjoy the arts with your kids, as well as encouraging them to have fun on their own. Enjoy both actively and passively: that is, singing or playing music as well as listening; enjoying the visual arts, and drawing, painting, playing with clay yourselves. Read stories and make them up. Have fun experimenting with materials; books with art activities for preschoolers have lots of good ideas. Make bath time fun with soap "crayons" that wash off the tub surround; fingerpaint with pudding mix; drum with wooden spoons on pots and pans.

Think carefully before offering formal lessons. Some kids will want to enjoy themselves without being told what to do, while others might enjoy lessons as a way to learn new techniques.

Role-playing can help your child find the courage to do something scary or develop a new skill. For example, it's a thrill for a 4- or 5-year-old to be entrusted with the responsibility of answering the phone. Practice with a script:

PARENT: Ring! Ring!

CHILD: Hello. Who's calling please?

PARENT: Is Ms. Matsumura there?

CHILD: I'll see. Can I ask who's calling?

Take inspiration from silly fantasies in children's stories. For example, in *The Wonderful O,* James Thurber imagines the consequences when a king bans the use of the letter "O"—among other things, Ophelia Oliver doesn't want to say her name any more! What would happen if we dropped the letter "A"? If rivers ran backwards? If people could walk on the ceiling like flies (especially if they were trying to wear hats)?

Differentiating fantasy from reality is a common concern of humanist parents. Remember that serious imagining can be the first step to a marvelous goal. You can talk with your child about the difference between pretend ways to make something happen and real ways to make it happen. There are many stories of people flying by flapping their arms or tying on imitation bird wings. Then there are the stories of experiments that led to the invention of airplanes and even human-powered flight (the original "Gossamer Condor" is on display at the Smithsonian Institution, and there are books and DVDs about it.)

Listen to your kids' fantasies as a way of learning about their feelings. For example, while having an imaginary friend may just be a fun game, it may mean your child wants more chances to play with other kids.

Resources
Happiness and Flow
Authentic Happiness

> *www.authentichappiness.com*

Maintained by the Positive Psychology Center of the University of Pennsylvania, this website includes such self-assessment tools as a survey of individual strengths for adults and a shorter questionnaire that helps kids about 10 and older identify their individual character strengths. Children under 13 must be registered by their parents. It's a site you will want to revisit from time to time as interesting research reports accumulate. Imagine how helpful it will be to know the outcome of a research project on teaching ninth graders positive psychology. **Special feature:** Articles by Ben Dean on "Open-Mindedness," "Love of Learning," "Persistence," and "Integrity" in the *Authentic Happiness Coaching Newsletters.*

Greater Good Science Center: The Science of Raising Happy Kids

> *www.greatergoodscience.org* > Click on FOR PARENTS

Affiliated with the University of California, Berkeley, this is a rich, varied, and accessible treasury of resources for parents. Focus is on "the scientific understanding of happy and compassionate individuals, strong social bonds, and altruistic behavior." Parenting videos, the "Half Full" parenting blog, and *Greater Good Magazine* are just a few of the offerings. **Special feature:** Wonderful, engaging, down-to-earth videos on raising happy kids.

Seligman, Martin. *Authentic Happiness: Using the New Positive Psychology to Realize Your Potential for Lasting Fulfillment* (New York: Free Press, 2004). A readable overview of scientific research on what really makes people happy, including short self-tests and practical tools to use in daily life, lightened up with personal anecdotes. There is one chapter on parenting, so you might prefer to get the book from the library (although many tools appropriate for adults can be extrapolated to kids.)

Carter, Christine. "The Childhood Roots of Adult Happiness," a research report for the Greater Good Science Center at the University of California, Berkeley. *http://peacecenter.berkeley.edu/research_families_carter.html*. This chapter draws on research in the field of positive psychology, and this article summarizes some of its findings. Written for parents, it helps sort out nature and nurture and summarizes research on what we can do to help our kids grow into happy adults with the skills to lead a fulfilling life.

Csikszentmihalyi, Mihaly. *Finding Flow: The Psychology of Engagement with Everyday Life* (New York: Basic Books, 1998). The definitive work on the subject.

Creativity
Writing with Writers

www.teacher.scholastic.com/writewit

Affiliated with Scholastic Books, this wonderful website includes ideas for many kinds of writing (for example, biography, descriptive, myth) and places that publish kids' writing. **Special feature:** A "Brainstorming Machine" for writing myths. Click on WRITING MYTHS > Myth Brainstorming Machine.

Perry, Susan K. *Playing Smart: The Family Guide to Enriching, Offbeat Learning Activities for Ages 4–14,* revised ed. (Minneapolis: Free Spirit Publishing, 2001). Now available at the author's website at *www.bunnyape.com/other_books .htm*. I wish I'd had this book when my kids were little; I'll make sure my grandchildren's parents have it. Where else would you find a book with a list of dozens of books for children written by famous adult authors (Maya Angelou, David Mamet, Isaac Bashevis Singer), *and* chapters on fun in the kitchen, a backyard, in cemeteries, *and* a chapter on how kids can learn about their own psychology and other peoples'. Definitely a life-enricher.

Gould, Roberta. *The Kids Multicultural Craft Book: 35 Crafts from Around the World* (Charlotte, VT: Williamson Publishing, 2004). Why this book, out of the countless arts and crafts books that are available? Instructions are clear and thorough, always letting kids know if an adult should be available; many of the projects really can and will continue to be used (like the musical instruments); the ideas for using recycled materials are well calculated to inspire your kids to find more uses for everyday objects; another layer of excitement is added by the author's stories about how she learned various crafts, and her explanations of their cultural context. (An inset at the beginning of each project locates its origin on a map of the home continent.)

Character, Reflection, and More

Lewis, Barbara A. *What Do You Stand For? A Kid's Guide to Building Character* (Minneapolis: Free Spirit Publishing, 1998). Preteens and teens enjoy taking quizzes and surveys that help them understand themselves better. The survey on page 7 of this book helps them identify the ethical strengths they already have and where they would like to grow. *And then* the following chapters offer probing questions and practical exercises for helping your kids become the people they would like to be.

Comte-Sponville, Andre. *The Little Book of Atheist Spirituality* (New York: Viking Adult, 2007). A marvelous, thought-provoking new book addressing one of the most common concerns about a world without religion.

Grayling, A.C. *The Meaning of Things: Applying Philosophy to Life* (London: Phoenix, New Ed edition, 2002). One of the great living writers exploring meaning from the humanist perspective.

Winell, Marlene. *Leaving the Fold: A Guide for Former Fundamentalists and Others Leaving Their Religion* (Berkeley: Apocryphile Press, 2006). Written as a guide for people who have left fundamentalist religion and are going through major emotional changes, this book will also be helpful to parents who want to give their children an upbringing different from what they experienced. The book contains practical exercises and chances for reflection that can help you become the parent you want to be, or give your kids useful guidance.

Especially relevant to meaning and purpose: Chapter 13, "Living Life Now" (especially the sections on pleasure and humor); Chapter 14, "Thinking for Yourself"; and Chapter 15, "Choosing and Creating."

Notes

1. *Ecclesiastes* 8:15 (King James version). Yes, *really*! What a humanistic statement! No wonder commentators have pointed out that Ecclesiastes is very different from the rest of the bible.

2. Russell, Bertrand. Quoted at *www.wisdomquotes.com* (WQ), a reliable source maintained by Ethical Culture Leader Jone Johnson. Accessed March 4, 2008.

3. Roosevelt, Franklin D., First Inaugural Address. Saturday, March 4, 1933.

4. George Sand.

5. Ingersoll, Robert G., in the course of a discussion on The Limits of Toleration (1888). For the full text of this statement by the "Great Agnostic" of the 19th century, visit *www.secularweb.org*. Accessed March 4, 2008.

6. Keller, Helen, Wisdom Quotes. *www.wisdomquotes.com*

7. One method these researchers have used is The Experience-Sampling Method (ESM), in which participants keep a log in which they describe specific activities they were engaged in and accompanying moods on a detailed list provided by researchers. Tens of thousands of people have participated in such studies, which in turn served as the basis for numerous scientific studies.

8. Csikszentmihalyi, Mihaly, *Finding Flow: The Psychology of Engagement with Everyday Life* (New York: Basic Books, 1998), pp. 28–29. Other aspects of this discussion have been taken from pp. 23–34. See also "Flow vs. Its Opposite" (*www.daddy-dialectic.blogspot.com/2007/01/flow-vs-its-opposite .html*) and "Outside Room 15" (*www.greatergoodscience.blogspot.com/ 2007/01/outside-room-15-chocolate-ice-cream-vs.html#links*) for two brilliant blog excursions on flow. Both sites accessed April 28, 2008.

9. For example, Dweck, C.S., and M.L. Kamins, "Person Versus Process, Praise and Criticism: Implications for Contingent Self-Worth and Coping," *Developmental Psychology, 35*(3) (1999), 835–847; and Dweck, C.S., and M.L. Kamins, "Praise for Intelligence Can Undermine Children's Motivation and Performance," *Journal of Personality and Social Psychology, 75*(1) (1998), 41. These and similar research results are described at *http://greater good.berkeley.edu/half_full/?p=49*. Accessed April 28, 2008.

10. Peterson, C., and M. Seligman, *Character Strengths and Virtues, A Handbook and Classification* (New York: Oxford University Press, 2004). This is the academic text. A list of the "twenty-four strengths" is at *www .viastrengths.org*, along with a brief summary of how the classification was developed and how it is used in research. Accessed May 4, 2008.

11. Park, N., C. Peterson, and M.E.P. Seligman, *Strengths of Character and Well-Being Among Youth*. Unpublished manuscript, University of Rhode Island, 2005. Abstract accessed May 4, 2008, from *www.viastrengths.org/ Research/Abstracts/tabid/63/Default.aspx*

12. "History of the [VIA] Classification and Survey." Accessed May 4, 2008, from *www.viastrengths.org/AboutVIA/ClassificationOverview/tabid/66/ Default.aspx*

13. According to a research overview at *www.viastrengths.org/Research/tabid/ 57/Default.aspx*, "Much of the early research . . . [on] the association between character strengths and life . . . point[s] in particular to the strengths

of love, hope, gratitude, curiosity, and zest as robust contributors." (This overview includes citations of scholarly literature). Site accessed May 4, 2008.

14. "A study with more than 4000 participants revealed that five key strengths—gratitude, optimism, zest, curiosity, and the ability to love and be loved—are more closely and consistently related to life satisfaction than the other strengths." Dean, Ben, PhD, "The Five Key Strengths" adapted from the *Authentic Happiness Newsletter*, 2(7), and posted at *www.viastrengths.org/VIAClassification/MoreOnStrengths/FiveKeyStrengths/tabid/116/Default.aspx*. Note that these lists of key strengths are overlapping, but not identical. Accessed May 4, 2008.

15. Csikszentmihalyi points out that, "The most positive experiences people report are usually those with friends. This is especially true for adolescents . . ." (p. 81). He continues on pp. 85–88 to discuss how friendship has become an important part of modern family life, and how friendships within the family work differently from friendships outside the family.

CHAPTER 6

Celebrating Life

Jan Devor

The world that we live in too often seems filled with very serious business. Grim news, grim rules for children ("Don't leave my sight at the mall or someone will kidnap you!")[1] and grim expressions on our faces. Teachers, parents, and coaches are constantly telling children to "Get serious!" You have to be a serious student, a serious worker, a serious musician, or a serious athlete to get ahead.

There is indeed a lot to be serious about, from economic concerns to violence and injustice to the seemingly intractable problems of poverty, starvation, and war. That's why nonreligious people are involved in so many social and civic actions: We realize that our efforts in the here and now are the one shot we have at making this world a better place. There is so much to do, so much to work on, so much to think and talk about.

But just as we have only one life, our children have only one childhood. It would be a shame to allow the amazing joy of being alive to be consumed by the grim and serious side of things. So how can you lighten up your children's experience of the world? How do you give them a shot of hope, fun, and excitement, a feeling that growing up is an adventure, imbued with meaning and delight? How do you give them a sense of family and the continuity of time? One great way is through rituals, celebrations, and holiday festivals.

Ritual is something that you do repeatedly. It offers that feeling of continuity to life and to your family. Celebrations are occasions to have a party! You can combine ritual and celebration, of course. Birthday celebrations provide a perfect example. They vary from year to year but usually include some element of tradition as well, some golden thread connecting each individual celebration with those that have passed. Perhaps the parents always read a poem that they've written about the birthday person. Maybe you always slept over at Aunt Meg's house on the last day of school.

Holiday festivals are those cultural and religious celebrations that come around once a year—and usually mean some time off from school! These include both religious and nonreligious holidays, as well as religious holidays with fully formed secular expressions, like Easter and Christmas.

Which brings us to heart of the matter for nonreligious parents. The idea of parallel secular expressions of religious holidays is key to the nonreligious experience of cultural celebrations. That most holidays have religious roots, even those we think of as entirely secular, should come as no surprise, since the church controlled the calendar and traced the rhythms of the year for so many centuries. Both Valentine's Day and St. Patrick's Day were originally the feast days of saints, after all. Does that have to interfere with our expressions of love or Irishness?

One way or another, nonreligious parents must come to terms with the religious holidays. Kids don't like to feel out of sync with the majority of their friends who are celebrating, for example, Christmas or Easter. Don't be the parents who make your child say, "Happy Spring" instead of "Happy Easter." Instead of discarding religious holidays, make them your own. Many of us were celebrating Christmas as kids long before we even knew that Jesus was involved! Look beyond the religious underpinnings to the human meaning surrounding each holiday and the human needs that are satisfied by it. Generosity, kindness, peace on Earth, the uniqueness of every child—these are values not just for the religious!

There is a wonderful new movement called Krismas that captures all the warmth, spirit, and fun of Christmas but focuses on Kris (Kringle) and his spirit of giving. Many secular families have found Krismas the perfect solution to the conundrum of that particular holiday, bellowing out "Merry Krismas!" to friends and neighbors and meaning it with all their hearts.

This chapter includes many more suggestions on how to reframe holidays to a more secular view. Also, holidays such as the Fourth of July, Earth Day, and Thanksgiving are perfect opportunities to invite religious relatives over for a celebration unburdened with religious expectations.

Creative rites of passage are meaningful ways to recognize the development of your child. These rites can acknowledge movement between school levels—preschool to kindergarten, middle school to high school, and so on—or a way to remember someone who has died. Some mothers want to recog-

Santatheology

GRANDMA: Oh, look, here's another one: "To Delaney, from Santa!"

DELANEY (5): EEEEEE, hee hee hee! (*rustle rustle*) Omigosh, new PJs!! With puppy dogs!!

GRANDMA: Now, if they don't fit, we can exchange them. I have the receipt.

DELANEY, *with accusing eyebrows:* What do you mean, you have the receipt? How could *you* have the receipt?

GRANDMA: Oh, I mean . . . well, Santa leaves the receipts with the gifts.

DELANEY, *eyebrows still deployed:* Uh huh.

CONNOR (11): Laney, be careful. If you don't believe in Santa even for one minute, you'll get coal in your stocking.

DELANEY: I don't think so.

CONNOR: Well, you better not doubt him anyway, just in case it's true!

DELANEY: I think Santa would care more that I was good than if I believe in him.

It was the whole history of religious discourse in 15 seconds. Reread it, changing "Santa" to "God" and "get coal in your stocking" to "burn in Hell." For the finishing touch, replace Connor with Blaise Pascal and Delaney with Voltaire.

—*Dale McGowan, from the blog* The Meming of Life

nize the maturing of a daughter who has begun menstruation, while some parents mark the fifteenth or sixteenth birthday as significant.

Creating a rite of passage doesn't have to be a big deal—just a meaningful one! All that is required is some kind of public or private recognition of an important event in your child's life. You won't be disappointed by your child's reaction to a rite of passage if you just put some kind of effort into making it personal to them. A personal statement of appreciation is always a keepsake for your child. A handmade gift shows how much care and thought you have put into the celebration. Making a child's favorite meal and saying a few words is making a family dinner a simple rite of passage! It is the recognition of the accomplishment and not the gift that is important.

This chapter will help you to navigate some situations that might come up around holidays and celebrations within our religiously diverse society and, perhaps, family. It will give resources for nonreligious families to create your own meaningful rituals, celebrations, and holidays and suggest activities that could create fun and memories for nonreligious families. Remember that religious families do not have the corner on family values and family fun. Nonreligious families have many opportunities to make special times with special meanings for their families!

Questions and Answers

Q: I loved the sights and sounds of Christmas and Easter when I was a kid, but now as an adult, I don't want to build it around the Christian message for my kids. Is there a way to get around the religious meaning and still celebrate the holidays without them becoming just commercial celebrations?

A: There are countless ways to celebrate Christmas and Easter, and most fall well between devout religious observance and crass consumerism. Celebrating Christmas as the possibility of every child and Easter as the renewal of spirit and the earth are certainly ways to frame these holidays in a nonreligious way. There is a wonderful website that suggests that we celebrate the Christmas holiday as Krismas and frame the holiday around the celebration of Kris Kringle. You can find more information on this at *http://krismas.org.*

Many of us have been celebrating these holidays in secular ways from the beginning, focusing on the warmth of the human spirit and community, the renewal of hope and the fun activities that surround the day. The website *www.tetrakatus.org* offers a list of the Twelve Days of Secular Christmas. These include Winter Solstice, Human Light, Krismas, Crispness, World Week, Boxing Day, Kwanzaa, and New Years. *Parenting Beyond Belief* includes some great chapters such as "To Easter Bunny or Not to Easter Bunny?" and "The Question of Claus—Should the Santa Story Stay or Go in Secular Families?" which gives a point/counterpoint format to this age-old discussion.

Looking for something to do together on Christmas or Easter morning? Unitarian Universalist congregations are an excellent option, or seek out any liberal religious institution such as the Ethical Cultural Society. As fundamentalists point out, to their chagrin, there is no shortage of utterly secular celebrations around these holidays as well, from Christmas morning ice skating parties to Easter egg rolls and egg hunts. Check your local paper or Chamber of Commerce website.

Q: How can I create some family traditions of my own for the month of December?

A: December is rich with possibilities for family traditions. What appeals to you? Family dinners in candlelight? Perhaps creating a decorative paper chain where one link is taken off each day until Christmas morning or the solstice? Look in the Activities section of this chapter to see about creating your own specialized advent wreath. Singing is a wonderful way to cheer up a dark evening. Is there one recipe that you can save and only bake during December? Take a car ride with the whole family and look at holiday lights. Making a tradition doesn't have to be elaborate. It has to do with the family gathering for a purpose and that can be around whatever you wish. Do it twice and it's a tradition!

Q: Christmas Eve is always a strain on our family. We travel to my parents' house and they insist on the whole gang going to our old family church for services. The memories of that place are not pleasant for me and I hate going, but I've done so anyway to please my parents. Do you think that I should keep up this charade?

A: Participating in some religious rituals—baptism and communion, for example—can raise serious issues of integrity and give the impression that you endorse specific ideas (such as original sin) that you do not. But simply going to your parents' church on Christmas Eve need not carry the same weight. You have already chosen not to participate in the family religion, which is statement enough that the religion holds no value for you. You don't have to re-emphasize that by refusing to accompany the family to church, and going can be a sign of respect on your part for them, even if not for the church itself.

I would explain it this way to my children: "While I do not agree with the teachings of this church, I do respect the fact that the church is important to Grandma and Grandpa, and I am going for them. We can talk about the service afterwards and how you felt about it. I do not expect you to kneel or bow your head during prayers unless you feel like it, and none of us will be taking communion, since that means you are part of the church. I do expect that you sit quietly and to be respectful of the people who are there."

Q: My relatives insist on sending my kids very religious cards and presents for birthdays and holidays. This really annoys me—but no one wants to rip a new book out of a young child's hands and refuse to read it! How should I handle this?

A: Communicating about religious gifts ahead of time is important. Waiting until a religious gift is opened and then voicing disapproval simply teaches rudeness. I would approach the giver and ask if, for the joy of the occasion for everyone, the gifts given could be of a secular nature. If the person disagrees, you will simply have to talk with your children ahead of time about what you think and decide on how to handle the situation. In a similar vein, I will never forget my son getting a huge war toy for Christmas. Toys like this were not allowed in our home. My son looked at it and said, "You don't like this kind of toy, do you, Mom?" So while I didn't have to rip it out his hands, I felt confident that my values were there, and it gave us a chance to talk about it. (He played with it for about two days and then forgot about it!)

Q: My family has been invited to our niece's first communion. It seems like a big party to my daughter, and she wants to know when her first communion is! What can I do to help her feel special?

A: That's just the right way to phrase the question. Children who feel envious of the religious rituals of their peers are often seeking the same sense of specialness—something that doesn't remotely require pledges of devotion to God or the memorization of scriptures. First communion represents a child's reaching what Catholics call the "age of reason." Traditionally around age 8, this is the point at which the child is said to be sufficiently mature to understand the nature of the Eucharist, to enter into a relationship with Christ, and to take personal responsibility for her sins.

Without debating these (highly debatable) theological points, parents can create a similar humanistic event for a child—a kind of first step, perhaps, on the way to the traditional coming of age at 13.

Invite friends and family to dress up for a special recognition event at your house. Create a short ceremony—10 minutes, perhaps—that focuses attention on how fast and well your daughter is growing up. Show a few slides of her early days. Have one friend, one parent, and one grandparent each say a few words about her special qualities. Have her recite a poem from memory (or some similar accomplishment to mark the day). End with a song, then bring out the food!

These same ideas can be adapted and made age-appropriate for a coming-of-age ceremony at 12 or 13. In either case, you will have created a wonderful event that your child will always remember without all that scripture and talk of sin.

Q: Are there any existing secular coming-of-age ceremonies I can look to as models?

A: There are indeed. Ethical Societies are a good place to begin. The Ethical Society of St. Louis, Missouri, has a well-developed coming-of-age program. Their eighth grade Sunday School class is entirely structured as a coming-of-age transition from childhood to adolescence. They address such questions as "Who am I and what do I believe?" (discussing the existence of God, the fact of death, the reality of suffering, and other such topics), "Where do we begin?" (a joint effort between the student and his or her opposite-sex parent in community-building and cooperation), "What is happening to me?" (a parent-teen negotiation workshop focused on dating and sexual responsibility), "How can I make a difference?" (group participation in service to the community) and finish with an opportunity for each student to address the congregation.

Unsurprisingly, Europe is well ahead of the United States in this regard. National humanist associations in the United Kingdom, Germany, and throughout Scandinavia have developed extensive coming-of-age programs, sometimes referred to as "civil confirmations." An excellent summary of these, including links for further information, is available on Wikipedia at *www.en.wikipedia.org/wiki/Secular_coming_of_age_ceremony*.

Q: My sister-in-law says that Halloween is evil and won't let her children do anything around this holiday. It is really confusing to my children. Is there any legitimate basis to my sister-in-law's claims?

A: To their credit, most Christians roll their eyes at this kind of fearful response to Halloween, but there are some who consider the holiday some sort of embodiment or celebration of evil. I have even heard it claimed that Halloween is the birthday of Satan—a particularly strange idea, since Satan/Lucifer was originally an angel and was therefore created, not born!

Also common among conservative Christians is the erroneous idea that Halloween was born in the worship of "Samhain, the Celtic God of Death." Among the many problems with this idea: There is no Celtic god named Samhain.

Celts recognized only two seasons: summer (life) and winter (death). Samhain (pronounced "sow-en" and meaning "summer's end") is the name of a *month* corresponding to November. The "feast of Samhain" on October 31 marks the end of summer and the last harvest of the year. It was symbolized in Celtic mythology as the death of a god, who would then be resurrected six months later at the feast of Beltane (April 30–May 1). Samhain, then, is not about the God of Death, but the death of a god.[2] In this way, Halloween is rooted in the same mythic impulse as the Christian Easter.

Like the Mexican Day of the Dead, Samhain is a recognition of the relationship between life and death. By equating death with evil, conservative Christianity recoils from and fears it.

By instead recognizing death as a natural part of the cycle of life, nonreligious parents can find endless fascination in the holiday's origins. At Samhain, the boundary between the worlds of the living and the dead was said to become thinner, and the ancient Celts believed the spirits of beloved ancestors could cross that boundary and walk among the living. Food would be set at the threshold for the departed spirits.[3]

Kids are fascinated to see how the tradition of dressing as spirits and going from door to door for treats grew out of this ancient Celtic idea of caring for and remembering departed loved ones.

Q: I feel that our relationship with our planet is more important than ever and would like to weave that awareness into our family traditions. What are some ideas for more earth-centered celebrations that we could participate in?

A: The national and international celebration of Earth Day (April 22) has taken on greater significance since concerns about global warming have entered popular attention. It is now common for communities to launch environmental projects and celebrations on Earth Day. Check your local paper or the websites at the end of this chapter for Earth Day activities.

Also, pagan groups celebrate not only the four festivals of the solar cycle, but the four belonging to the agricultural cycle. These are Imbolc or Oimele on February 1–3, Beltane on April 30–May 1, Lammas July 31–August 3, and Samhain on October 31.[4] For pagan news, tools for activists, and more features, visit Pagan Institute Report at *www.paganinstitute.org/PIR/contents.shtml*.

Q: My children recently experienced the first loss of someone close to them when my father died. They want to go to the funeral, but I know that it will be filled with religious messages, and it might be scary for them. Should I take my children to the funeral? Can you suggest an alternative way to honor their dead grandfather?

A: Taking children to a funeral is a family decision, one that should include the child's opinion if possible. There is no set age before which a child should not attend a funeral—in fact, some developmental psychologists point to a possible lack of closure for children who do not attend. If your children have expressed a desire to go, bring them—but talk in advance about what they will see and what the ceremony is for. Most of all, listen to their feelings about death, loss, and the person who has died, and talk about your own.

Remember that it doesn't have to be all or nothing. A child can decide that he wants to attend certain parts of the service, or that he will try it, and you can have a plan for what to do if he feels uncomfortable.

If you decide not to include children in the funeral, you might plan some kind of ceremony at home. Create a place in your home where pictures of the person are displayed and the children can talk about pleasant memories about the person, share a funny story, or perhaps light a candle in that person's honor. You could bake the person's favorite food or do an activity that the person enjoyed.

This might also be a great time to introduce the Day of the Dead celebration that takes place in Mexico each year around the first part of November. This celebration focuses on remembering the dead, cleaning graves, fixing foods that the dead person enjoyed, and decorating with colorful marigolds. There are many excellent books focusing on this tradition, some of which are listed in the resources section of this chapter.

Explain that you honor the person who died every time you remember her, and that holding her in your memory is a very meaningful way to carry that person with you throughout life.

(See also Chapter 7, "Death and Life," for a more extensive look at the Day of the Dead. Also see the essay "Dealing with Death in the Secular Family" by Kendyl Gibbons in *Parenting Beyond Belief* for further thoughts on approaching death while celebrating life.)

Q: We are about to have our first child. Are there nontheistic traditions for welcoming a baby into this world?

A: Congratulations! What a special time for you. There are so many wonderful ways to welcome children into the world, including many without reference to a deity. The activities section in this chapter provides some specific ideas, but you can also create a personal ceremony very easily. I think the most touching thing that you can do for your child is to write a message to her on the day she is born expressing what you are feeling about her on that day. Mount it on special paper and save it in a safe place to be given to her at a coming-of-age ceremony, on her sixteenth birthday, or some other special time. If you are a songwriter, create a song; if you are a potter, make a special pot. The birth of a child is a tremendously personal event and should be celebrated thoughtfully. You can create a special blessing for her that is read at every birthday celebration. Let your imagination be your guide.

Unitarian Universalist congregations offer warm and meaning-filled dedication ceremonies. The wordings of these dedications vary but are reliably "God-free." Many UU ministers use a rose with the thorns removed as a symbol of the unfolding promise of the child. Later a rose can be given to the adolescent child in a Coming of Age ceremony with the thorns on the stem as recognition that he now has to handle the "thorns" in life himself!

The wording of UU dedications generally focuses on the mystery and wonder of life, the role of the parents to teach with respect and love and to model how they want their child to be in the world, to listen carefully for the natural spirit of the child, and to tend that spirit with love and care.

You can also look into the wonderful and growing tradition of humanist naming ceremonies. Both the British Humanist Association (*www.humanism.org.uk*) and the Institute for Humanist Studies (*www.humaniststudies.org*) include resources for planning a naming ceremony. The IHS site even includes the complete text of a sample ceremony. A naming or welcoming ceremony can take place anywhere and at any age, although birth to age 2 is most common. Typical elements include readings (anything from Maya Angelou to Dr. Seuss), songs, stories, a description of the origin of the child's name and its family significance, and the naming of one or two special adults in the child's life—often called "mentors" rather than godparents—who pledge to support and encourage the child's engagement with life and entrance into the human community.

An additional plus: These ceremonies can often partially satisfy religious grandparents who want their grandchildren baptized. Although the promise of religious faith and loyalty is not present, many such grandparents express pleasant surprise at the evident warmth, love, and beauty of nonreligious naming or dedication ceremonies.

Activities

Celebrate Birth: Helping Siblings Welcome a New Child

- *Make a small, simple quilt* with your children out of leftover material for the newborn baby. Read *The Quiltmaker's Gift* by Jeff Brumbeau (Orchard Books, 2000) with your children and talk about how people are happiest when they are helping others and giving instead of receiving. This can also help prepare them for the helping role of older siblings. *See also:* Polacco, Patricia. *The Keeping Quilt* (New York: Aladdin, 2001).

- Read Charlene Costanzo's *The Twelve Gifts of Birth* (New York: HarperCollins, 2001) to your children. Twelve gifts are given to every child at birth: strength, beauty, courage, compassion, hope, joy, talent, imagination, reverence, wisdom, love, and faith (leaving open-ended what to have faith in). Talk about what the baby might need strength, beauty, wisdom, and other attributes for. Are there other attributes that your children think that the baby needs to get through life that aren't listed?

- In honor of the new baby, *make simple baby blankets* out of fleece to give to a local shelter. An easy way to make the blankets is to cut two identical squares of fleece, cut in on each side three inches, place the pieces on top of one another, and then tie the two corresponding cut tabs together to bind the two pieces of cloth into a blanket! Kids love to do this project!

- *Create a special poem* for the new child. Write it on special paper for a keepsake. Use the newborn's name and make a special wish for the child for every letter of the name. You could even frame this and decorate the frame.

- To celebrate the adoption of a child from another country, *put a color with a special meaning* from the country of origin into the outfit for the day. Red, for example, is the color of celebration in China.

Celebrate Earth—on Earth Day or Any Day!

- *Make pinecone bird feeders.* Just spread some peanut butter on a pinecone, roll it in some bird seed, attach a piece of yarn to hang it up and you have a bird magnet! *Plant a tree,* flowers, or a vegetable garden.

- Check out Kaboose (*http://holidays.kaboose.com*) for wonderful Earth-centered activities!

- *Do a guided meditation* with your children. Ask them to relax and close their eyes, then take them on a journey through a world without nature.

Ask them to imagine waking up in a world of only concrete, glass, and brick, walking out the front door to find no trees, no flowers, no green grass. Where would they play? Where would they get shade? Where would beauty come from? Ask them how they would begin to rebuild the natural world.

- *Make a new Ten Commandments for the earth:* "Thou shalt not dump garbage into the waters; Thou shalt ride your bike whenever possible; etc."
- *Raise money for a local environmental project* by baking and selling cookies or organizing a raffle or neighborhood rummage sale.
- Have the whole family *take a hike* and pick up any trash that you see along the way.
- Read *Earth Tales from Around the World* by Michael J. Caduto (Golden, CO: Fulcrum, 1997), and talk about the many ideas that different cultures had about how the world began. Your children could come up with a creation story of their own!
- Get the book *Keepers of the Earth* by Michael J. Caduto and Joseph Bruchac (Golden, CO: Fulcrum, 1988). This is a great book that combines creation stories with environmental projects. You can read a creation story, then the book gives you discussion questions and activities to do to help understand the story.

Celebrate the Rhythms of the Year: Winter Solstice

The winter solstice is the meeting point of opposites: night and day, darkness and light, cold and warmth. Find activities to explore these contrasts and to reconnect with an earlier time when humans eagerly anticipated and celebrated the slow return of the sun at the darkest and coldest moment of the year.

- Design different symbols of the sun and color them. *Make a mobile* from the designs.
- *Rewrite the lyrics of familiar songs or poems* to fit the themes of the solstice, including the return of light, the retreat of night, or an awareness of our humbling place in nature.
- If you live in an area with snow in the winter, *make a large sun sculpture* out of the snow in your yard. Use food coloring to decorate the sculpture with bright colors.
- *Explain the concept of seasons* by putting one toothpick in the top of an orange (Earth) and another in the bottom. In a dark room, shine a flashlight (the Sun) directly at the middle of the orange. Tilt the North Pole toothpick slightly toward the light and note that most of the light shines

on the top of the orange/Earth during the Northern Hemisphere summer. Keeping the poles at the same angle, orbit your orange/Earth to the other side of the flashlight and turn the light to continue facing the orange. The North Pole will now be tilted slightly away from the light—the position of the Earth at the time of the Northern Hemisphere's winter solstice when it receives less sunlight than the Southern Hemisphere. Note that people near the Equator really don't have true seasons because the amount of light and temperature is usually about the same year-round.

Celebrate a Secular Advent

In December, instead of focusing on the weeks until Jesus' birth, why not take Advent and reshape it into your values system? Instead of an Advent Wreath, take a log (images of Yule Log!) and drill four holes in the top. Place a candle in each, one for each week in December. Use a permanent marker to label each candle with something that you want to focus on for a week. My family uses Love, Hope, Peace, and Joy. For the first week in December at dinnertime, we light the first candle and talk about how love can help the world and this family. The next week we light the two candles and talk about what we hope for— and so on, for the four weeks of December. You can pick your own words (Reason, Humor, Compassion, and Fun, perhaps) and begin a holiday advent tradition of your own. The colors of the candles can also be your choice, with your choice of meaning attached to each one: In the book *A Grateful Heart,* M.J. Ryan suggests "White for spiritual truth and household purification, Green for healing, prosperity and luck, Red for physical health and vigor, and Yellow for charm and confidence.[5]

Other Adapted Advent Activities

- *Kindness Calendar.* Make up an advent calendar with the days of December. On each day of December, write something kind that you will do for one family member as an expression of your family's humanistic priorities. Put flaps over the activities so your family will be surprised what each day will bring.
- *Cosmic Advent Calendar* (from Friendly Humanist Timothy Mills).[6] The advent calendars of my youth had little windows for each December day, behind each of which was a tiny toy or stale bit of chocolate. Imagine instead a Cosmic Advent Calendar paying homage to the landmarks of evolution! First, read about Carl Sagan's Cosmic Calendar (back in Chapter 1,

Activities section, Analogy 1), which compresses the history of the universe into a single year. Then Google "Cosmic Calendar" for the daily details of December. Arrayed through that cosmic "month" are great steps in evolutionary history. Worms evolve on the cosmic equivalent of December 16—so imagine an advent calendar with gummy worms on the 16th! Put gummy fish on the 19th, Pop Rocks to represent the dinosaur-smacking asteroid on the 28th, chocolate monkeys on the 29th . . . and Flintstones vitamins on the 31st! (Okay, it needs some refinement. So refine it, and drop Dale an email at *dale@parentingbeyondbelief.com*!)

- Contribute money each day for something that you have in the house and then give the money to a charity of your choice. Example: Day One, put $1 into the pot for every TV that you have; Day Two, put 5¢ into a collection box for every can of soup that you have in the house—and so on, throughout the month.
- Make holiday cards with your kids that reflect your family's holiday values. You could focus on peace, kindness, or other secular values associated with the December holiday season. Remember to save those holiday cards that you get so that you can cut them up next year and make your own cards or wrapping paper.
- Talk about the mainline holidays in ways that make you comfortable and your children at ease about joining in the cultural traditions: Christmas = the gift of birth and the promise of each child that is born; Easter = the wonder of natural cycles and life itself; Hanukah = the idea that light is a miracle; solstice = the cycles of nature and life.

Explore Other December Traditions

As a family, make a recipe from the Kwanzaa tradition and talk with your children about the principles put forth with this celebration: unity, self-determination, collective work and responsibility, cooperative economics, purpose, creativity, and faith. Do they understand these concepts, and why do you think that African Americans chose these principles? What principles would your family think would be ones that they would include in their lives?

Cosmic Holidays

Related to the Cosmic Advent Calendar idea above: Why not let Sagan's Cosmic Calendar also generate some cool new humanist holidays? In the compressed cosmic year, the Milky Way came into being on May 1—so celebrate

May 1 as Milky Way May Day! September 9 is Sun Day, for obvious reasons. November 1 is Sex Day (evolution of sexual reproduction, 2.5 billion years ago). Kudos again to Friendly Humanist Timothy Mills for this one.

Celebrate Peace

The values of peace and nonviolence are a wonderful fit with the values of humanism. Two international holidays draw particular attention to these values: **United Nations Peace Day** (September 21) and **International Day of Nonviolence** (October 2—Gandhi's birthday). Some ways your family can observe and celebrate these holidays:

- Write letters to the leadership of your country about your desire for peace in a certain part of the world.
- Have a neighborhood picnic for peace.
- Make a banner or poster and place it on your front lawn.
- Create your own video project of people talking about their hopes for peace.
- Light a candle for peace and place it on the table while you eat.
- Mail out Peace Cards to family and friends.
- Buy Peace Bonds to support the work of Nonviolent Peaceforce (*www.nonviolentpeaceforce.org*).
- Visit the "One Safe Generation" webpage at the Institute for Humanist Studies (*www.humanistparenting.org* > One Safe Generation) for ideas about protecting children from violence at all levels.

(See the Resources section for websites with resources for celebrating and promoting peace and nonviolence.)

Celebrate the Cycle of Life and Death: Day of the Dead

It sometimes takes a bit of doing to get beyond our traditional aversion toward death. Day of the Dead is a terrific way to do it. Create an altar in your home. Place on it pictures of the person who has died, flowers, and candles. Talk about what good memories you have of that person and what he or she was like as a person. You can place a mirror on this altar in remembrance that we will all die someday. Google the recipe for sugar skulls! Buy wooden skeletons at a local craft store and decorate the skeleton like a person who has died and talk about the memories you have of that person. Visit the graves of loved ones to clean, sweep, and weed the area—and to tell stories about the person.

Celebrate Coming of Age: Rites of Passage

This is a time to use some creativity and insight about what your child turning into an adolescent or your adolescent turning young adult might like. One thing I think that is universal to any Coming of Age ceremony is the planning of special time with an adult or adults in the child's/youth's life. Planning a special dinner with just the teen or a camping trip is a way to say that we recognize the passage of time and that the child is growing up. There are huge celebrations planned in some religious traditions, but don't be intimidated by those big celebrations into doing nothing! A quiet and meaningful time can be as simple as a dinner at home with special readings. The book *Coming of Age, A Treasury of Poems, Quotations and Readings on Growing Up* collected by Edward Searl is a great place to get such readings.

I love this quote from Mary Pipher: "Maturity involves being honest and true to oneself, making decisions based on a conscious internal process, assuming responsibility for one's decisions, having healthy relationships with others and developing one's own true gifts. It involves thinking about one's environment and deciding what one will and won't accept." Decorate a frame for your child and frame this or another special quote that captures your feelings about maturity.

Coming of age is also a great time to pass down special keepsakes from family members—a true statement that the maturing young person represents the future.

Many Unitarian Universalist churches have Coming of Age programs for teens where they look at themselves and the big questions in life. It would worth looking into for a group experience for your youth.

This is also the perfect time to write your growing child a letter telling how you treasure him or her, your hopes for the future, and what values you hope your child will have. It should be a time to talk about how far he or she has come and how far is still left to go! Talk to your child about the life lessons you have learned that might help along the way. Present this at a special time in a special envelope.

Adapt Existing Ceremonies

Choose a traditional coming-of-age ceremony, such as a Mexican Quinceanera. Adapt it by substituting your values and symbols for the traditional elements.

(Also see the Appendix for great movies with themes related to coming-of-age and other issues of finding one's identity.)

Celebrate Rebirth: Spring

Try having a hunt with plastic eggs filled with varying amounts of money. When the children have gathered up all of the eggs, do some math and count the total amount collected and then decide to which charity you want to donate the money.

Instead of the traditional Easter Egg Hunt, have the children "hunt" for canned goods by doing a collection of canned goods in the neighborhood the week before Easter and then organize the canned goods and donate them on Easter morning to some charity.

Take this morning to go walking and to see what is starting to bloom and be "reborn," or visit a farm to see what animals are being born.

Resources

Planning Celebrations—General

Lang, Virginia, and Louise Nayer. *How to Bury a Goldfish and Other Ceremonies and Celebrations for Everyday Life* (Boston: Skinner House, 2007). New traditions to commemorate the special moments and milestones in life. More than 100 rituals for everything from holidays and birthdays to teen's first job and a woman's midlife journey. All ages.

Cox, Meg. *The Book of New Family Traditions: How to Create Great Rituals for Holidays and Everyday* (Philadelphia: Running Press, 2003). A compilation of interviews with diverse families about family rituals and celebrations. Adult.

Rites of Passage

Wall, Kathleen. *Rites of Passage: Celebrating Life's Changes* (Hillsboro, OR: Beyond Words Publishing, 1998). Provides a very good description of how to create ritual/traditions for various times in life. The chapter on Ritual for the Healthy Family includes insights on such issues as communication, mealtime, and holidays. Definitely on the "spiritual but not religious" side of the spectrum. Adult.

Searl, Edward. *A Treasury of Poems, Quotations and Readings on Growing Up* (Boston: Skinner House, 2007).You can get it at the Unitarian Universalist bookstore, *uua.org/bookstore*. This small book gives poems, quotations, and readings from around the world on growing up from adolescence to adulthood. All ages.

(See the first Appendix for an extensive list of movies with coming-of-age themes.)

Special Occasions

Seaburg, Carl. *Great Occasions: Readings for the Celebration of Birth, Coming of Age, Marriage and Death* (Boston: Skinner House Press, 2003). Words from many traditions to celebrate life passages, including Christian traditions. All ages.

Solstice

Pfeffer, Wendy. *The Shortest Day* (New York: Dutton Juvenile, 2003). Ages 4–10.

Shragg, Karen. *A Solstice Tree for Jenny* (Amherst, NY: Prometheus, 2001). Ages 4–8.

(Both reviewed in *Parenting Beyond Belief.*)

Martin, Jacqueline Briggs. *Snowflake Bentley* (New York: Houghton Mifflin Company, 1998). A winner of the Caldecott Medal, this is the true story of Wilson Bentley, who used a microscopic camera to photograph the wonders of snow, showing that no two flakes are alike and that each has stunning beauty. Ages 4–8.

(See also the marvelous *In Nature's Honor* in the Earth Day section, below.)

Expressing Thanks

Wood, Douglas. *The Secret of Saying Thanks* (New York: Simon and Schuster, 2005). A nonreligious look at how to give thanks without giving thanks to God. Ages 4–8.

London, Jonathan. *Giving Thanks* (Cambridge, MA: Candlewick Press, 2005). A moving nonreligious approach to giving thanks for the nature that is all around us. Ages 4–8.

Christmas

Waldron, Jan. *Angel Pig and the Hidden Christmas* (London: Puffin Books, 2000). Shows the joy of turning away from commercialism and making your own gifts. Ages 4–8.

Robinson, Jo, and Jean Staehel. *Unplug the Christmas Machine* (New York: William Morrow Publishing, 1991). A classic for parents (now in its thirteenth printing) on ways to decommercialize Christmas. Special attention is paid to the nonreligious. Adult.

Elliot, Jock. *Inventing Christmas: How Our Holiday Came to Be* (New York: Harry N. Abrams, 2002). A great, easy-to-read historical look the beginnings of the Christmas holiday and its traditions. All ages.

Krismas: *http://krismas.org*

The Twelve Days of Christmas: *www.tetrakatus.org*

EvolveFISH.com has some interesting and unique secular holiday greeting cards ranging from combative to inspirational and from naughty to nice. Choosing the right one might be an interesting discussion opportunity for your family.

Earth Day

Brisson, Pat. *Wanda's Roses* (Homesdale, PA: Boyds Mills Press, 1994). The story of a little girl who has the imagination and hope to turn an old, run-down lot into a garden, creating community at the same time.

Montley, Patricia. *In Nature's Honor, Myths and Rituals Celebrating the Earth* (Boston: Skinner House Books, 2005). Gives the background of winter solstice, Imbolc, Purification and Candlemas, Spring Equinox, Beltane and May Day, Summer Solstice and Midsummer, Lughnasa and Lammas, Autumn Equinox and Samhain, All Souls Day and Day of the Dead, as well as descriptions of contemporary celebrations, readings, and ways for individuals and families to celebrate these holidays.

Birth/Adoption

Costanzo, Charlene. *The Twelve Gifts of Birth* (New York: HarperCollins, 2001). Simple exploration of gifts you could give a new child, such as courage, hope, and beauty.

Searl, Edward. *Bless This Child: A Treasury of Poems, Quotations, and Readings to Celebrate Birth* (Boston: Skinner Publishing, 2007).

Kranz, Linda. *Only One You* (New York: Rising Moon Publishers, 2006). "There is only one you in this great big world. Make it a better place."

Table Reflections and Blessings

Ryan, M. J. *A Grateful Heart: Daily Blessings for the Evening Meal from Buddha to the Beatles* (Newburyport, MA: Conari Press, 2002). A marvelous source of diverse reflections and meditations from diverse sources both religious and nonreligious.

Easter

Berenstain, Stan and Jan. *The Berenstain Bears and the Real Easter Eggs* (New York: Random House, 2002). An Easter Egg hunt shows the Bears that new life is the real message of Easter. Ages 4–8.

Barth, Edna. *Lilies, Rabbits, and Painted Eggs: The Story of the Easter Symbols* (New York: Clarion Books, 2001). A great reference book for Easter with clear explanations for many Easter customs and symbols. Ages 9–12.

Peace and Nonviolence

Munson, Derek. *Enemy Pie* (San Francisco: Chronicle Books, 2000). An enemy is turned into a friend through the actions of a very insightful parent.

Rice, David. *Because Brian Hugged His Mother* (Nevada City, CA: Dawn, 1999). One act of kindness ricochets into a whole day of kindnesses.

Pearson, Emily. *Ordinary Mary's Extraordinary Deed* (Layton, UT: Gibbs Smith, 2002). How one good deed leads to another.

MacLean, Kerry Lee. *Peaceful Piggy Meditation* (Morton Grove, IL: Albert Whitman and Co., 2004). Teaches children how to meditate when they are feeling stressed.

Websites to celebrate and promote peace and nonviolence
www.internationaldayofpeace.org
www.peaceoneday.org

Miscellaneous Resources

Pagan Institute Report
www.paganinstitute.org/PIR/contents.shtml

British Humanist Association
www.humanism.org.uk

Institute for Humanist Studies
www.humaniststudies.org

Secular Seasons
www.secularseasons.org

Notes

1. In 2005, violent crime in the United States across the board reached its lowest level *ever*—yet our hysteria about violent crime has never been more extreme (U.S. Bureau of Justice Statistics, *www.ojp.usdoj.gov/bjs/glance/viort.htm*).

2. See Robinson, B.A. "The Myth of Samhain." Accessed February 11, 2008, from *www.religioustolerance.org*

3. Danaher, Kevin. *The Year in Ireland: Irish Calendar Customs* (New York: Mercier, 1972); O'Driscoll, Robert (Ed.), *The Celtic Consciousness* (New York: Braziller, 1981).

4. Landon, Christa. The Pagan Institute (*www.paganinstitute.org*)

5. *The Grateful Heart*, p. 62. Full citation in Resources.

6. Visit Friendly Humanist Timothy Mills at *www.friendlyhumanist.blogspot .com.* Accessed August 17, 2008.

CHAPTER 7

Death and Life

Dale McGowan

Of the hundreds of questions about nonreligious parenting I've fielded from reporters and audiences, one stands head and shoulders above the rest for its ability to amaze, amuse, and confound me: *"Without heaven, how will you make your kids okay with death?"*

I can't get used to it no matter how often I hear it. No fewer than three myths are embedded in those eleven words—three common misunderstandings that must be unpacked before we can get a handle on this topic. Let's look at those three myths, as well as the two obligations that nonreligious parents have to their children regarding the subject of death.

Three Myths, Two Obligations
Myth 1: Religion Cures the Fear of Death

Given the overwhelming evidence to the contrary, I'm baffled whenever I hear it implied that religion cures the fear of death. I know many deeply religious people, all of whom work hard at delaying their demise. They look carefully before crossing the street. They watch what they eat, follow doctor's orders, shrink in terror when given a troubling diagnosis, pray for the recovery of seriously ill friends, and weep as uncontrollably as the rest of us when someone close to them dies. They are every bit as dissatisfied with company policy as I am.

If not more so. I also know some who worry themselves to distraction over whether they've satisfied the requirements for entrance to Paradise. One woman I know lost sleep for weeks after her husband died, convinced that he had gone to hell for missing too many Masses.

Some comfort.

When it comes to comforting children in the face of loss, most mainstream parenting experts find the invocation of heaven problematic at best. In *Guiding Your Child Through Grief,* James and Mary Ann Emswiler caution against such wincers as "God took Mommy because she was so good," or "God took Daddy because He wanted him to be with Him," for reasons that should be obvious. "Don't use God or religion as a pacifier to make grieving children feel better. It probably won't work," they continue. "Do not explain death as a punishment or a reward from God."[1] By the time they and most other child development experts are done, the single greatest supposed advantage of religion lies in tatters.

> If we are immortal, it is a fact of nature, and that fact does not depend on bibles, on Christs, priests or creeds. It cannot be destroyed by unbelief.
>
> —Robert Green Ingersoll, orator, "The Great Agnostic"

We've now set the bar more reasonably. Our goal as parents is not to somehow cure the fear of death, but to keep that natural and unavoidable fear from interfering overly much with the experience of life.

Myth 2: Children Are Less Able Than Adults to Think About Death

We grownups flatter ourselves by suggesting that we are in a position to comfort our children when it comes to thinking about and dealing with death. If anything, the opposite is true. Compared to their parents, children have a greatly reduced grasp of death. As Emory University psychologist Melvin Konner notes in his brilliant classic *The Tangled Wing,* "From age 3 to 5 they consider it reversible, resembling a journey or sleep. After 6 they view it as a fact of life but a very remote one."[2] Although rates of conceptual development vary, Konner places the first true grasp of the finality and universality of death around age 10—a realization that includes the first dawning deep awareness that it applies to them as well.

Critics of approaching the topic of death straightforwardly with children assume that nonreligious parents are telling their children, in essence, "deal with it." This is a willfully ignorant critique. Nonreligious parents are every bit as concerned for the comfort and happiness of their children as religious parents. They simply recognize that an early, naturalistic engagement with the topic makes it easier to come to terms this most difficult of human realities, not harder.

The fact that children tend not to fully "get" death during the early years has its downside—crossing the street would be easier, for example, if they did—but it also has a decided advantage. These are the years during which they can engage the idea of death *more* easily and *more* dispassionately than they will as adults. And such early engagement can only help to build a foundation of understanding and familiarity to ease and inform their later encounters with this most profound of all human realities.

Myth 3: We Can, Even Should, Be Comfortable with the Idea of Death

Fear of death is among our healthiest and most desirable fears. Natural selection put it there, after all, and for good reason. Imagine two early ancestors crossing the savannah. One has a genetically endowed fear of death, while the other is indifferent to it. A predator sprints their way. All other things being equal, which of these guys will survive to pass on his attitude toward death?

The desire to live is also a helpful social regulator. It has been noted by several commentators that only by using the promise of a glorious afterlife to suppress the simple and natural fear of death were the attacks of September 11 made possible.[3] Membership in the ranks of those who stand fearless in the face of death is not something we should wish for our children.

So perhaps we can agree that curing our children of the fear of death is off the table. But then what are our obligations to our children regarding mortality? I would suggest two: to provide reasonable comfort and to encourage thoughtful engagement.

Obligation 1: To Provide Comfort

Although we can't cure our kids of the fear of death, it's important to keep that fear from overwhelming them.

Even when it does not involve death, loss is a difficult issue for kids, especially in their first few years. Peek-a-boo is riveting for infants precisely because the parent vanishes *and then returns*—a kind of mini-resurrection worthy of a squeal of delight. A toy that rolls under the crib gives rise to a keening wail worthy of an Irish widow. Only after a good deal of experience and development does the child begin to learn that things that go away continue to exist out of sight—and generally return.

It's hardly surprising that the child's first confrontation with death is such a cruel blow. After that long, hard climb out of her early misconceptions about loss, she suddenly learns that Mr. Skittles the hamster is gone and *not* coming back. Little wonder that we create safe and happy places in our imaginations for our loved and lost ones to continue running on the exercise wheel.

Fortunately, there are genuinely comforting ways to help children accept the finality of death—both of others and of themselves—without the need for afterlife fantasies. This chapter will offer several ways to provide that honest comfort, as well as additional resources for further exploration.

■ ■ ■ ■

The Buddha and the Mustard Seed

When I lost a baby in an ectopic pregnancy, it was a sad and scary time for my 5-year-old. Just a couple of weeks earlier, we had been happily making up songs about the new baby we would be welcoming into our family. But then her mommy spent three days in the hospital for surgery. When I came home, I had to tell my daughter that our baby was not going to be born, and I was too sore to take her on my lap and comfort her.

We could still snuggle, though, and a few days later, as we cuddled on the sofa, I impulsively asked her, "Have I ever told you the story of Buddha and the mustard seed?"

When she shook her head, I told her, "Once there was a great teacher called Buddha. Some people thought he could do magic. One morning, a mother came to him carrying the body of her dead child. She said, "I've heard that you can do miracles. Will you bring my child back to life? My heart is broken without him.""

He answered, "If you can bring me a mustard seed from a house where no one has died, bring it back to me at the end of the day, and I will use it to revive your child."

Then I said to my daughter, "We can act out the story of what happened then. Knock on the wall, and I'll pretend to open the door, and you be the mother asking me for the mustard seed."

She knocked. With a door-opening gesture, I said, "Yes?" She explained, "If I can bring the Buddha a mustard seed from a house where no one has died, he will use it to bring my baby back to life." I answered, "I'm sorry. I wish I could help you, but my grandfather died just last week. He was very old and it was time, but we miss him anyway."

I said, "Now let's try another house." This time, the story I told was that, just a month before, my husband had been run over by an ox cart, and my family didn't know what we would do. I told her that the two women talked for a while, comforting each other.

We imagined a few more visits. At one, the man who answered the door commented, "You've been walking a long time. You look tired and thirsty. Would you like to come to rest and have a drink of water?"

Eventually, I ended the story, "At the end of the day, the woman went back to Buddha and said, 'Now I understand,' and he helped her bury her baby."

Each day for the next few days, we reenacted the story, sometimes making up different incidents in the lives of the people we visited. Then one day, my daughter said, "You be the mommy, and knock at my door."

So I did, and when I told her my story, she answered, "I can't give you a mustard seed, because we were going to have a baby, but the baby died. But my mommy and daddy are going to try and have another baby, maybe you could, too."

"That's a good idea," I said. "Thank you for telling me that." And we hugged.

As it turned out, I never did have another baby. But my daughter had learned valuable lessons about creating meaning from painful experiences. She learned that we are not alone with our problems, and there is comfort in knowing that. She learned how people in pain and need can comfort each other by giving each other compassion and support. She built a network of friends who were like brothers and sisters. Some of them even call me "Ma." That's a lot of emotional nourishment from one little mustard seed!

—Molleen Matsumura

■ ■ ■ ■ ■

Obligation 2: To Help Our Children Engage a Most Profound Concept

Someone once said that the single most significant and profound thing about our existence is that it ends, rivaled only by the fact that it begins.[4] One of my objections to the idea of an afterlife is that it deflects our attention from the deep and honest consideration of mortality by pretending that, what do you know, we aren't really mortal after all.

Nonreligious parents are in a unique position to help their children begin a lifetime of powerful reflection on death and life, dipping their minds into the deepest and richest streams of thought. It's not always easy to be mortal, but do we really want to limit our children's experience of the world to those things that are "always easy"? Haven't we discovered by now that the most meaningful engagement in life includes challenges?

I wax rhetorical.

Michel de Montaigne, my favorite philosopher, said that "to philosophize is to learn how to die." And Montaigne wasn't the only one to put the contemplation of death at the center of our intellectual universe. As parents, one of the greatest gifts we can give our children is a healthy start on the honest engagement with the biggest idea they will ever confront. The choice, after all, isn't between helping them confront death and helping them avoid it. They *will* encounter it. And just as with sexuality, alcohol, religion, drugs, and all sorts of other things they will eventually encounter, the worst thing we can do is strive to keep them as ignorant as possible of the subject. The longer they are kept from thinking about these things, the more dysfunctionally they will confront them once they finally do. That doesn't remotely imply a "deal-with-it" approach to death. On the contrary: Talking openly, honestly, and compassionately about mortality is the best way to protect our children from being painfully blindsided by it later in life.

> We pause to ask ourselves the questions that human beings have always asked, questions that help to define what a human being is: "Why am I here?" "What is death?" "How should I be living now?" These are not morbid reflections; they throw life into perspective. If we had a thousand years to live, such questions would lack urgency. It is death, ironically, that prompts us to learn how to live.
>
> —Eknath Easwaran,
> Hindu author and professor
> of English Literature

Parenting Beyond Belief laid the foundation for a healthy consideration of death and the way it frames and makes precious our life. In this chapter we hope to translate that philosophy into practical, concrete ideas for approaching and embracing the stunning fact that one day we will cease to be—and the equally stunning fact that we first have the opportunity to *be*.

Questions and Answers

Q: How can a nonreligious person comfort a child who has experienced a devastating loss?

A: Nonreligious parents who suffered the loss of a close relative when they were young often tell of the well-meaning but very unhelpful things that were said to them: "I know your mother is in heaven with God." "Jesus took her because she was so good." ("Now be a good girl and eat your peas.")

It's hard to find a mainstream expert on grief who considers religious consolations useful or even advisable when comforting a bereaved child. After offering many of the suggestions listed below, such experts will typically include an apologetic coda— something like, "Depending on your family's religious tradition, you may wish to explain a person's death to your children in terms of God's will or an afterlife. But be aware that such statements as 'she went to be with Jesus' can lead to feelings of confusion and abandonment, while 'God took her to be with him' can cause feelings of anger followed by guilt and fear."[5] Worst of all is any suggestion that the child should not be sad ("You should be happy! She's with Jesus now"), which discounts and invalidates the child's natural grief.

> " Death is a fact of life. As rational adults we all know this. As anxious parents, however, we also want to deny it and to protect our children from the painful reality, especially when someone close to them is dying or dies. But as we have learned from the mishandling of subjects like sexuality with children, ignorance and avoidance of a mysterious, frightening or emotionally charged issue can breed needless fears and anxieties, inappropriate behavior and persistent psychological trauma. "
>
> —Jane Brody, Personal Health column, *New York Times*, August 12, 1987

That's what *not* to say and do. So what do grief specialists across the board recommend?

- **Be honest.** Don't pretend that anything less than the worst event of her life has happened. Validate her pain and grief. Tell the child it is not just "okay" to be sad: It's good. Her sadness honors her mother, showing that she loved her very much, and expresses real feelings instead of keeping them locked inside.
- **Share emotions.** Keeping a stiff upper lip in front of the children is of no help whatsoever for a grieving child. Let her know that you are grieving too—or better yet, *show* it.

- **Be patient.** There is no healthy or effective way to rush a grief process. The suggestion that "it's time to move on" should come only from the griever, not from the outside.
- **Listen.** Invite the child to share what she is feeling *if she wants to*. If not, respect her silence. Listen without judgment.
- **Reassure.** You can't bring back the deceased parent, nor can you pretend he or she is somewhere else. But you can and should do everything possible to make the child feel personally safe, loved, and cared for.
- **Speak openly.** The absence of the parent is the single most painful element of the loss. Avoiding the parent's name or discussion of the person can often make that sense of absence more painful and more acute. Share memories of the person and use her name or "your mom." If tears result, remember: the goal is not to avoid sadness, but to help the child work through the intense grief. Let her be the one to tell you if a conversation is too painful.

Outstanding resource: Trozzi, Maria. *Talking with Children About Loss* (New York: Perigee Trade, 1999).

Q: What about the reverse? A friend of mine who is a nonreligious parent recently lost her daughter to leukemia. I cannot even imagine the pain she's feeling. All I want to do is take that pain away. Is that even possible without the promise of heaven?

A: No, it isn't possible without heaven—nor is it possible with it. Even religious parents who have lost a child still suffer an immense and consuming blow. Some even describe feeling guilt on top of the grief as they are reminded, repeatedly, that all is well in heaven and feel no better for it.

I agree that the loss of a child must surely be the most incomprehensible pain possible. One of the best things you can do is acknowledge that. Never say, "I know how you feel." You don't. Better by far to phrase it just as you have: "I cannot even imagine the pain you're feeling."

Although you can't remove the pain, there are ways to help your friend *through* the pain of the grief process:

- **Be there.** Your presence can't fill the void left by the lost child, but bereaved parents often describe that void becoming overwhelming when the parent is alone. Offer a hug, conversation, and the simple expression "I am so sorry." Listen. Avoid all judgments.

- **Relieve everyday burdens.** Don't wait to be asked. Take over bill payments, household chores, running the other children to school or sports, running errands—so long as such help does not leave the parent alone and isolated.
- **Pay special attention to surviving siblings,** many of whom will suppress their own grief to avoid burdening the parents. Talk to them and acknowledge their own loss.
- **Talk about the child.** As in the case of a parent's death, avoiding the mention of the deceased can make the absence more intense.
- **Stay in touch.** Things will never be the same for a bereaved parent. Don't assume that a return to work or the passage of a set amount of time represents the end of a need for support.[6]

Outstanding organization for bereaved parents: The Compassionate Friends (*www.compassionatefriends.org*), with more than 600 chapters in the United States and United Kingdom. "Espouse[s] no specific religious or philosophical ideology."

Q: I have heard of the Day of the Dead celebration from Mexico. What is it? Would it be a good way for secular parents to help our children think about death?

A: The Day of the Dead (celebrated November 1–2) is a fascinating example of the syncretism found in many cultures with colonization in their past. The practices and beliefs of the invading culture (in this case Catholic Spain) are melded with local practices and beliefs (in this case the ancient Aztec festival of Mictecacihuatl, queen of the underworld and guardian of the dead) to produce new traditions.[7]

Like the Celtic festival of Samhain,[8] the Day of the Dead recognizes the moment when summer turns to winter as a time when the worlds of the living and the dead are in close proximity. People build altars to draw visits from their beloved dead, filling them with flowers and the loved ones' favorite foods.

Visits are made to cemeteries to communicate with the dead. Towns hold macabre processions of people dressed as skeletons or as deceased relatives, rattling beads and shells to wake the dead.

Many U.S. communities now hold Day of the Dead celebrations, especially those with large Mexican expatriate populations. Although the Virgin Mary is now woven into the celebration in place of Mictecacihuatl, there are many elements of the holiday that secular families can adopt, enjoy, and use to reflect on death and the preciousness it lends to life.

(See Chapter 6, "Celebrating Life," for more on the Day of the Dead.)

Q: My son is in preschool and hears all of the time from his friends that their dead grandparents go to heaven after they die and that they will see them when they die. My son has now decided that that is the truth. How can I get him away from this position? Or should I?

A: Don't think of a preschool dalliance with belief as "deciding the truth." You should expect your child to try on different religious hats along the way, declaring this or that belief, then switching a week later. It is part of a very healthy process of making up his own mind about religious questions. Simply:

- Let him know what you believe and why.
- Encourage him to question his own beliefs and the beliefs of others, including yours.
- Engage in broad-based comparative religious education as described in Chapter 3.
- Let him know that he can change his mind a thousand times and (most important) that the final decision is entirely his—*and mean it.*

Q: Should my children (ages 6, 8, and 10) attend the funeral of their grandmother?

A: Although this depends largely on the emotional makeup of each child, I strongly recommend allowing any child who wishes to attend to do so. In addition to the emotional benefits of closure, the children will have an opportunity to observe a family and community in the process of grieving and saying goodbye and to be a part of that process. They will hear their grandmother being eulogized and remembered by those who loved her, and they will have an opportunity to begin a lifelong contemplation of

❝ Every now and then I think about my own death and I think about my own funeral. And then I ask myself, "What is it that I would want said?" If any of you are around when I have to meet my day, I don't want a long funeral. And if you get somebody to deliver the eulogy, tell them not to talk too long . . . . Tell them not to mention that I have a Nobel Peace Prize, which isn't important. Tell them not to mention that I have three or four hundred other awards, that's not important. . . . I'd like somebody to mention that day, that Martin Luther King, Jr., tried to give his life serving others. I'd like for somebody to say that day, that Martin Luther King, Jr., tried to love somebody. I want you to be able to say that day, that I did try to feed the hungry. . . . I want you to say that I tried to love and serve humanity. Yes, if you want to say that I was a drum major, say that I was a drum major for justice; say that I was a drum major for righteousness. And all of the other shallow things will not matter. I the deepest questions surrounding life and death.

Ideally, you will have prepared them for years by talking about death in naturalistic and unforced ways as described throughout this chapter, from the dead bird in the backyard to walks in cemeteries. Given this preparation, the funeral of a loved one is a natural and good step forward in the process of pondering the imponderable.

won't have any money to leave behind. I won't have the fine and luxurious things of life to leave behind. But I just want to leave a committed life behind. **"**

—Dr. Martin Luther King, Jr.,
from an address at Ebenezer
Baptist Church, February 4, 1968

Q: A friend of our family died recently, and now my daughter is really worried that her dad or I will die. She keeps asking me what will happen to her if we die. How do I answer her in a way that is realistic but also reassuring?

A: The fear that his or her parents will die very often precedes and overshadows any fears a child has about his or her own mortality. Among other things, there is a sense that the older generation stands between us and death—that you are shielded from it so long as your parents are still around.[9]

Let your child know of the many ways in which you take care of yourself and each other. No need to pretend that this is certain protection. In fact, your question implies that she has already begun to consider the aftereffects of such an event. Take the time to consider and plan for this eventuality yourself, designating a guardian or guardians, and letting your child know that even this unlikely possibility has been thought through, and that she would be safe and cared for.

Q: We need to decide who will care for our child if something should happen to us but are having some difficulty making the decision. Our siblings and parents are all very religious, have parenting views very different from our own, and live in other states. What can we do about this decision?

A: This is a difficult but important decision, one that all parents must take the time to make.

One of the best ways to proceed is to consider the hypothetical situation as concretely as possible. Your children have lost both parents, presumably without warning, throwing their world into a tailspin. Everything will have changed for them. The two most important considerations in this case are security and continuity. In other words, you want your children to end up in the

■ ■ ■ ■ ■

No doubt about it: We were on a Seussian bender. For three weeks, every bedtime story had been from the gruffulous world of Dr. Seuss. Then one night, in the middle of *Oh, The Places You'll Go!* we ran smack into mortality.

ERIN (9): Is he still alive?

DAD: Who?

ERIN: Dr. Seuss.

DAD: Oh. No, he died about fifteen years ago, I think. But he had a good long life first.
I suddenly became aware that Delaney (6) was very quietly sobbing.

DAD : Oh, sweetie, what's the matter?

DELANEY: Is anybody taking his place?

DAD : What do you mean, punkin?

DELANEY: Is anybody taking Dr. Seuss's place to write his books? *(Begins a deep cry.)* Because I love them so much, I don't want him to be all-done!

I hugged her tightly and started giving every lame comfort I could muster—everything short of "I'm sure he's in Heaven writing *Revenge of the Lorax.*"

I scanned the list of Seuss books on the back cover. "Hey, you know what?" I offered lamely. "We haven't even read half of his books yet!"

"But we *will* read them all!" she shot back. "And then there won't be any more!" I had only moved the target, which didn't solve the problem in the least.

Laney wants to be a writer. I seized on this, telling her *she* could be the next Dr. Seuss. She liked that idea, and we finished the book. The next day she was at work on a story called "What Do I Sound Like?" about a girl who didn't know her own voice because she had never spoken.

My instinct whenever one of my kids cries—especially that deep, sincere, wounded cry—is to get her happy again. This once entailed nothing more than putting something on my head—anything would do—at which point laughter would replace tears. It's a bit harder once they're older and, instead of skinned knees, they are saddened by the limitations imposed by mortality on the people they love.

But is "getting them happy again" the right goal?

Death is immensely sad, even as it makes life more precious. It's supposed to be. So I shouldn't be *too* quick to put something on my head or dream up a consolation every time my kids encounter the sadness of mortality. Let them think about what it means that Dr. Seuss is all-done, and even cry that deep, sincere, heartbreaking cry.

■ ■ ■ ■ ■

care of someone who will keep them safe (physically and emotionally) and provide the least jarring transition.

Religious expressions vary considerably, so you would need to consider where in the spectrum your family members fall. Moving children from a freethought home to a conservative religious home, even with well-meaning guardians, can be quite unsettling to the children at precisely the moment they need stability. If, on the other hand, a home is of a progressive religious orientation, it's entirely possible that a stable transition could be negotiated. Many liberal religionists would be perfectly willing to raise your children in an open questioning environment. Ask the person you are considering how he or she would handle questions about religion, about authority, and about the boundaries of inquiry.

Child welfare advocates also recommend minimizing other disruptions as much as possible, such as moving to another city or state or changing schools.

If you have family friends who you know well, whose parenting style and beliefs are a better fit with yours, who live locally, and are willing to take on the responsibility, such considerations can and should trump family relationships. That's a lot of ifs, but they're worth weighing. And once you've decided on the best situation for your kids (and confirmed it with the person you've chosen), put it in writing. Consult a legal professional for advice on creating a binding document.

Q: My husband and I disagree about the importance of making advance plans for our own funerals. He wants us to write out detailed plans, but I just don't care. I'll be gone! Bury me, burn me, shoot me into space, whatever turns you on! Am I missing something?

A: Well, yes. You are making the false assumption that funerals have more to do with the dead than the living.

As far as you are concerned, it may indeed matter not one bit what your funeral is like. But think of your survivors, those who loved you and knew about your beliefs. Unless you've made it quite clear what you want, or equally clear that you don't care, they will immediately have to wrestle with massive uncertainty. *Should we have a clergyman officiate? Can it be in a church, or is that inappropriate? Will Aunt Gladys blow a vein if we hang a picture of Andromeda over the crucifix? Is "Ave Maria" too religious to have sung?*

You get the idea. The nonreligious have an even *greater* responsibility to be explicit because there's no institution spelling it out for their survivors. Many religious expressions have the same basic interchangeable funereal elements, but a nonreligious service has to be planned from scratch. If you do wish to keep religion out of it, use the books in the Resource section to spell out your wishes, right down to the music and readings. Or, if you truly don't care, make that absolutely explicit to spare your heirs from infighting, guilt, and uncertainty.

Q: Neither of my kids (3 and 6) has ever had to deal with death, but they have several older relatives to whom they are very close. How can I prepare my kids as well as possible for their first encounter with death?

A: The first way is to naturalize the topic from the very beginning. We have an almost unlimited ability to accept things, even incredibly strange and difficult things, if they are presented to us as normal form the start. Next time you talk to your mother, flash on the fact that *you emerged into the world through her body.* It doesn't get stranger than that—but because (storkists aside) we have always known this, we simply talk to her as if she were another person in the world instead of our portal into it. We accept something transcendently strange as normal because it has never been otherwise. The inimitable Douglas Adams captured this nicely when he said, "The fact that we live at the bottom of a deep gravity well, on the surface of a gas-covered planet going around a nuclear fireball 90 million miles away and think this to be *normal* is some indication of how skewed our perspective tends to be."[10]

The same applies to mortality. If children start out with the knowledge that we genuinely die, they will think this to be normal. Not exciting, not even easy, perhaps, but they are much more likely to accept the reality and actually get on with the lifelong work of understanding it if they *begin* with it. They might even see how it makes every moment of life itself so much more fantastically precious. So never treat death as an untouchable subject. Touch it all over. The more familiar, the less frightening. It's a lifelong challenge to come to terms with death, but our kids will be all the further along if they don't have to waste time and effort erasing heaven and hell from their conceptual maps.

Pets can also contribute, however unwillingly, to our lifelong education in mortality. Although we don't buy pets in *order* for kids to experience death (with the possible exception of aquariums, *aack!*), most every pet short of a giant land tortoise will predecease its owner. The deaths of my various guinea pigs, dogs, fish, and rabbits were my first introductions to irretrievable loss. At their passings, I learned both how to grieve and the depth of love I was capable of feeling. And I am certain they helped prepare me for the sudden loss of my father. It didn't make the loss itself any easier, nor did it shorten my grief, which continues to this day. But the grief didn't blindside me in quite the way it would have if my father's death had been my first experience of profound loss.

Q: I can understand that the experience of a pet's death helps to prepare a child for even more traumatic losses to come, but how can I help my kids weather the loss of the pet itself? We have a much-loved older dog, and I'm concerned as I think of the huge impact his death will have on my kids. What should I say? What should I do with the body? I want this to be a healthy experience for all of us about handling our emotions and the logistics of death.

A: The death of a pet can be nearly as devastating to a child as the death of another member of the family. The first priority is to recognize that and to be certain you are taking the loss just that seriously. That said, here are a few of the guidelines agreed upon by child development specialists:

- **Prepare well in advance.** Talking about the fact that your dog will not live forever can help them to make the most of their remaining time with him and to feel that they have properly said goodbye. Take photos and videos with the pet. If they wish, have children write a letter to the pet while still living expressing their love for him.
- **Be honest.** Just as in the death of a person, it is important to be honest about what has happened. Don't say that Prince has gone on a trip or (yikes) that he fell asleep and didn't wake up. Take advantage of the opportunity to gently introduce the reality of death while reassuring the child of the many consolations that can help us through our grief.
- **Involve the child—up to a point.** If you do plan to bury the pet (and yes, that is an acceptable option if City Hall allows it), give the child the option

of attending. Announcing that the pet has been buried after the fact can seriously impede the grieving process, delay a sense of closure, and fracture the child's trust in you. Have everyone tell stories about the pet over the grave, sing a song, leave a toy, say goodbye. It is *never* appropriate, however, to involve a child in the decision to euthanize a pet. Such a complex and multilayered ethical decision is agony even for adults. In most cases it is also not advised that young children be present for the euthanasia, although teens may wish to decide for themselves. It can be helpful to the grief process for the children to see the pet once more after the euthanasia is completed. It's a moment guaranteed to break any parent's heart, but many parents report that the closure process is more difficult without that final visit.

- **Validate their sadness and encourage their thinking.** As with the death of a person, it's important to validate their pain and grief, to give them permission to cry, and to allow them to see and hear your own feelings. Invite questions and answer them gently but honestly. This will often be your child's first engagement in a lifelong inquiry. Honor that process by attending to it.

These early experiences can literally teach children how to grieve—a nonnegotiable part of every life. In the process, they can learn much about themselves and their own emotions while moving forward in their reflections on the fact that everything that lives also dies.

Q: My 7-year-old daughter has recently been expressing fears about her own death. How can I comfort her when I don't believe in an afterlife?

A: Philosophers throughout the ages have grappled with the idea of death and produced some genuine consolations for the more mature mind, several of which are discussed below. As for the youngest kids, there are two main ways to relieve immediate fears:

1. **Distance in time.** It make seem like a cheap sleight-of-hand, but simply assuring the youngest children that they will live a long, long time before dying is quite effective. When at the age of 7 my daughter Erin first said, "I don't want to die," I simply replied, "I know what you mean. I don't either! But you're gonna live a hundred years first. You'll be older than Mom, even older than Grandma before your life is done!" To a 7-year-old, "older than Grandma" is close enough to immortal to alleviate fear (at least until the midlife crisis).

2. **Correct misconceptions of death.** When I was a kid trying to conceive of death without an afterlife, I got a truly terrifying image—let's call it "me-floating-in-darkness-forever." Compared to that (and compared to the terror of hell and the boredom of heaven), genuine nonexistence is downright lovely.

Q: So how *do* you conceive of nonexistence? I have a devil of a time grasping it myself.

A: You do, eh? Then I'm guessing you are a conscious being. There's nothing harder for a conscious being to conceive than *unconscious nonbeing*. It's entirely outside our experience because it is the absence of experience, the absence of perception.

That's the flaw in "me-floating-in-darkness." Darkness must be *perceived*. Instead, you have to grasp nonexistence. And there's one great way to do this: by recognizing that you "nonexisted" before—and for quite a long time at that.

This idea, variously attributed to the philosophers Epicurus and Lucretius, is called the "symmetry argument." Your life is bounded not by one period of nonexistence, but two: the period after your death and the period before your birth. If a child—or an adult, for that matter—expresses fear at the idea of death, ask if she was afraid a hundred years ago. When she laughs and says "Of course not! I wasn't *anywhere!*" explain that the time after her life is done will be exactly the same. There is literally no difference. There's some real consolation there.

Q: What other consolations of philosophy and science can help nonreligious people come to terms with death?

A: Different people find consolation in different ideas and at different stages in their consideration of mortality. Here are three others to try on for size:

1. **Conservation.** National Public Radio commentator Aaron Freeman offered a thought-provoking consolation in the form of an essay titled "You Want a Physicist to Speak at Your Funeral." An excerpt:

   You want a physicist to speak at your funeral. You want the physicist to talk to your grieving family about the conservation of energy, so they will understand that your energy has not died. You want the physicist to remind your sobbing mother about the first law of thermodynamics; that no energy gets created in the universe, and none is destroyed. You want your mother to know that all your energy . . . every wave of every particle that was her beloved child remains with her in this world. . . .

There may be a few fanning themselves with their programs as he says it. And he will tell them that the warmth that flowed through you in life is still here, still part of all that we are, even as we who mourn continue the heat of our own lives.

And you'll want the physicist to explain to those who loved you that they need not have faith; indeed, they should not have faith. . . . The science is sound. . . . According to the law of the conservation of energy, not a bit of you is gone; you're just less orderly. Amen.[11]

Some will find physical conservation to be irrelevant and unconsoling. Others, myself included, see a door to a greater appreciation for our part in the continuing cosmos. Every atom of your body has been around since the dawn of time and will continue to the end of time. That they assembled to form you for a little while is astonishing and wonderful. That "you" continue to exist, albeit in greater disarray, is a point well worth pondering.

2. **The inversion of death and life.** We tend to think of life as our natural condition and death as some sort of affront to that condition. But seeing your existence in the longer view can flip that on its head. Since the stuff that makes you up has always been here and will always be here, nonexistence can be seen as our normal condition. But for one short blip in that vast nonexistence, pop—here you are. Existing. Conscious. Instead of seeing death as an outrage, this view allows us to see death as the universal norm and *life* as the giddy exception.

Arthur Dobrin puts it this way: "I think there are two ultimate sources of comfort for the bereaved. The first is the recognition that the great mystery is not death but birth, not that someone loved is now gone but that the person was here at all."[12] By really grasping this inverted view, our mourning of death can be converted to gratitude for life.

3. **How amazingly unlikely was your birth.** Closely related to the above is the contemplation of the incredible odds against each of us ever existing. For billions of years, you were simply stuff—a lot of dissociated elements. Most of the universe—99.999999+ percent of it—remains insensate, unconscious, inert. But you got lucky. Out of all the quadrillions of possible combinations of elements and DNA, and despite the infinite number of things that could have kept all of your direct ancestors from meeting, from finding each other attractive, from mating (at precisely the right time) and

from raising you to adulthood—despite all of that incredible improbability, here you are. Congratulations.

In the light of that incredible good fortune, whining about the fact that life doesn't go on forever begins to seem incredibly piggy, don't you think?

These are some of the consolations I find meaningful. Others find consolation in art, in music, in transcendent poetry—or in the mythic imagination. Take your pick.

Q: My 10-year-old nephew was recently struck by a car and killed. How can I help my children deal with their cousin's sudden death at so young an age?

A: There is no denying that the death of a person so young—which feels like such a subversion of the natural order—brings a terrible additional burden to those who grieve. Rev. Dr. Kendyl Gibbons noted that "When a sibling or friend near the child's own age dies, it often feels more tragic and wasteful to the adults, and bewildering to the child, because such things are not 'supposed' to happen."[13] In addition to all of the same comforts described for more "ordinary" bereavements, children in these situations need to be particularly reassured that they themselves are not at any increased risk as a result of the tragedy. At the same time, it would not be inappropriate to underline the ways in which they can ensure their own safety (seat belts, caution, etc.). If a child seems especially affected by a tragic death, professional counseling is an option worth investigating.

Although nonreligious parents will not have access to religious comforts in these situations, they do have one notable advantage: They are freed from the unenviable task of explaining how an all-good and all-powerful god can allow such things to happen.

"I Guess We'll Never See You Again"

Our success as parents of a grieving child is not measured in inverse proportion to the number of tears or the depth of sadness. The most loving approach is often the most honest—one that looks mortality in the eye, affirms and validates sadness, and lets the griever find the voice of his grief.

When 4-year-old Lucas began to ask about death, his father Andrew loved and respected him enough to take his questions seriously. What follows is a moving and heartfelt account by Andrew of his son's early grapplings with mortality, brought to the fore by the death of a beloved pet. It was first posted on the discussion forum at www.AtheistParents.org on April 30, 2008.

Today our cat Seymour gave up the ghost. He was 17 years old and his kidneys failed.

After he died, I went out back to dig a grave for him, with Lucas in tow. Lucas was very excited to dig the grave. He has this interest in graveyards and cemeteries. Part of it is that he likes "spooky things," and part of it is his questions about death. About five months ago he started to ask me about death. I told him, "Everything that is living will someday die." One night he asked if an old lady on TV was going to die, and I said "Everything that is living will someday die." He then asked, "Will *I* die?"

I told him with a measured voice, "Everything that is living will someday die."

"I DON'T WANT TO DIE!" he said. "I WANT TO STAY HERE ALL THE DAYS! I WANT TO PLAY WITH ALL THE CARS! I WANT TO GO TO ALL THE RESTAURANTS! I WANT TO READ ALL THE BOOKS! I DON'T WANT TO DIE!" After some explanations and some more tears, he seemed to calm down.

Since then, "spooky things" and cemeteries have become more prevalent in his play. And then, Seymour was gone.

After April came home and I consoled her, we made our way out to the meager grave. Lucas was ahead of us, almost skipping, "We dug a grave, and we are going to put Seymour's body in it." We laid his body down in the hole, and Lucas gave a giggle or two as we put the first shovelful of dirt on top of our departed cat. By the second shovelful, tears were streaming down the boy's face.

"Goodbye, Seymour," he said. "I guess we'll never see you again," and swallowing the words faster then he could say them—"I love you."

He picked some dandelions and wild violets and placed them on top of the dirt pile. "I loved him too much. I hope he is not sick in my memories." He put a big cinderblock at one side of the hole and asked April to write "Mommy, Daddy, and Lucas Loves Seymour."

—*Andrew d'Apice*

■ ■ ■ ■ ■

Activities

Whistling Through the Graveyard

All ages

Some of the most meaningful and profound conversations I've had with my kids have been in cemeteries. No long car trip is complete in our family without pulling over at a roadside cemetery to stretch our legs and ponder the amazing situation we're in.

Choose well—at least a century of age and a good variety of headstones is best. No need to script it. A kid who has never heard that death is "morbid" or otherwise been shielded from healthy engagement will immediately begin to shout out discoveries. There will be tragedies—the 19-year-old who died in 1944, most likely a soldier; the wife followed just weeks later in death by her husband; a father and his 7-year-old son gone on the same day; infants and young children; a dozen dead in a single winter, perhaps from an epidemic. But there will also be the 108-year-old matriarch whose name matches that of the town, expressions of familial love, and endless evidence of lives well-lived.

If you've found a cemetery that includes epitaphs—*Beloved Mother, Artist and Visionary, He Made So Many People Happy,* etc.—muse aloud on what you'd like your own to be. What brief sentence sums up the life you hope to be remembered for? The kids will need no invitation to chime in with their own—or to suggest what yours should *really* be!

If you find yourself thinking these activities are somehow too ghoulish, snap out of it! Give the cemetery walk a try, then drop me an email of thanks.

Related topic of conversation:

Imagine your own funeral. What would you want said of you? What do you fear *might* be said? What can you do right now to change the "script"?

Talking About "Right-to-Die" Issues

Age 8+

Find age-appropriate ways to discuss a story in the news that involves "right to die" issues. Let your kids know your own wishes regarding your end-of-life treatment and WRITE IT DOWN in an easily accessible place.

Other End-of-Life Issues

Age 6+

Casually talk about your own preferences (cremation, burial, etc.) and where you would like to be buried, scattered, etc. Modeling comfort with the discussion can help kids. Ask them where they would like to be buried or have their ashes scattered. Again: If you find yourself recoiling at the idea of such a conversation, reread this chapter. Kids tend to deal with these issues *more* matter-of-factly than adults.

The Buddha and the Mustard Seed

Ages 4–8

This activity (described by Molleen Matsumura earlier in this chapter—see box) is especially useful when your family has experienced a loss. Act out the story of Buddha and the mustard seed. A woman goes to see a great teacher (the Buddha) and asks him to bring her child back to life. He tells her to bring him a mustard seed from a house in which no one has lost a child, a spouse, a parent, or a friend. After spending the day looking for such a house, she comes back empty-handed, but with the understanding that death and grief are universal.

To act out the story, have your child knock on the wall or a table and ask for a mustard seed, each time, make up a different story of a death in that house, like, "My grandfather was very, very old, and he died last week," or, "My dog ran into the street and got hit by a car." Each time, mention that the two people comfort each other somehow (e.g., by talking, or offering something to eat). Finally, knock on the wall and say, "Now the mother is knocking on *our* door." Have your child pretend to answer the door. Take the role of the grieving mother as your child explains who your family has lost and what you are doing about it. This activity goes beyond the original story's message that death comes to us all by highlighting the ways that people can support each other.

The Memory Candle

All ages

On the birthday of someone who has died, or on the anniversary of the person's death, light a 24-hour memory candle (in a glass container). Share stories of the person as you light it. Caring for the flame creates a pleasant sense of caring for the person, and the slowly disappearing candle serves as a poignant reminder of the cycle of life and the power of memory.

The idea of a "deathday" observance was popularized, but not invented, by J.K. Rowling for the Harry Potter series. Jewish tradition includes the Yahrzeit, precisely this kind of commemoration. Search for "Yahrzeit candle" online to find 24-hour commemoration candles.

Talking About Death Won't Kill You[14]

All ages

Because we are surrounded by life, we are also surrounded by death. Adults tend to stop noticing the dead bird in the backyard, the fly on the windowsill, the opossum by the roadside. Take advantage of a child's ability to see and comment on these things by engaging the questions around it. How do you think it happened? Do you think she's feeling any pain now? What do you think will happen to the bird's body in a week, a year, ten years? Where will the molecules of the bird's body be a thousand years from now?

If a small pet dies, and if you have a yard, bury your pet (or spread its ashes) together. Plant it under a small fruit tree or flowering shrub, or plant flowers over it; your child will have the experience of the pet literally turning to something wonderful.

Day of the Dead

All ages

Create a Day of the Dead altar with your child and talk about the memories that you have of a loved one. (See more about Day of the Dead activities in Chapter 3).

The Bucket List

All ages

Make a list with your children of what they want to do *and be* before they die— a list of "A Life of No Regrets."

Resources

Planning Nonreligious Funerals/Memorials

York, Sarah. *Remembering Well: Rituals for Celebrating Life and Mourning Death* (San Francisco: Jossey-Bass, 2000). The author, a Unitarian Universalist minister, clearly has both experience with and concern for the nonreligious bereaved. An outstanding resource.

Bennett, Amanda, and Terence Foley. *In Memoriam: A Practical Guide to Planning a Memorial Service* (New York: Fireside, 1997). Includes over eighty pages of suggested readings, many nonreligious.

Munro, Eleanor. *Readings for Remembrance* (New York: Penguin, 2000). Includes many wonderfully unconventional readings from philosophy, fiction, oratory, and poetry, from such minds as Joyce, Homer, Lao-Tzu, Ovid, Tolstoy, and Dante, and from sources as divergent as Buddhism, the Aztecs, and postmodernism.

Willson, Jane Wynne. *Funerals Without God* (Amherst, NY: Prometheus Books, 1991). Still the last word in last words.

For the Grieving Child

Silverman, Janis. *Help Me Say Goodbye: Activities for Helping Kids Cope When a Special Person Dies* (Hudson, NY: Fairview, 1999). An art therapy book with activities for grieving kids. Ages 4–8.

Dennison, Amy, Allie, and David. *Our Dad Died: The True Story of Three Kids Whose Lives Changed* (Minneapolis: Free Spirit, 2003). Dad died unexpectedly in his sleep from arrhythmia. Mom had the kids (8, 8, and 4 at the time) journal for two years. Although the family is Jewish, there is very little reference to or reliance on religious ideas. Quite simply, there is no other book like this. Powerful, moving, compelling. Age 8+.

Romain, Trevor. *What on Earth Do You Do When Someone Dies?* (Minneapolis: Free Spirit, 1999). Honest, compassionate, original. Highly recommended by grief therapists. Ages 9–12.

When a Pet Dies

Rogers, Fred. *When a Pet Dies* (New York: Putnam Juvenile, 1998). Ages 3–6. Thank goodness for this gentle, intelligent soul (who was also an ordained Presbyterian minister, by the way).

Wilhelm, Hans. *I'll Always Love You* (Albuquerque: Dragonfly, 1988). An unbeatable, classic tearjerker about the loss of a pet and the continuity of love. Ages 4–8.

Viorst, Judith. *The Tenth Good Thing About Barney* (New York: Aladdin, 1987). A little boy thinks of nine good things about his cat Barney, who died last Friday. But after the burial, he thinks of a tenth good thing—a naturalistic and wonderful thing that nonreligious parents will appreciate. Ages 4–8.

For the Grieving Teen

Fitzgerald, Helen. *The Grieving Teen: A Guide for Teenagers and Their Friends* (New York: Fireside, 2000).

Gootman, Marilyn, and Pamela Espeland. *When a Friend Dies: A Book for Teens About Grieving and Healing* (Minneapolis: Free Spirit, 2005).

Dougy Center. *Helping Teens Cope with Death* (Portland, OR: Dougy Center, 1999).

For the Bereaved Parent

Mitchell, Ellen, et al. *Beyond Tears: Living After Losing a Child* (New York: St. Martin's Griffin, 2005). Nine mothers who lost children co-authored this powerful and effective guide for surviving the ultimate loss. Adult.

The Compassionate Friends

www.compassionatefriends.org

A wonderful international support organization for bereaved parents and their supporters. "Espouse(s) no specific religious or philosophical ideology."

Helping Kids Think About Death

Hill, Frances. *The Bug Cemetery* (New York: Holt, 2002). Kids find a dead ladybug and conduct a mock funeral, then another and another for all the dead bugs in the neighborhood. All is fun and games until Billy's cat is hit by a car, and sadness becomes real. Not unlike Margaret Wise Brown's classic *The Dead Bird,* but the twist makes it even more powerful. Ages 4–8.

Brown, Laurie Krasny, and Marc Brown. *When Dinosaurs Die: A Guide to Understanding Death* (New York: Little, Brown Young Readers, 1998). "No one can really understand death, but to children, the passing away of a loved one can be especially perplexing and troublesome." Chapters include "What Does Alive

Mean?" "Why Does Someone Die?" "What Does Dead Mean?" "Saying Good-bye," "Keeping Customs," "What Comes After Death?" and "Ways to Remember Someone". "My family thinks Mom's soul is with God," says one character, "but I'm not sure." What better recommendation for freethinking families than that single sentence. Ages 4–8.

Buscaglia, Leo. *The Fall of Freddie the Leaf: 20th Anniversary Edition* (Thorofare, NJ: Slack, 2002). One of the great beloved classics, Freddie follows a single leaf through spring and summer and into fall. As he watches other leaves fall, he realizes and eventually comes to terms with the fact that the same will happen to him. Ages 6–12.

Schweibert, Pat, and Chuck DeKlyen. *Tear Soup*, 3rd ed. (Portland, OR: Grief Watch, 2005). Hard to imagine a more beautifully conceived and written affirmation of grieving. Simply perfect. Ages 4–8.

Movies Exploring Death and Loss

See Appendix 1 for a complete table of suggested films including ratings and age appropriateness.

Three Best Works of Kid Lit Exploring the Topic of Death

White, E. B. *Charlotte's Web* (New York: HarperCollins, 1952, renewed 1980). Ages 6–12.

Babbitt, Natalie. *Tuck Everlasting* (New York: Farrar, Straus, & Giroux, 1985). Ages 6–12.

Paterson, Katherine. *Bridge to Terabithia* (New York: HarperTeen, 2004). Age 9+.

Reflections for Adults and Young Adults

Dobrin, Arthur. *Love Is Stronger Than Death* (1986). A beautiful, moving, thoughtful piece of work, now out of print but available online at *www.ethicalunion.org/loveis/index.html*

Willson, Harry. *Myth and Mortality—Testing the Stories* (Albuquerque: Amador, 2007). This engaging and thoughtful book looks at thirty-two beliefs dealing with death and assesses their helpfulness in confronting mortality. Willson is a former missionary pastor who is now a secular humanist social justice activist.

Wilson, Robert Anton. "Cheerful Reflections on Death and Dying." Google it, or brave the long URL: *www.deepleafproductions.com/wilsonlibrary/texts/raw-dying.html*

Morris, Virginia. *Talking About Death Won't Kill You* (New York: Workman, September 10, 2001). A wonderfully healthy and candid look at death and our tendency to avoid the topic. The publication date alone is enough to grab one's attention.

Montross, Christine. *Body of Work: Meditations on Mortality from the Human Anatomy Lab* (New York: Penguin Press, 2007). Not for everyone, but for those interested in a very (very) direct look at mortality through the lens of the physical, this is worth looking into.

Enright, D.J. (Ed.). *The Oxford Book of Death* (London: Oxford University Press, 2002). A magnificent anthology of writings on death and dying.

Nuland, Sherwin. *How We Die: Reflections on Life's Final Chapter* (New York: Vintage, 1995). A brilliant and important contribution to the literature, written from the perspective of a physician with the heart of a sage.

Byock, Ira, M.D. *Dying Well* (New York: Riverhead Trade, 1998). A book lauded for its "humanistic soul," *Dying Well* is a clear-eyed, thoughtful excursion through the process of decline and death, built around the author's experience of his own father's death.

See also the following reviews in *Parenting Beyond Belief*:
Emswiler, James, and Mary Ann. *Guiding Your Child through Grief* (New York: Bantam, 2000).

Arent, Ruth P., MA, MSW. *Helping Children Grieve* (Belgium, WI: Champion Press, 2005).

Thomas, Pat. *I Miss You—A First Look at Death* (New York: Barron's, 2000). Ages 3–8.

Bryant-Mole, Karen. *Talking About Death* (Redwood City, CA: Raintree, 1999). Ages 4–8.

Rothman, Juliet Cassuto. *A Birthday Present for Daniel: A Child's Story of Loss* (Amherst, NY: Prometheus, 2001). Ages 7–10.

Trozzi, Maria, M.Ed. *Talking with Children About Loss* (New York: Perigee Trade, 1999).

Notes

1. Emswiler, James, and Emswiler, Mary Ann, *Guiding Your Child Through Grief* (New York: Bantam Books, 2000), p. 112.

2. Konner, Melvin, *The Tangled Wing* (New York: Holt Paperback, 2003), p. 369.

3. Dawkins, Richard, "Religion's misguided missiles." *The Guardian* (UK), September 15, 2001.

4. Oh . . . that was me: Accessed August 2, 2008, from *http://parentingbeyond belief.com/blog/?p=71*

5. See Emswiler, James, and Emswiler, Mary Ann, *Guiding Your Child Through Grief* (New York: Bantam, 2000) for an excellent example of a mainstream parenting book with similar caveats.

6. These same suggestions are offered by many grief practitioners and authors, but few as clearly and concisely as The Compassionate Friends' website. Accessed July 8, 2008, from *www.compassionatefriends.org*

7. Several other cultures in what is now Mexico and Central America observed festivals with similar rituals and iconography, including the Maya, Olmec, Zapotec, and Mixtec.

8. See the entry on Halloween and Samhain in the Q&A section of Chapter 6, "Celebrating Life."

9. This was not the case in earlier historical periods when child and infant mortality were significantly higher.

10. From an impromptu address at Digital Biota 2, Cambridge, UK, September 1998. Full text available at *www.biota.org/people/douglasadams*. Accessed March 22, 2008.

11. Freeman, Aaron. "You Want a Physicist to Speak at Your Funeral," National Public Radio, June 1, 2005. Available in podcast at *www.npr.org/templates/story/story.php?storyId=4675953*. Accessed March 22, 2008.

12. From Chapter 1 of *Love Is Stronger Than Death* (1986). Accessed May 4, 2008, from *www.ethicalunion.org/loveis/index.html*

13. *Parenting Beyond Belief*, pp. 170–171.

14. See the book of the same name in the Resources section.

CHAPTER 8

Finding and Creating Community

Amanda Metskas

When the secular parenting discussion forums at ParentingBeyondBelief.com opened in February 2007, a single comment, phrased various ways, was posted over and over: "It's so nice to talk to other secular parents out there dealing with similar issues." The comments were often followed with stories of isolation, feelings of uncertainty—and the desire for community.

There are literally millions of families in the United States with nonreligious worldviews, but too often they feel as if they are going it alone. By contrast, religious families usually have a nearby church community offering Sunday school, parent groups, and organized family outings—all in addition to the weekly worship service.[1] Secular families seldom have the same built-in access to communities where they can congregate, share ideas, and pass along values to their children. This might explain why getting married and having children are the two key factors that bring people back to church.[2] The readymade community is one area where it is safe to say that religious parents have a real advantage.

A Caveat for Community-Builders

In our rush to create and embrace community, an important caution must be sounded. A community can quickly turn into a gated enclave, an "us" that not only binds its members together but also excludes and even demonizes "them"—those who are on the outside of our defining wall.

We live in naturally concentric circles of community. The inner circle is often our immediate family, those with whom we feel the most connection. Around that circle runs the larger circle of extended family, followed by other affinities like regional, cultural, and language groups; our ethnicities, regions, and nations; our worldviews; even our species. Each of these concentric circles defines a community, linking us to those with whom we share something significant.

In addition to these concentric circles, we also have cross-cutting community memberships and identities—we may be similar to others in one way, and different in others.[3] For example, a doctor may belong to a community of medical professionals, but may be different from many other members of that community in terms of her race, religious views, or other characteristics. She may also belong to an empowerment group for African American women, but differ from many members of that group in her religious views or her occupational identity.

Our connection, our compassion, and our empathy often drop as we move outward through concentric communities, or interact with those who are different from us in more of our important identities, across what has been called an "empathy gradient." We tend to feel closest to and most protective of those who are closely related or otherwise similar to us—natural selection at work—followed by those who live nearby but are less similar. By the time we have moved outward to people living far away, or those who are unlike us in other ways, we tend to feel a reduced empathy. It's easier to feel compassion for the neighbor child with leukemia than the child in a distant country with the same condition.

Merely spending time with people who are different than you doesn't always lead to increased empathy and understanding. It helps a lot to have a common goal, as Muzafer Sherif found out in his famous "Robbers Cave Experiment" in 1954.[4] In the experiment, two groups of boys at a summer camp were organized into competing teams. The experimenters tried to break down the animosity between the groups by having the boys spend time together, but instead of decreased animosity, they got food fights in the dining hall. What succeeded in breaking down the barriers between the groups were situations in which both groups had to work together to accomplish something that everyone wanted. It took work from both groups, for example, to pull the camp truck when it wouldn't start.

Several more recent studies have come to similar conclusions.[5] For example, recognizing our cross-cutting social identities and recognizing larger shared identities have both been shown to lead to more cooperation and fairer outcomes in social dilemma situations, where there is a limited resource that people have to allocate and share.[6]

As humanists, our goal should be not just building the inner circles of community, but pushing that sense of connectedness out across as many of boundaries as possible. The community of freethinkers should be just one of *several* communities of which we consider ourselves to be a part. It's one of the nine "best practices" for nonreligious parenting mentioned in the Preface: *Encourage the widest possible circles of empathy.* As we define our immediate communities, it's important to recognize and reinforce the communities of which we are already a part, all the way out to the widest circle of all: the community of life on Earth.

We can take a page from the atheists, agnostics, and freethinkers at the University of Illinois who went on a spring break community service trip together with members of their school's Campus Crusade for Christ group to help with rebuilding in New Orleans. As we seek to form communities with other freethinking families, we can and should also join together with other groups to make our broader community a better place.

What Human Community Is (Really) All About

Freethought groups and freethinkers around the country are working to create viable, satisfying, multigenerational communities—and meeting with varying degrees of success. Some have forged a connection with young people and families, even starting humanist children's programs and parent support groups. Others, however, find their membership numbers frozen year after year as the average age of their members drifts slowly upward. What makes the difference between a thriving, growing community and a stagnant one?

The answer lies in an understanding of community itself. You can't choose your family, but membership in a community is largely voluntary. Give me what I'm looking for and I'm likely to stay. Give me something less and I'll go elsewhere. It's just about that simple.

Freethought communities stagnate when they fail to work hard enough at understanding what people are seeking—what human needs have spurred their search for a community in the first place. Too many freethought communities have drawn their purposes too narrowly. They are about inquiry, reason, the search for truth, and the rejection of religion. They don't want to attend churches because they don't want a community that's centered on gods and theologies.

What they fail to realize is that theology is less important to most church-goers than a number of other benefits. In many cases, they attend *despite* the theology.

It is telling that only 27 percent of churchgoing U.S. respondents to a 2007 Gallup poll even mentioned God when asked for the *main* reason they attend church.[7] Most people go for personal growth, for guidance in their lives, to be encouraged, to be inspired—or for the community and fellowship of other members. These, not worship, are the primary needs fulfilled by churches.

If freethought communities wish to build their memberships well beyond the 60ish white male demographic that currently dominates the rolls (God bless 'em!), they must begin considering the real reasons people flock to church. It's not about theology. It's about belonging. It's about acceptance. It's about mutual support and encouragement. Most of all, it speaks to needs beyond the intellectual into the emotional.

This chapter will offer several specific ways in which freethought communities can speak more directly to these needs. Organizing freethinkers has been compared to herding cats, and there's merit in the metaphor. Nonetheless, nonreligious families are clearly looking for community. This chapter is about helping freethinking families find and build the communities they seek.

Questions and Answers

Q: My partner and I are not religious, but now that we have kids, we really feel the need for a community to reinforce the values we teach at home. We've been talking about going back to church. Are there alternatives?

A: There are indeed, and those alternatives are increasing in number and in variety. The resources section of this chapter contains websites for organizations with local chapters or congregations, some of which might be a good fit for your family. Not all are available in all areas, and some of them offer more for children and families than others, but this should provide a place to start looking for an existing community that you can join.

Nonreligious families vary considerably in the communities they seek. Some like the congregational model, which can provide many of the positive emotional and social benefits of religion without supernatural claims and dogma. Here are three options on the "congregational" end of the spectrum:

Unitarian Universalist Fellowships

Unitarian fellowships are "creedless," meaning they require no expression of shared dogmas, doctrines, or religious beliefs. In lieu of doctrines, the denomination is organized around Seven UU Principles (outlined in the Appendix). The majority of Unitarian Universalists identify as atheists or agnostics, and an even larger percentage (91 percent) include "humanist" as one of their self-identities.[8] Unitarian Universalist congregations have a well-developed religious education program for kids, focusing on comparative religion and ethics, as well as a highly regarded sex education program. There are currently over 1,040 UU fellowships in North America, so the odds are good that you will find one or more in your area.

UU fellowships vary widely in their approach and atmosphere depending on the minister and the makeup of the congregation. Some continue to use Christian language and symbolism, while others have a more completely nontheistic flavor. If there is more than one UU in your area, compare them to see which suits your family the best. If the services are not for you, there may still be other programmatic offerings that are appealing.

In addition to visiting fellowships, many answers to common questions about Unitarian Universalism can be found at *www.uufaq.com*.

Ethical Societies

There are currently twenty-five Ethical Societies in the United States organized around the principles of Ethical Culture, as well as a web-based "Ethical Society Without Walls" (*www.eswow.org*) for those without a local Ethical Society. According to the American Ethical Union, "Ethical Culture is a humanistic religious and educational movement inspired by the ideal that the supreme aim of human life is working to create a more humane society."[9] Unlike Unitarian Universalist congregations, which have people of many different religious and nonreligious beliefs, Ethical Culture groups have a core set of beliefs. Although they are nontheistic, many people in the movement consider Ethical Culture to be their religion. Ethical Societies offer religious education programs for young children up through college students. The American Ethical Union also offers yearly youth conferences for middle school, high school, and college students. There are a lot of curriculum resources for Ethical Culture children's programs available on its website at *www.aeu.org*.

Humanistic Jewish Congregations

For those who are nontheistic but remain committed to cultural or ethnic Jewish identity and tradition, there are twenty-nine congregations in North America identified with Humanistic Judaism. Humanistic Jewish congregations celebrate Jewish holidays and practice Jewish traditions in a way that is free of supernatural elements. The congregations offer programs for children, and the Society for Humanistic Judaism offers youth conferences.

To learn about their youth programs, go to *www.shj.org*. There are also cultural and secular Jewish groups that belong to the Congress of Secular Jewish Organizations (*www.csjo.org*), and some of these groups have schools or other programs for children.

For nonreligious parents interested in a less "congregational" option for a community of shared values, the freethought group model may be appealing. Such groups to date have seldom had programs for children and families, but this is changing rapidly. The Humanist Community in Palo Alto, California, for example, offers a humanist Sunday school program that was profiled in *TIME*,[10] committed to ethics education. Similar programs are starting up at local humanist groups in Phoenix, Albuquerque, Colorado Springs, and Portland.

In addition to these regular, local opportunities to find a community and pass on values for your freethinking family, there are opportunities like Camp Quest (*www.camp-quest.org*). Camp Quest offers week-long summer camp programs that combine traditional summer camp activities like swimming, arts and crafts, and canoeing with educational activities focused on secular ethics, critical thinking, freethought heroes, and scientific inquiry. Kids have an opportunity to meet other kids from freethinking families, and the friendships that they form are often long-lasting. For many kids, the community they find at camp lets them know that their family isn't alone, and the opportunity to interact with other kids their own age about these topics helps them develop their values and beliefs.

Q: My partner and I attended a local freethought group in our town when we were first together. But we stopped going once we had kids because they don't offer any kids programs or activities, and we don't want to have to get a babysitter to go to the meeting. What can we do to make our local freethought group more family-friendly?

A: When it comes to serving families, a lot of local atheist, freethought, and humanist groups have a "chicken and egg" problem. They don't offer programs for children because no families with children are members of the group, and no families are members because they have no children's programs.

Before heading out on your own, I'd recommend trying to create a children's program at the meetings of the local group. Ask the group organizers if there are families who are members of the group or former members of the group who are still on the mailing list but no longer attend. There's your core group! Get in touch with those families. Find out if they would be interested in coming back to the group if there were a kids' program at the same time as the regular meeting. If you get some interest from these families, present that information to the group organizers and ask them to commit to the idea.

If the organizers don't know of any families on the mailing list, put out a sign-up sheet at meetings for parents. Also, see if you can get an announcement on the group's website and in the group's newsletter asking for those interested in a children's program to email you. Post notices on *www.craigslist.com* and *www.meetup.com*.

Once you've found some interested folks and secured support from the group's leadership, it's time to start planning the program. A common mistake people make in this phase is trying to do too much too fast. You and the other families interested in this group are probably very busy people without the time to write a whole Sunday School curriculum or plan elaborate events. There may also not be enough demand to justify that kind of program at the beginning.

It's generally best to start a program in small, simple steps. If the interested families have mostly younger children, start with something like a storytime, some drawing and coloring, and a simple song. The purpose of these first sessions to build some momentum, let people know that there is a children's program, and have the kids and parents get to know each other. If you have three families with kids who are interested in the program, perhaps each family can plan and lead every third session. This spreads out the work and (equally important) builds a community in which all the parents are involved.

Q: How can I get a nonreligious parenting group started in my area? There aren't many organized secular groups where we are, and the ones that do exist don't really work for us.

A: A number of nonreligious parenting groups have begun to form nationwide in recent years. Shortly after the release of *Parenting Beyond Belief,* a "Meetup" group by the same name formed in Raleigh, North Carolina. Within three months the group had over fifty members. In early 2008, the Center for

Inquiry (CFI) began forming nonreligious parenting groups in cities including Austin and Portland, just as a "Perplexed Parenting Circle" for secular parents began meeting in New York City. If you are planning to start a group of your own, you are in good company and have a number of existing groups to use as models.

First, determine what purpose or purposes you are hoping that the group will serve. Are you interested in finding other secular parents to share advice and ideas? Are you looking to help your kids connect with other kids from a similar background? Are there topics like ethics that you want your kids to learn about in groups larger than the family?

Deciding on the purpose of the group and stating that purpose up front is a crucial foundation for long-term success. The purpose can certainly evolve over time, but it's important to begin on the same page.

If you are looking for a playgroup for your kids with likeminded families, and some fellow secular parents to get to know and swap ideas with, you might be best served by creating something informal. Planning and organizing a more formal group can be burdensome and unnecessary if your goals are that simple.

The online secular parenting communities in the resources section often allow people to list their city or state and provide a way to send targeted or private messages. Find some secular parents who live in your area and have kids of similar ages and suggest going to a local museum, zoo, swimming pool, park, or other nearby attraction for families. Meet the parents and kids, and if things go well, suggest a regular every-other Saturday outing, or a weekly rotating playdate/parent get-together. No need to complicate your life by creating a website, doing promotions, and creating an organization with officers and budget in this case.

If, on the other hand, your goals are to create a group that has more formal educational outcomes—like teaching ethics, critical thinking, comparative religions, freethought history, scientific inquiry, etc.—then you may indeed want and need the group to be more formalized. You'll probably be crafting some lesson plans and buying supplies for lessons, so you want to know how many kids are coming ahead of time. You may need to work with a more specific age group, and if you're going through this effort, you may want to promote your group to the broader community.

This is a great goal, but it's best to start small and build your program and activities over time. Start with meeting other interested parents and kids through outings or playdates, and get to know the other parents. Find out if they are interested in working on a "freethought Sunday school" project and how they would envision such a thing. Get a sense of how much time your fellow parents can commit to the project, and what their areas of expertise are. It's important to spread out the work of running the program to avoid burning yourselves out and so that other families are invested in the program and don't take your hard work for granted.

As your group grows, remember to keep in mind why you started the group in the first place. Don't let organizing and planning the group get in the way of the real purpose—creating a community for your family. The educational activities should be fun, not something the kids dread and have to be coerced and cajoled into attending. The group should provide parents with support and ideas rather than being a burden to plan that overshadows the benefits.

Check out the Activities section for some activities that are good for larger groups of kids. Look in the Resources sections for freethought curriculum ideas.

Q: We don't have any local groups in our area (or the local groups in our area don't fit in our schedule or work for our family), and I just don't have the time to start a new group. What are our options?

A: Even if you don't have a local group in your area there are still several ways for you to find a freethinking community for your family.

There are online resources for freethinking families—*Parenting Beyond Belief* has a website (*www.ParentingBeyondBelief.com*) with a forum in which parents can talk about secular parenting issues, swap stories, get ideas, and find support.

The Ethical Society Without Walls (*www.eswow.org*) and the UU Church of the Larger Fellowship (*http://clf.uua.org*) have religious education materials that you can use with your family. (Remember that for Ethical Culture and UU groups "religious education" is worlds away from "bible study.") The Institute for Humanist Studies has a website section on parenting (*www .humaniststudies.org/parenting/*) with resources of interest to humanist and freethinking parents.

There may also be groups in your local community that aren't explicitly nontheist but share your tolerant values and are welcoming to freethinking families. Look around for groups that lead kids' science activities or have programs for kids who are intellectually curious and/or gifted, or volunteer opportunities for families. A welcoming group focused on compassion, creativity, and critical thinking is a great place for your family no matter the religious or nonreligious preferences of most members. In fact, this kind of environment may be the best place for kids to explore a variety of worldviews in a non-indoctrinating setting.

Annual conferences, retreats, and summer camps can also expose your kids to a community of freethinkers. Although these options don't give you a local community to meet with regularly throughout the year, they can supplement what's available in your area. Camp Quest offers week-long summer camp programs in several locations around North America.

A few organizations offer conferences specifically aimed at youth: The American Ethical Union offers youth conferences for middle school, high school, and college-aged kids. The Secular Student Alliance (*www.secularstudents.org*) offers conferences aimed primarily at college students, although some high school students participate as well.

Some informal family camping opportunities and other retreats are also springing up in some areas. Check out the Lake Hypatia event hosted by the Alabama Freethought Association and the Freedom from Religion Foundation (*www.ffrf.org/lakehypatia/*) every year over the July 4th weekend for a fun freethought event that is combination conference and campout. It includes some whimsical events like the annual Atheists vs. Agnostics Softball Game.

Q: Is it really that important for children to know other freethinking families, or will the influence of our family be enough exposure to freethought ideas?

A: While I'm sure your kids will turn out just fine either way, a community of freethinking families can help in some very important ways.

As Bobbie Kirkhart explains in *Parenting Beyond Belief*, while a lot of freethinking adults may tend not to be "joiners," kids are often looking for ways to belong. Most of your kids' friends will be members of a church or other religious group with their families, and your child may feel like he or she is missing out. There is also the possibility that kids without the context of a community of shared values will find ways to belong, one way or another, and may end up in "communities" built around risky behaviors.

Kids learn a lot from each other, and it is important that they have people their own age who they can talk to about their worldview and their ideas. These don't necessarily all have to be kids from freethinking families—in fact, it's best if they can share ideas with kids from a variety of perspectives. I remember having great conversations with my friends about all sorts of questions related to religion. Even though most of my friends had Christian parents, they were trying to figure out what they thought about the world, just like I was. (Of course, sometimes their parents were not thrilled when they found out about such discussions.)

Most freethinking families seek a community with similar values *not* to cut their children off from other points of view but to reinforce the ethical lessons they are trying to impart at home. While there is a lot you can do to teach values like compassion and critical thinking in the home, kids inevitably compare their families to other families they know. It lends your teaching credibility if your kids know other families who share a similar worldview and discuss the same issues.

One more reason to find a freethought community beyond the family: Depending on where you live, your family's beliefs may be controversial among the parents of your children's schoolmates and peers. Some children from free-thinking families are singled out for harassment at school, told they are untrustworthy, evil, or damned to hell. Coaches, teachers, or activity leaders have been known to punish children who don't participate in a team prayer or religious activity that "everyone else" is doing. For kids facing prejudices or bullying because of their beliefs, it is especially important to have a network of other freethinkers in their lives. Knowing that there are others like them and their families can help kids understand that they aren't alone and serve as a source of support as they seek to stand up for their beliefs and educate their classmates about who they are and what they think.

Q: Boy Scouting was a great community for me growing up, but they seem to have taken an intolerant turn in recent years. Can you tell me exactly what the BSA's policy is regarding religion? Are atheists actively prohibited, or is it a "don't ask, don't tell" policy?

A: The most accurate way to phrase the policy is that religious belief is required. If atheists were prohibited, an "unlabeled" child would be permitted. But the Boy Scouts organization requires the declaration of religious belief. From the BSA's Declaration of Religious Principle:

> The BSA maintains that no member can grow into the best kind of citizen without recognizing an obligation to God. The recognition of God as the ruling and leading power in the universe and the grateful acknowledgment of His favors and blessings are necessary to the best type of citizenship and are wholesome precepts in the education of the growing members.

The Scout Oath also begins with "On my honor I will do my best to do my duty to God and my country."

So no, it is not passive. A Boy Scout is required to actively and repeatedly affirm belief in God.

Q: But all of my son's friends are joining Scouts, and he wants to sign up. Should I let him join?

A: This is essentially an ethical question, one you can and should discuss with your son. But since the issue often arises at the age of 8, it will ultimately be up to you as parents to decide.

The Boy Scouts of America has a national policy that bans atheists (and gays) from membership. Certain troops may not enforce the policy, but (as noted above) members must repeatedly affirm religious belief in the Scout Oath. Scouts who do not believe—and note that this includes "unlabeled" children, who have not yet decided the question of belief—must lie when speaking the Oath, unless their troop leader is willing to let them modify the Oath. We'll call that Ethical Issue number one.

The second ethical issue: Such a policy, if enforced, demands that children take a religious stand—something directly opposed to the "best practice" of leaving children free of labels.

Third issue: Membership in an organization implies a certain level of endorsement of the group's policies. Some feel that being a Boy Scout (or allowing your son to join) lends some support and credence to discrimination based on religious belief and sexual orientation.

This doesn't add up to a slam dunk decision. Different parents can reasonably come to different conclusions about whether to join. If you are unsure of your decision, talk with the local troop leader who would be working with your son. Explain your concerns and see how he or she reacts. Look over the materials that your son would be using and see if the troop leader is willing to let your son say modified versions of oaths that mention God and do modified activities for merit badges that have a religious component if they make you uncomfortable. Let the troop leader know that you are committed to letting your son make his own decisions about religious ideas as he grows up, but you don't want him to be in an environment where he is taught (implicitly or explicitly) that nonreligious people are lacking in moral values or are somehow morally inferior to religious people.

Talk with your son as well. Let him know about the policy and see what he thinks. The attractions of joining will generally outweigh an ethical argument at this age. If he still wants to join after your discussion, and you agree, let him know that he should keep thinking about it while a member. Make sure that he knows he is not required to participate in oaths or activities that he disagrees with and that he can always talk to you about any problems that arise. And if you are not comfortable letting your son join, explain why and help him seek out other activities.

Additional Resources

- Margaret Downey's essay "Teaching Children to Stand on Principle" in *Parenting Beyond Belief.*
- Scouting For All (*www.scoutingforall.org*), an organization committed to reforming the Boy Scouts of America into a nondiscriminatory organization.

Q: My daughter is interested in Girl Scouts. Does Girl Scouting have the same discriminatory policies?

A: No, it doesn't. Despite the presence of "God" in the Girl Scout Promise, the Girl Scouts organization (which is entirely independent of the Boy Scouts) has gone out of its way to spell out nondiscriminatory policies. The results have not been perfect—there have been local reports of discriminatory acts contrary to the organization's principles—but that's to be expected in a group of this size.

The attitude of Girl Scouts USA regarding religious belief is summed up in a landslide 1993 vote by which the organization adopted a measure to permit its members to substitute another word or phrase for "God" in the Girl Scout Promise. A 2003 statement titled "What We Stand For" included this outstandingly clear passage:

> The Girl Scout organization does not endorse or promote any particular philosophy or religious belief. Our movement is secular and is founded on American democratic principles, one of which is freedom of religion.[11]

A 1991 policy letter also clarified the policy on sexual orientation:

> As a private organization, Girl Scouts of the USA respects the values and beliefs of each of its members and does not intrude into personal matters. Therefore, there are no membership policies on sexual preference."[12]

Q: Are there alternatives to the traditional scouting organizations?

A: Partly as a result of the discriminatory policies of BSA and other concerns with traditional Scouting (including reinforcement of gender roles, the emphasis on obedience, and other issues), several alternatives have recently developed, including:

- Earth Scouts (*www.earthscouts.org*): "Earth Scouts is an inclusive, co-educational scouting program . . . [emphasizing] sustainability, equity and nonviolence."[13]
- Spiral Scouts (*www.spiralscouts.org*): "SpiralScouts thrives on . . . religious tolerance and interfaith cooperation, personal responsibility, and ecological education and conservation, in order to help our children learn to grow into . . . citizens of the world."[14] The Spiral Scouts grew out of a pagan religious tradition, and some of the terms they use like "circles" and "hearths" for their troops reflect that tradition, but their activities are meant to be for kids from any tradition. Their website provides more information and a way to find a circle near you.

Q: I want my kids to be part of a freethinking community, but I don't want them labeled as atheists before they've had a chance to think through their ideas for themselves. How can I expose them to a freethought community without them being labeled or indoctrinated?

A: You've got exactly the right idea. There's a consensus emerging among freethinkers that children need to come to their own conclusions about their religious (or nonreligious) beliefs, and concern about labeling and indoctrination is taken very seriously. Freethinkers by definition have come to their beliefs due to their own thinking, reading, and reflection, and most understand that their kids are entitled to no less. Many freethinkers had negative experiences with religious indoctrination in childhood and understand that the best way to turn a child off to an idea—any idea—is to force-feed it to her.

One of the core missions of The Richard Dawkins Foundation for Reason and Science (*www.richarddawkinsfoundation.org*) is raising awareness about the problem of labeling children based on the religious (or nonreligious) beliefs of their parents. Camp Quest also avoids labeling children and instead seeks to create a place where children can explore their developing worldviews free of the negative stereotypes and controversy that may be leveled at their families back home due to their parents' beliefs.

Even though the vast majority of freethinkers are on the same page regarding this issue, not everyone is. Check out the children's freethought activities that your child is involved in just as vigorously as any other activity. Talk to the activity leaders about any concerns you have.

While most freethinkers won't try to label a child based on the parents' beliefs, your child may be facing such labeling from others in the community. Talk with your child about this, and help her to have ready responses, such as, "Why do you think I believe that just because my parents do? Do you always believe the same thing as your parents?" Remind your child that she is free to change her mind about her beliefs as often as she wishes, and that you recognize she has her own beliefs even if sometimes other adults may forget that. When other adults label your child based on your beliefs, gently correct them: "Well, that's what *I* believe, but if you want to know what my *son* believes, you'll have to ask him."

A nonreligious mom in Ohio answers questions about homeschooling for the nonreligious.

Q: Why did you decide to homeschool?
A: My daughter, Allison, was in second grade and having a hard time. She wasn't clicking with her teacher or her school. She was also being bullied about her nontheism. Two girls cornered her in the bathroom and told her she was going to hell because she doesn't believe in God. Many other similar incidents happened. I talked to her teacher and the principal. Since the students were doing this of their own accord, the school wouldn't interfere. They said that if they put a stop to it, they would be violating those students' right to free speech. Rather than face a lengthy battle, I decided to pull her out to homeschool.

Q: Aren't all homeschoolers religious fundamentalists?
About three in four homeschoolers in the United States are evangelical Christians, but there are also a lot of nontheist homeschoolers. We're just a bit harder to find! We are becoming more vocal, though. Our main way of connecting is through email groups [see the Resources section]. We support each other and help find secular school materials.

Q: So there are secular homeschool curricula?
A: Yes—we just have to be really careful what we buy. Most religious publishers are proud of their theism and make it clear that their materials

217

are not secular. But some are sneaky. When I first began homeschooling, I thought I could use their books and just ignore the religious sentences, but I quickly realized their whole worldview is different from mine. Many homeschool supply companies are openly Christian but do sell some secular materials. If I see a warning that a book is by a secular publisher and may be offensive, that's the book I buy!

Q: Where do you find secular resources?
A: If you do an Internet search of secular homeschool resources, you'll find lots of links. Some people research and review materials and post lists. I recently ordered textbooks used in public schools. I've found them all secular. They're expensive, though. You can also find slightly older editions on eBay at a large discount. I also order books from Great Britain and have been very pleased with them.

Q: What about socialization?
A: This is the most common question homeschoolers hear. Socialization can be particularly tough for nontheists. I've been to many gatherings where people assume I'm religious. I had a choice: Proclaim my Humanism, possibly alienating my daughter and myself from the group, or I could keep quiet and scream later. When Allison was younger, I chose to bite my tongue. We were new to homeschooling, and she needed all the playmates she could find.

Now I'm more open. Also, since Allison is older, she's more forthright herself with her friends. Luckily, a wonderful woman in town started a secular homeschooling group. We're the Mid Ohio Secular Homeschoolers. We finally have a place to fit in and be completely ourselves! We sometimes discuss secular materials, but mostly we get together just for support and friendship. Allison feels so free now that she can openly discuss her nontheism. The kids encourage each other to stand up for freethought. They also help each other deal with harassment about their lifestyles.

Q: What are the pros and cons of homeschooling?
A: For us, the biggest benefit of homeschooling has been the lifestyle. We are free to go where we please, and we find learning experiences everywhere. Learning doesn't just take place in four walls of a schoolroom! We are trying to raise Allison as a citizen of the world, and we are able to do that through homeschooling. We travel as much as possible, paying lower off-season prices. We choose our own materials and style of learning. Also, my daughter is no longer bullied for being a Humanist.

The main "con" of homeschooling is that we have to actively seek out social experiences. Allison loves being around kids, and sometimes she misses being around classmates all day. Occasionally, we get on each others' nerves since we're together most of the time. We work it out through open communication. We feel learning to get along and talk things out is an important life skill for kids. Also, we have to deal with the stereotype of homeschoolers being religious. We like to open people's minds and let them know all kinds of people homeschool.

Don't let being a nontheist stop you from homeschooling. We can support each other and make our voices heard. As the number of nontheist homeschoolers grows, publishers will see the need in the market and publish more materials for us.

Deciding to homeschool can be a scary decision. I was really nervous at first, but now I'm absolutely sure it's the right decision for our family.

—*Amy Page, Mid Ohio Secular Homeschoolers,*
ohiohomeschoolhumanist@yahoo.com

Activities

This Activities section includes ideas for finding communities, building communities, and exploring the idea of community.

The Belief-O-Matic™ Quiz

www.beliefnet.com > Belief-O-Matic

Age 12+

Have friends and family take the Belief-O-Matic Quiz at *www.beliefnet.com*. Answer twenty multiple-choice questions about your beliefs and receive a list of belief systems and your percentage of agreement with each. A fascinating exercise in community building and in demonstrating the common ground among belief systems.

Hit the Road to Find Freethought Communities

All ages

Visit local freethought groups, UU congregations, or Ethical Societies. Learn about what they have to offer and look for ways your family can get involved.

Famous Freethinkers, Humanist Heroes

All ages

Most kids grow up completely unaware of the many contributions made by the nonreligious. Just as the theistic worldviews of Martin Luther King and Mahatma Gandhi informed and energized their work and character, so nontheistic, humanistic values informed the lives and work of such towering figures as John Stuart Mill, Susan B. Anthony, Jane Addams, Albert Einstein, Thomas Edison, and countless others. Next time your child is choosing a famous subject for a book report or project, why not suggest a freethinker? Check out *www.celebatheists.com* for a list of several hundred atheists and agnostics, and pick out a few with your child about whom she is interested in learning more.

The Community Mural

All ages

> *Materials:* butcher paper and crayons, markers, or paint

Start by brainstorming what a community is. Help kids to move beyond the physical community into the concept of shared values and traditions. Have the kids draw or paint a mural with their own vision of community. Ask that they include pictures of people doing things that help to bind a community together. Follow up by talking about ways to support each other and keep communities together.

Guru2Go

All ages

(Works best in groups of twelve or more, in relatively small age range)

1. Tell the children you are looking for four "gurus"—kids who can teach something they know in 3 to 4 minutes. (Help them brainstorm ideas: Have you been to another country? Do you know how stars form? Can you explain how trees turn sunlight into food?)

2. Have the four gurus spread out in the room. Divide the remaining kids into groups of three.

3. One from each group goes to a guru, who then teaches what he or she knows. The learners listen, ask questions, and take notes.

4. The learners come back to their groups and teach what they learned.

5. Repeat with new gurus.

Common Bonds

All ages, groups of eight or more—the more, the better

Materials: scratch pads, pens, butcher paper, markers

1. Have kids pair up.

2. Each pair talks to discover something they have in common (an interest, a preference, a talent, an experience, etc.), then writes it down.

3. Each pair then finds another pair. Kids determine something that all four members have in common and write it down.

4. Each group of four then finds another group of four and determines something all eight have in common.

5. Continue to entire group.

6. Make a mural illustrating each level of community.

All My Friends and Neighbors

All ages, groups of ten to sixty or more. Kids and adults can play this game together.

> *Materials:* open field or floor space and enough chairs for everyone in the group minus one.

This is a game we play at Camp Quest to help everyone get to know each other.

Set up the chairs in a circle, with one chair fewer than the number of participants. The person starting the game stands in the middle and says something true about him- or herself, beginning with the phrase "All my friends and neighbors . . ." Example: "All my friends and neighbors like math class the best." Everyone in the circle for whom that statement is true, and the person in the middle, runs and finds a new chair somewhere else in the circle (usually they aren't allowed to take the chair right next to them). The new person who is left without a chair goes to the middle and says something true about him- or herself, like "All my friends and neighbors know how to knit." Repeat until you're ready to move on.

Tips: Try to discourage merely visible attributes. You don't learn nearly as much about each other if most of the rounds are, "All my friends and neighbors are wearing blue jeans." Encourage people to be careful not to collide with each other or tip over their chairs when sitting down. If some of the younger participants are getting in the middle over and over, help them get to a chair, or have them swap with someone who hasn't been in the middle yet.

"Yeah, But . . ."

Ages 8 and up. Groups of two to eight. If more are participating, break them into a few groups.

> *Materials:* Topics for argument appropriate to the age group.

This is an activity used at Camp Quest to encourage kids to think on their feet and argue both sides of an issue. It's adapted from an activity called "Chain Debate" that is used as a warmup for high school policy debate teams. It's good for small groups of kids ages 8 and up. It can also be used as a way to air a disagreement in the group and get the issues on the table. The lesson here is that there are multiple sides to issues. Understanding the arguments of people who disagree with you can help you make better arguments for your own position—or may even change your mind. When you are working with a group, you may not agree, but you can find a way to discuss the issue and work together.

1. Sit in a circle with the group.

2. Explain that you're going to start a topic, and each person has to respond to the argument made by the person who went directly before her. No matter what her personal beliefs are, she should argue *against* the point made by the person immediately before her.

3. Start a topic by stating a position and giving a reason. For example, "Kids should wear uniforms to school because then they don't have to compete with each other over whose family can afford the coolest designer clothes."

4. The person next to you then responds. For example, "Kids shouldn't have to wear school uniforms because wearing their own clothes allows them to express their individuality, which they can do even with inexpensive clothes."

5. The next person argues against the person immediately before him. It's important to point out that this person should respond to the *new reason* being offered, rather than just restating what the first person said. For example, "Individuality can be expressed by kids in other ways at school, and since the school should be an environment where kids focus on learning, they should wear school uniforms so that they aren't distracted by clothes."

6. Go around until everyone has had at least one turn. In smaller groups you may want to go around the circle with the same issue more than once. If you have an odd number of participants in the circle, the second time around everyone will argue the opposite side as before. You can achieve this with an even number by having the organizer pass to the next person when it comes back around to his or her turn.

Tips: Selecting topics that are relevant and approachable to kids in the age group you are working with helps make this activity a success. Ideas include school uniforms, curfews, household chores, homework. Pick something that kids will know enough about that they can come up with reasons and something that clearly has two points of view that can be defended somewhat equally. For older participants, choose topics that are more complex or abstract. Have several topic choices written down when you start the activity, and if one topic isn't working well, move on to something else.

Group Story
All ages, for groups of any size

> *Materials:* none needed; can use paper and pencils or markers

Gather the group together and let everyone know that you're going to be telling (or writing) stories. But there is a catch: You're going to tell them together. Form a circle. The first person in the circle offers a single word to begin the story. Each person adds just one word to the story when it comes around. The word has to fit grammatically with what has been said before—otherwise it can be anything you want. Keep going until the story comes to a natural stopping point.

Alternative 1: Instead of going around in a circle, have someone act as the "pointer" and point to whomever they want to add the next word.

Alternative 2: Pass around a piece of paper and have each person add his or her word in writing, then at the end have someone read the whole story aloud. This way no one knows what is happening in the story until the paper reaches him or her, and no one knows the whole story until the end.

Alternative 3: Instead of adding just one word, have participants add a certain number of words or a whole sentence.

Blob Tag
All ages; best for ten or more participants

> *Materials:* an open, space safe for running around

One person starts out "it" and tries to tag others. When someone is tagged, instead of just that person being it, that person joins hands with the person who is it. Together they try to tag more people. The "it" blob grows until everyone has been tagged.

Alternative: If playing with a large group, you can have the "it" blob break in half and form two blobs once you reach a certain number.

Team Spirit

All ages, for groups of 3 or more

Materials: big paper, markers, scrap paper, pencils, or pens

In this activity kids create a team name, team chant, and team logo. A great activity to use on the first meeting of a group that will be together for some time or will meet repeatedly. Depending on the size of the group, you may have all the kids work together to create one team identity, or you may group the kids into a few separate teams and have each group create an identity. Smaller teams can be especially good if you have a large group and wish to rotate between activities or have ready-made teams to play team games later. If you are creating several teams, have the groups number off randomly or have the adults create the groups so that people mix together with folks they don't know as well.

1. Give each group pencils or pens and some scrap paper. Give groups 15 minutes to come up with a team name. Remind the groups that they can use whatever method they want to for coming up with a name but should agree on the method (for example: voting, consensus, or picking from the best choices out of a hat) and the team name should be something that the people in the group like being associated with.

2. Once the group has come up with a name, give it another 10 minutes to come up with a chant or a cheer for the group. Let groups know that the chant should be something to cheer on the group, not something that puts other teams down.

3. Then give the group another 15 minutes to come up with a logo for the team using the scratch paper to work out a design.

4. Once each group has a logo design, hand out markers and big sheets of paper so that each team can draw and color in its logo. The logos can hang in the common meeting room or identify places in the room for teams to gather.

5. At the end have each team present its name, chant/cheer, and logo to the other teams. If there is only one team, have members present it to the group leader.

Tips: You may wish to adjust the times for these steps depending on the total size of the group and how long the group will be using these teams. You can omit the logo portion if you just want to do names and chants and then move on with another activity.

Human Knot

All ages; best for groups of eight to fifteen. Can be used with multiple groups of that size at once.

     Materials: an open floor space or field

1. Have everyone in the group stand shoulder to shoulder together in circle facing each other, tightly together.
2. Each person reaches both hands into the circle and grabs two other hands. You may not grab the hands of the people right next to you, and you can't grab both hands with the same person.
3. The group tries to disentangle the knot into a circle without letting go of any hands so that at the end each person is standing between the two people whose hands they are holding. Note that in the final circle some people will be facing to the inside and others will be facing out.

Alternatives: To make this activity more difficult, have some or all of the members of the group not be allowed to talk during the activity.

Resources

Finding Existing Nontheistic Communities in Your Area

American Humanist Association List of Chapters

www.americanhumanist.org/chapters/

American Atheists Affiliate List

www.atheists.org/affiliation/

Atheist Alliance International Member Groups

www.atheistalliance.org/aai/members.php

American Ethical Union Ethical Societies

www.aeu.org/index.php?case=members

Society for Humanistic Judaism Congregations

www.shj.org/CongList.htm

Congress of Secular Jewish Organizations Affiliates

www.csjo.org/pages/affiliates.htm

Unitarian Universalist Congregations

www.uua.org/aboutus/findcongregation/index.php

Center for Inquiry Communities

www.centerforinquiry.net/about/communities

Secular Student Alliance Campus Affiliates

www.secularstudents.org/affiliates

The Brights Local Constituencies

www.the-brights.net/community/blc/list.html

Camp Quest

www.camp-quest.org

Meetup Groups

>Atheists: *www.atheists.meetup.com*
>Humanists: *www.humanism.meetup.com*
>Brights: *www.humanism.meetup.com*
>Parenting: *www.parenting.meetup.com*

The Freedom From Religion Foundation has a few local chapters as well but no online list. Go to *www.ffrf.org* for more information.

Alternatives to Traditional Scouting

Earth Scouts

>*www.earthscouts.org*

Spiral Scouts

>*www.spiralscouts.org*

Curricula

American Ethical Union

>Sample curriculum: *http://64.118.87.15/~aeuorg/library/articles/Love_Your_Neighbor_exploration.pdf*

The American Ethical Union publishes some of its religious education curricula for kids on its website. The Love Your Neighbor curriculum is its ethics and values curriculum for preschool through early elementary school. If you are starting a children's program, you may find some of the stories and activities useful. If you are considering an Ethical Society, you may also find this curriculum interesting as an example of the children's programs offered.

OABITAR (Objectivity, Accuracy, and Balance In Teaching About Religion)

>*Different Drummers curriculum: www.teachingaboutreligion.com/new_dd.htm*

Different Drummers is a curriculum on the role of freethinkers in history, produced by OABITAR. Designed for use in public schools, this resource focuses on the important societal roles played by people who think differently from the mainstream. Some parts of this curriculum may be helpful if you are starting a children's program. You may also want to suggest it to your child's school, especially if you are looking for a way to help remedy a bias toward Christianity or conformity in the classroom.

Ethical Society Without Walls

www.eswow.org

Ethical Culture

www.aeu.org

Society for Humanistic Judaism

www.shj.org

Congress of Secular Jewish Organizations

www.csjo.org

The Unitarian Universalist Association Tapestry of Faith curriculum

www.uua.org/religiouseducation/curricula/tapestryfaith/index.shtml

Some of the stories and lessons in this curriculum are available online. Some sections would be relevant for humanist children's programs.

Resources for Secular Homeschoolers

Secular Homeschoolers' Personal Web Pages

www.geocities.com/hs_hopeful/personal_pages/Secular.html

Secular Homeschool

www.atheistview.com/secular_homeschool.htm

Secular Homeschooling Magazine—a new resource

www.secular-homeschooling.com/

General homeschooling information

http://homeschooling.about.com

Lawrence Hall of Science, the public science center of the University of California, Berkeley, produces pre-K through high school science and math education materials, some of which are aimed at homeschoolers. *www.lhs .berkeley.edu*

Yahoo! Groups for Freethought Homeschoolers (all membership totals as of May 2008)

Secular homeschoolers group (1520 members)

www.groups.yahoo.com/group/secular_homeschoolers

Atheist homeschoolers group (729 members)

www.groups.yahoo.com/group/homeschool_atheists

UU homeschoolers group (995 members)

www.groups.yahoo.com/group/UUHomeschoolers

Freethinking HomeEducators group (270 members)

www.groups.yahoo.com/group/FreeThinking-HomeEducators

Freethinking Unschoolers group (582 members)

www.groups.yahoo.com/group/freethinking_unschoolers

Many smaller groups are available, including some on the state or city level. Enter appropriate search terms (e.g., secular homeschool Georgia) at *www.groups.yahoo.com.*

Miscellaneous

Pollack, Stanley, and Mary Fusoni. *Moving Beyond Icebreakers* (Boston: Center for Teen Empowerment, 2005). A great resource for organizing groups and meetings with kids, teenagers, and adults. Contains more than 300 exercises, but unlike many other resources, it also gives helpful guidance on *why* to integrate these activities, creating buy-in and overcoming resistance of group members, plus tips regarding how best to select activities that will work well with your group's membership and purposes.

This book would be useful to those who are trying to start a new group, whether the group is aimed at kids, teens, adults, or families participating together. It would also be a helpful tool for those who are trying improve the dynamics and community feeling of an existing group. If your local freethought group consists of a monthly lecture with Q&A and then everyone disappears, this book can provide insights into how to build a more robust community in your group by making meetings more interactive. The book is produced by a nonprofit organization called Teen Empowerment (*www*

.teenempowerment.org) and is available from its website or from your favorite online bookstore.

Unitarian Universalist FAQ: *www.uufaq.com*. Several exciting new resources for nonreligious parents are currently in development, including a "Secular Parenting Wiki" of activities related to critical thinking, ethics, meaning, and inquiry and a humanist Sunday school curriculum from the American Humanist Association. For continuous updates on new resources for nonreligious parents, visit the *Parenting Beyond Belief* homepage at *www.parentingbeyondbelief.com*.

Notes

1. Church and Sunday School are the terms used by the majority Christian religious communities in the United States. I will use those terms for convenience. Other religious groups use different terms that refer to similar practices. Jewish families often belong to a synagogue or temple, for example, and their children may spend Saturdays going to Hebrew School.

2. From a study conducted by W. Bradford Wilcox, reported by PBS on October 19, 2005, in its *Religion and Ethics Newsweekly*. The analysis is available at *www.pbs.org/wnet/religionandethics/week908/analysis1.html*. Table 1, which includes the relevant findings, is available at *www.pbs.org/wnet/religionandethics/week908/Wilcox_Data.pdf*. Both accessed May 20, 2008.

3. Roccas, S., and M. B. Brewer, "Social Identity Complexity," *Personality and Social Psychology Review 6* (2002), 88–106.

4. Sherif, Muzafer, O. J. Harvey, B. Jack White, William R. Hood, and Carolyn W. Sherif (1954/1961), "Intergroup Conflict and Cooperation: The Robbers Cave Experiment." Available online here: *http://psychclassics.yorku.ca/Sherif/index.htm*. Accessed April 13, 2008.

5. Gaertner, S. L., J. F. Dovidio, P. A. Anastasio, B. A. Bachman, and M. C. Rust, "The Common Ingroup Identity Model: Recategorization and the Reduction of Intergroup Bias." In W. Stroebe & M. Hewstone (Eds.), *European Review of Social Psychology*, 4 (1993), 1–26.

6. Witt, A. P., and N. L. Kerr, " 'Me Versus Just Us Versus Us All': Categorization and Cooperation in Nested Social Dilemmas," *Journal of Personality and Social Psychology*, 83 (2002), 616–637.

7. Accessed May 14, 2008, from *www.gallup.com/poll/27124/Just-Why-Americans-Attend-Church.aspx*

8. Based on several internal and external UUA surveys, including the Casebolt survey (2001) and the FACT survey (2000). The Casebolt survey offered seven labels and allowed respondents to select as many as they felt applied to them. "Humanist was a clear choice (54 percent), but agnostic (33 percent) beat out earth-centered (31 percent). Atheist was picked by 18 percent and Buddhist by 16.5 percent. Pagan and Christian tied at 13.1 percent." The UUA's 1997 in-house survey asked members to choose only one label. "The top choices were humanist (46 percent), earth/nature-centered (19 percent), theist (13 percent), [and] Christian (9.5 percent)." Quotes from Dart, John, "Churchgoers from Elsewhere," *The Christian Century* (December 5, 2001).

9. Accessed May 14, 2008, from *www.aeu.org*

10. Lee-St. John, Jeninne, "Sunday School for Atheists: An Oxymoron? Nope—Nonbelievers Need Places to Teach Their Kids Values Too," *TIME Magazine* (December 3, 2007), 99.

11. Accessed June 4, 2008, from *http://en.wikipedia.org/wiki/Girl_Scouts_of_the_USA*

12. Accessed June 4, 2008, from *www.bsa-discrimination.org/html/gsusa.html*

13. Accessed June 4, 2008, from *www.earthscouts.org*

14. Accessed June 4, 2008, from *www.spiralscouts.org*

CHAPTER 9

The Grab Bag

Dale McGowan

It'd be lovely if everything in life fit into neat little well-defined packages. Wait—no it wouldn't. That would be terrible. This chapter, then, is a celebration of the untidiness of it all, a place to put questions, answers, statistics, quotes, dialogues, resources, and other miscellany that didn't bloody well feel like conforming to any of the other chapter topics. I've done my best to eliminate any semblance of order, and in some cases, of relevance. Enjoy.

Twelve Blogs for Us
Motherhood Uncensored

www.motherhooduncensored.typepad.com

Kristen Chase is a foul-mouthed, cynical, cut-the-crap mother of two with no sense of propriety or common decency. I adore her. Like me, she is also a former music professor recently relocated to the Deep South.

The Friendly Atheist

www.friendlyatheist.com

If you are allergic to wit, intelligence, and friendly but firm commentary on the religious and nonreligious worlds, avoid Hemant Mehta's blog. Otherwise, come on in.

Pharyngula

www.scienceblogs.com/pharyngula

P.Z. Myers, a biologist at the University of Minnesota, Morris, writes the smartest and funniest science blog on Earth.

Bad Astronomy

www.badastronomy.com

Author/astronomer Phil Plait (apparently his real name)[1] blogs about astronomical misconceptions, hoaxes, and other silliana.

Atheist Ethicist

www.atheistethicist.blogspot.com

The ethico-philosophical blog of Alonzo Fyfe. For the quiet reflectors among us.

Friendly Humanist

www.friendlyhumanist.blogspot.com

The blog of a smart and (yes) friendly Canadian humanist in Scotland. One of my favorites for quiet intelligence.

Rant & Reason

http://blog.thehumanist.com/

"Humanist perspectives on breaking news and politics."

Half Full Blog

http://greatergood.berkeley.edu/half_full/

Subtitled "The Science of Raising Happy Kids." Doesn't get better than this.

New Humanist

http://blog.newhumanist.org.uk/

Blog of the British magazine of the same name.

The Meming of Life

www.ParentingBeyondBelief.com/blog

You honestly thought I had the maturity to not mention my own secular parenting blog. And you call yourself a rationalist.

Bligbi

www.bligbi.com

"The ramblings of a non-apologetic militant atheist mom."

Daddy Dialectic

www.daddy-dialectic.blogspot.com

A blog by *Greater Good* editor and secular dad Jeremy Adam Smith and others that is smarter and better than my blog in every way. So what's your point?

Q: How would you respond if one of your children became religious?

I asked each of the four co-authors of this book to provide a short (150-word) answer to this very common question. The result:

JAN DEVOR: First, make sure that your teen is not just following the pack to a local "in" religious community or youth program. *Gently* ask why he or she has made the decision and listen to the answer. He or she probably knows what you think about religion and might be reluctant to have this conversation.

You may spot weakness or flaws in his thinking, but jumping on him about these things is not the way to go. Allow your teen to follow his thinking in this area.

Ask if you can research the religion's theology and have open discussions with her about what she is learning and doing in this community as time goes by. You might even ask if you could attend a service with her.

Most of all, remain calm. Teens often need to experience things to sort through their feelings about them. This religious exploration is not unusual.

MOLLEEN MATSUMURA: What to do depends on why your kid is interested, and how deeply. There are a lot of reasons to explore religions that are not anything to worry about—certainly not enough to fight about.

Your child may be interested in exploring his or her roots, particularly if your family comes from a minority faith or ethnic community. Often in the United States, people join faith communities for the ethnic connection. This doesn't necessarily mean he's adopting the belief-system, and if not, the best thing you can do is encourage his interest in other ways; for example, by studying your ancestors' language or cooking ethnic recipes together.

In families where members disagree about religion, your child might be trying to maintain a connection by, say, going to church with grandma; be careful about assuming that she is taking sides. Making the issue a test of loyalty could just put distance between you.

AMANDA METSKAS: Make it clear that you love him no matter what he believes. Take your child's ideas seriously. Treating him as though he is "going through a phase" or just parroting the ideas of someone else will damage your relationship and stifle communication.

Encourage your child to continue to explore, and ask questions yourself. Congratulate her for the seriousness with which she is taking these issues, and say that you look forward to continuing to talk about it. Remember that exploring beliefs is an important part of our development.

Call into question any ideas that are contrary to your values and those of your child.

If your child is joining a religion with especially troubling elements—refusing medical care, for example, or isolating its members—that is a different situation. Consider talking to a professional counselor. Try to find out if there is something going on in your child's life that prompted him or her to join this group.

DALE McGOWAN: I encourage my kids to try on as many beliefs as they wish and switch whenever they feel drawn toward a different hat. They'll end up better informed about the identity they eventually choose as well as those they declined.

My reaction would also depend on what is meant by "religious." Is it "Love-your-neighbor" religious or "God-hates-fags" religious? "Dalai Lama" religious, or "September 11 hijackers" religious?

If my kids do choose a religious expression, it's likely to be one that expresses the values of compassion and reason in which they've been raised. We could do far worse than a world of liberal Quakers, for example. If instead one of my kids identified with a more malignant religion, I'd challenge the negative *consequences* of the belief, not the fact that it is "religious." And my love for my child would remain completely unchanged.

■ ■ ■ ■ ■ ■

Six Things the Religious (Generally) Do (Much) Better Than the Nonreligious

One of the central messages of Parenting Beyond Belief *and* Raising Freethinkers *is that there are secular ways to achieve all the benefits of religion. It's true. I've even been so bold as to suggest we do some things better. Time to let that other shoe drop. Here are six things Christians in the United States on the whole do much better than the nonreligious.*

1. ***Give generously.*** Although the nonreligious outpace the religious in volunteerism once "church maintenance" volunteering is eliminated,[2] when it comes to actual giving of actual money, there's no contest: The religious have us licked. Regular churchgoers are more likely than secularists to donate money (91 percent versus 66 percent).[3] Obviously, there will be notable exceptions—three of the top four philanthropists worldwide are atheists or agnostics[4]—but the overall picture of giving by secular individuals needs improvement.

    Part of the solution is the systematizing of giving. That offering plate passing beneath one's nose on a regular basis has a certain loosening effect on the wallet.

2. ***Connect their good works to their beliefs.*** As noted above, the nonreligious are very good about rolling up their sleeves and volunteering, but abysmal at making it clear that those good works are a reflection of our humanistic values. As a result, the presence of nonbelievers doing good works is often overlooked. That's why Dinesh D'Souza was able to write the ignorant screed "Where Were the Atheists?"[5] after the Virginia Tech tragedy. Nonbelievers were present and active as counselors, rescuers, and EMTs at the scene, but because they were not organized into named and tax-exempt units, their worldview was invisible. We must do a better job of making it clear that we do good works not despite our beliefs, but because of them.

3. ***Build community.*** The nonreligious to date have been miserable at forming genuine community. We fret and fuss over the urgent need for more rationality in the world, completely ignoring more basic human needs like unconditional acceptance. Most people do not go to church for theology— they go for acceptance. They go to be surrounded by people who smile at them and are nice to them, who ask how their kids are and whether that back injury is still hurting. Until we recognize why people gather together—

and that it isn't "to be a force for rationality"—freethought groups will continue to lag light years behind churches in offering community.

4. *Use transcendent language.* There are many transcendent religious words without good secular equivalents. There is no secular equivalent for "blessed." I want one, and "fortunate" doesn't cut it. I also want a secular word for "sacred." I want to be able to say something is "holy" without the implication that a God is involved. I want to speak of my "soul," but do so naturalistically, and not be misunderstood. Miracle, spiritual—the list goes on and on. [Molleen Matsumura offered a thoughtful rebuttal to Salman Rushdie when he made a similar point. Visit *www.humaniststudies.org/ podcast* and scroll down to #19 for the podcast. *Ed.*]

5. *Support each other in time of need.* Individuals do a lovely job of supporting each other in times of need, regardless of belief system. But when it comes to the loving embrace of a *community*, the religious once again tend to do it much, much better than any nonreligious community I've seen. Yes, they have the numbers, and yes, they have the structure—but I'll also give them credit for recognizing the need and having the desire to fulfill it.[6]

6. *Own their worldview.* Yes, it's easier for the religious to be "out" about their worldview because they are everywhere. Guess what—we're everywhere too. Current estimates put the nonreligious at 18 percent of the U.S. population. There are more nonreligious Americans than African Americans. Think of that. Coming out of the closet and owning your worldview makes it easier for the next person to do so. So do it.

Need more incentive? Think of the children. I want my kids to choose the worldview that suits them best, and yes, I'd like secular humanism to be one they consider. The more visible and normalized it is as a worldview, the better chance that it will appeal to them. But in the meantime, it would also help if we gave more generously, connected our good works to our beliefs, built communities, learned to use transcendent language, and developed a better collective ability to support each other in time of need.

■ ■ ■ ■ ■ ■

Q: My wife and I are facing a dilemma as my son is moving into middle school next year. Our local public school system is significantly missing our expectations for both environment and academic standards. We have decided to enroll him in a local private school, but all of the good ones in our area are religiously based. The one we like best is a "multidenominational" Christian school with bible study

The Question of the Pledge

During her afterschool snack one day, Delaney (6) asked, "What does 'liberty' mean?"

I knew immediately why she would ask and was once again ashamed of myself in comparison to my kids. I don't think I pondered the meaning of the Pledge of Allegiance until I was well into middle school. When I was her age, I'm certain I thought "EyePlejjaleejins" was one word that meant something like, "Hey, look at the flag." I certainly didn't know I was promising undying loyalty to something.

"Liberty means freedom," I said. "It means being free to do what you want as long as you don't hurt someone else."

"Oh, okay." Pause. "What about 'justice'?"

"Justice means fairness. If there is justice, it means everybody gets treated in a fair way."

"Oh! So when we say 'with liberty and justice for all,' it means 'everybody should be free and everybody should be fair.'"

"That's the idea."

"Hmm," she said. "I like that."

I like it too. A fine, fine idea. I also like the idea that the next time Laney said the Pledge, she had a little more knowledge of just what she was pledging her allegiance to.

There's an email that circulates quite a bit during the times we are asked to stand united against [INSERT IMPLACABLE ENEMY HERE]—the text of a 1969 speech by the comedian Red Skelton in which he recounts the words of an early teacher of his. The teacher had supposedly noticed the students going through the rote recitation of the pledge and decided to explain, word for word, what it meant.

The idea of wanting kids to understand what they are saying is a good one. It solves one of the four issues I have with the Pledge of Allegiance. There is the "under God" clause, of course—but that's the least of my concerns.

Far worse is the fact that it is *mandated,* either by law, policy, or social pressure. No one of any age should be placed in a situation where a loyalty oath is extracted by force, subtle or otherwise.

Worse still is something I had never considered before I heard it spelled out by Unitarian Universalist minister and *Parenting Beyond Belief* contributor Kendyl Gibbons at the onset of the latest (at this writing) Iraq

War in a brilliant sermon titled "Why I'm Not Saying the Pledge of Allegiance Any More." At one point she noted how important integrity is to humanism:

> One of the most basic obligations that I learned growing up as a humanist was to guard the integrity of my given word. Who and what I am as a human being is not predicated on the role assigned to me by a supernatural creator . . . rather, I am what I say I am; I am the loyalties I give, the promises I keep, the values I affirm, the covenants by which I undertake to live. To give my loyalties carelessly, to bespeak commitments casually, is to throw away the integrity that defines me, that helps me to live in wholeness and to cherish the unique worth and dignity of myself as a person. . . . We had better mean what we solemnly, publicly say and sign.

And then, the central issue—that the pledge is to a flag, when in fact it should be to principles, to values. One hopes that the flag stands for these things, but it's too easy for principles to slip and slide behind a symbol. A swastika symbolized universal harmony in ancient Buddhist and Hindu iconography, then something quite different in Germany of the 1930s and 1940s. Better to pledge allegiance to universal harmony than to the drifting swastika.

The same is true of a flag—any flag. Here's Kendyl again:

> I will not give my allegiance to a flag. . . . I will not commit the idolatry of mistaking the flag for the nation, or the nation for the ideals. . . . My allegiance is to my country as an expression of its ideals.
>
> To the extent that the republic for which our flag stands is faithful to the premises of its founding, it has my loyalty. . . . But to the extent that it is a finite and imperfect expression of the ideals to which my allegiance is ultimately given, to the extent that it falls into deceit and self-deception, into arrogance and coercion and violence, into self-serving secrecy and double standards of justice, to that extent my loyalty must take the form of protest, and my devotion must be expressed in dissent.[7]

It remains to this day one of the most eloquent addresses I've *ever* heard. And it continues to motivate me to raise children who pledge their allegiances conditionally rather than blindly—something that will make their eventual allegiances all the more meaningful.

—*Dale McGowan, from the blog* The Meming of Life

■ ■ ■ ■ ■

every day. I'm happy with the idea of religious literacy but am worried about indoctrination into the religion itself. Should I be?

A: I'm a passionate supporter of public schools, but if they are too far gone in your area, there's no use making your child a martyr to principle. A child in a (genuinely) progressive religious environment at school and a freethought environment at home might just have the best of all possible situations for genuine freethought. Three questions to ask:

1. Is it really multidenominational? A broad identity requires a certain amount of flexibility and generally causes Hell to evaporate. But many schools make the claim to increase enrollment but are really founded and funded by a single denomination. Ask to see stats on the religious affiliations of the students. The more the mix, the better. If you catch a whiff of Baptist or Catholic affiliation, stay away. Neither denomination has covered itself with glory when it comes to genuinely open inquiry.

2. What is the attitude toward open questioning and religious doubt? Mission statements will often reveal at least the official posture. A conversation with the principal will reveal more.

3. Get a look at the science curriculum standards, and by all means, *get your hands on the eighth grade science book*. If the world is less than 10,000 years old, run screaming into the woods.

If you get good answers regarding affiliation, openness, and science ed, I'll bet you're fine. A low-key, brimstone-free exposure to religious ideas encourages cultural literacy and permits kids to think for themselves. Reinforce exactly that at home.

■ ■ ■ ■ ■ ■

Fun Finds

Godchecker.com—Your Guide to the Gods

www.godchecker.com/

A frankly incredible and nicely wry archive of deographical information on over 2,800 gods, subdivided by region and culture.

Blasphemy—the Game

www.blasphemythegame.com

Blasphemy™ is an amazingly clever, well-made, and carefully researched board game that manages to provide religious literacy and skewer the sacred at the same time. There was more than one claimant to the title of Messiah in ancient Judea. Each player maneuvers his would-be Messiah through six phases in the life of Jesus. Whoever can attain baptism in the Jordan, resist the devil in the wilderness, give the greatest sermons, perform the most impressive miracles, discredit his rivals, and make his way first to the cross wins the game. If you (or your teens) don't like complex, multilayered games that stretch into the wee hours of the night, this isn't for you. If, on the other hand, that last sentence made you drool, and you think of sacred cows as excellent skewer-holders, this is the game for you. Ages 13+.

■ ■ ■ ■ ■ ■ ■

Q: My daughter's public school is very small and has no auditorium. They hold the kindergarten graduation in the Baptist church across the street. Thoughts?

A: All church-state considerations should begin with a single question: Does the matter at hand negatively affect the religious freedom of the children by dictating a single "right" belief? The use of the building (especially when you have no other space) seems unlikely to meet this standard. Much more problematic are the invocations with which thousands of public high school graduations open every June. Next thing you know, they'll be putting religious phrases on our money. (*Sigh.*) If they open the kindergarten graduation with a prayer or include any other overt religious *content*, that's different, and I'd get very serious with them about that church-state line. As always, express any concern in terms of religious freedom for all, not the avoidance of "offense." The former is constitutionally guaranteed; the latter is not.

Q: One of my neighbors has been dropping hints to my 6-year-old son that she could take him with her to Sunday school so he "could be with the other children." She is a nice enough lady, but it seems manipulative to me. Should I say something?

A: Yes. Take advantage of the next time you see each other taking out the trash, getting the mail, etc.—avoid the door knock if you can. Simply say, kindly but quite firmly, that the decision to attend church is up to the parents, not the neighbors, and that it is inappropriate to direct such an invitation to a 6-year-old without the parents' knowledge. Strangers with candy, and all that. If she has a child herself, and you wish to make a firmer point, ask if she would be pleased to hear that you had offered to take her child to the local Humanist meetup. End with a smile and a change of subject: "I see your petunias are coming in beautifully again!"

■ ■ ■ ■ ■ ■

Nonreligious Parenting Discussion Boards

Parenting Beyond Belief Forums   *www.ParentingBeyondBelief.com/forum*
Atheist Parents   *www.AtheistParents.org*
Atheist/Agnostic Parenting   *http://messageboards.ivillage.com/iv-ppatheist*

Q: What's the best way to improve the religious climate in my extended family? We never talk about beliefs, yet they affect every aspect of everything we do as a family.

A: First and foremost, *be out.* Letting others know that there is a perfectly lovely nonreligious person in their midst is the single most powerful contribution you can make to an improved religious climate in the family.

Second, make beliefs a normal, natural topic. Do this by simply bringing up belief issues in conversation. Perhaps an Amish community is in the news, or FLDS,[8] or Tibetan Buddhism. "It's so interesting that they believe XYZ" can start a rich conversation. Strap in first, of course.

Third, work to uncover the religious diversity present in *every* family. Even if you see your Southern Baptist clan as a sea of monolithic religiosity around the Secular Island of You, it's an illusion. There is always some variety in openness, in actual beliefs, and in comfort with difference. Find those who are religious but open and engage in a fascinating and easily overheard conversation about religious beliefs at your next family reunion or Thanksgiving gathering. This is not a time for critical challenge, just wide-eyed interest in this wonderful tapestry of belief.

Finally, my favorite: Take the Belief-o-Matic Quiz at *www.beliefnet.com*, talk about your results, and invite other family members to do the same. The quiz asks twenty multiple-choice worldview questions, then spits out a list of belief systems and your percentage of overlap. I'm 100 percent Secular Humanist, 92 percent Unitarian Universalist, and 76 percent Theravada Buddhist. I'm less Jewish now (18 percent) than I was three years ago (38 percent) but slightly more Catholic (18 versus 16 percent). Now tell me that's not a fun and interesting conversation starter. ***Best idea:*** Email all family the link before your next gathering. Have the heart pills ready when Born-Again Grandma finds out she's 70 percent Islamic. And yes, that's the approximate result a conservative Christian will get. Go to *www.beliefnet.com* and click Belief-o-Matic in the upper menu. If it helps to open conversations in your family, I'd really like to hear about it at *dale@ParentingBeyondBelief.com*.

■ ■ ■ ■ ■ ■

Rule, Britannia!

According to the European Values Study, just 38 percent of residents of the United Kingdom currently self-identify as religious believers. By some estimates, fully half of British public figures (politicians, entertainers, academics, etc.) are openly nonreligious. A taste of the nonreligious perspective from Old Blighty:

British Humanist Association

www.humanism.org.uk

A large, active, healthy national humanist organization with a rich and useful website.

BHA public service announcement

www.youtube.com/watch?v=0OY3y_fBpAs

Just imagine such a thing in the United States as this elegant, witty 2-minute encapsulation of the humanist point of view.

Pat Condell's Godless Comedy

www.patcondell.net

If you like your (anti-)religious commentary breathtakingly intelligent, articulate, uncompromising, and funny, look no further than Pat Condell. Not for the fainthearted. At this writing, Pat has produced forty short commentaries (see www.youtube.com/patcondell) and a compilation DVD is available through his site.

Thought for the World

www.thoughtfortheworld.org

The BBC does not allow nonreligious thinkers on its "Thought for the Day" program of personal reflections. The Humanist Society of Scotland responded by creating this brilliant podcast featuring such British humanist thinkers as Stephen Law, Tim Mills, Nigel Warburton, A.C. Grayling, and Kate Hudson (no, not that one).

■ ■ ■ ■ ■ ■

Q: I know that religious fundamentalists are generally enthusiastic about corporal punishment. When it comes to freethought parenting, is there a right answer on the use of spanking for discipline? And if spanking is out, what's in?

A: You're right: Religious conservatives tend to be pro-spanking, often citing the biblical injunction "Spare the rod and spoil the child." There's something doubly funny about the invocation of that scripture. Funny Thing 1 is that it isn't scripture. Funny Thing 2 is its actual source—a (quite) bawdy poem by Samuel Butler intended to skewer the fundamentalists of his time, the English Puritans. But as tempting as it is to refrain from spanking just because fundamentalists spank, I have a better reason—*reason*.

In the interest of full disclosure, let me confess that I have spanked my kids. It was seldom and long ago, before I had my parental wings. I'm still ashamed to admit it. Every time represented a failure in my own parenting. Most of all, it demonstrated a twofold failure in my confidence in reason.

Every time a parent raises a hand to a child, that parent is saying you cannot be reasoned with. In the process, the child learns that force is an acceptable substitute for reason and that Mom and Dad have more confidence in the former than in the latter.

I now try to correct behaviors by asking them to recognize and name the problem themselves. Replace "Don't pull the dog's ears" with "Why might pulling the dog's ears be a bad idea?" and you've required them to reason, not just to obey. Good practice.

The second failure is equally damning. Spanking doesn't work. In fact, it makes things worse. The research—a.k.a. "systematic reason"—is compelling. A meta-analysis of eighty-eight corporal punishment studies compiled by Elizabeth Thompson Gershoff at Columbia University found that ten negative outcomes are strongly correlated with spanking, including a damaged parent-child relationship, increased antisocial and aggressive behaviors, and the increased likelihood that the spanked child will physically abuse her or his own children.[9]

The study revealed just one positive correlation: immediate compliance.

Fortunately, many other things get their attention equally well or better than spanking without the nasty side effects. A discipline plan that is both inspired by love and guided by knowledge finds the most loving option that works. Spanking fails on both counts.

Instead, keep a mental list of your kids' favorite privileges and make them contingent on good behavior. Given a choice between a quick spanking or early bedtime for a week, my kids would surely hand me the rod and clench. Too bad. The quick fix is not an option.

The key to any discipline plan, of course, is follow-through. If kids learn that your threats are idle, all is lost.

I hope it's obvious that all this negative reinforcement should be peppered—no, marinated, overwhelmed—with loving, affirmative, positive reinforcements. Catch them doing well and being good frequently enough, and the need for consequences will plummet. It stands to reason.

In the long run, if our ultimate goal is creating autonomous adults, we should raise children who are not merely disciplined but *self*-disciplined. So if your parenting, like mine, is proudly grounded in reason, skip the spankings. We all have an investment in a future less saddled by aggression, abuse, and all the other antisocial maladies to which spanking is known to contribute. Reason with them first and foremost. Provide positive reinforcement. And when all that fails—and yes, it sometimes does—dip into the rich assortment of effective noncorporal consequences. Withhold privileges when necessary. Give time-outs, a focused expression of disapproval too often underrated.

And don't forget the power of simply expressing your disappointment. Your approval means more to them than you may think.

Alternatives to Corporal Punishment

American Academy of Pediatrics

> *www.aap.org/publiced/BR_Discipline.htm*

What is the best way to discipline my child?

Center for Effective Discipline

> *www.stophitting.com* > Discipline at Home > ParentSupport

Ten guidelines for effective discipline of children.

Positive Parenting

> *www.positiveparenting.com/resources/articles.html* > Nine Things to Do Instead of Spanking

For more information on corporal punishment, visit *www.HumanistParenting .org* and click on One Safe Generation > Corporal Punishment.

■ ■ ■ ■

One Safe Generation

www.humanistparenting.org > click ONE SAFE GENERATION

From the website:

One Safe Generation is a humanist initiative to create a more humane, ethical, and reasonable world by breaking the chain of inherited violence and fear. Our goal is to make it possible for one generation to grow up free of violence. In support of this goal of "one safe generation," we are advancing initiatives to combat violence against children in the home, in the community, and on the fields of war.

Our reason, our judgment, and our ethics are all severely impaired when we are afraid. Examples of individuals, groups, and nations thinking poorly and acting immorally under the influence of fear are innumerable.

Violence and other social pathologies are perpetuated from one generation to the next, as victims of violence in childhood are likely to become the perpetrators of violence in the next generation. From corporal punishment and neglect on the individual level to the forced conscription of child soldiers and the disproportionate victimization of children in war, each generation of adults has a choice to pass on traditions of violence and fear—or refuse to do so.

By recognizing that all manner of social pathologies—from violent conflict to religious fundamentalism to the suppression of free expression—are ultimately rooted in fear, humanists can focus our energies on that root cause even as we work to lessen the damage done by its various expressions.

One generation liberated from violence and fear would be more rational, more compassionate, more confident, and far less likely to perpetrate violence on its own children. By allowing a single generation to grow up safely, the tradition of inherited violence can be broken and the future remade.

One Safe Generation gathers valid research and resources in a single, accessible location; counters the advocates of violence in public forums; advocates progressive public policies on related issues through op-eds and legislation; and encourages support for existing organizations and advocates in three areas: (1) nonviolent parenting; (2) advocacy of progressive child social policies; and (3) protecting children from the effects of war.

In identifying fear itself as the enemy, Franklin Roosevelt made a statement of greater lasting import than he knew. Go to **One Safe Generation** for information and resources in the service of raising a generation of children less fearful and more hopeful than their ancestors dared dream.

■ ■ ■ ■

Great Bedtime Songs for Freethinking Families

Imagine (John Lennon)—the anthem of idealism

Little Boxes (Malvina Reynolds)—in praise of nonconformity

Questions (Tom Chapin)—a hat-tip to the inquiring mind of childhood

Cat's in the Cradle (Harry Chapin)—a heartbreaking wakeup for busy parents

The Galaxy Song (Eric Idle/Monty Python)—for that cosmic perspective!

Advanced Reading for Freethinking Teens

Yes, there is the remarkable *His Dark Materials* trilogy, the astronomy of Tim Ferris, the physics of Brian Greene, and the provocative atheism of Harris, Dawkins, and Dennett. But here are three books less often cited in the lists of fabulous reads for freethinking teens:

Fiction

Haddon, Mark. *The Curious Incident of the Dog in the Night-time* (London: Jonathan Cape, 2003)

Foer, Jonathan Safron. *Extremely Loud and Incredibly Close* (New York: Houghton Mifflin, 2005)

Many commentators have noted the many similarities between these two astonishing novels. Each is narrated by a brilliant, science-minded boy who has lost a parent and sets out into the larger world to solve a mystery. Less often noted is that the two narrators both self-identify as nontheistic. The result is a profound pair of reflections on death, loss, meaning, and the power of personal will that should resonate with most freethinking teens. Both are also available on audio at *www.audible.com*. (I especially recommend *Curious Incident* for the unique perspective of the autistic narrator—and especially in audio.)

Nonfiction

Hitchens, Christopher. *Letters to a Young Contrarian* (New York: Basic Books, 2001)

Fiat justitia, ruat caelum, says Hitchens—"let justice be done, though the skies fall." This remarkable and unique book, a collection of letters written by Hitchens to a hypothetical student, advocates dissent as a high value and holds the dissenter up as a vital moral force. Written with his usual combination of blazing intelligence and refusal to mince words, *Young Contrarian* can serve as a seminal influence and a powerful affirmation for the young person entering an adult life in which courageous dissent will play a part.

■ ■ ■ ■ ■ ■

On Fear

One Safe Generation focuses on reducing real threats to the physical safety of children. But media coverage, Internet hype, and even many parenting books do their best to divert attention to threats that are statistically tiny by comparison.

Fear sells papers and drives online traffic, so half-overheard urban myths that "a child is abducted every 40 seconds" and "child abduction rates have risen 444 percent since 1982," always uncited, continue to make the rounds. Christian parenting books often seize this opportunity, sounding a frightening "values" alarm. Crime is spiraling out of control. Morality is on the retreat. Our children are at greater risk of teen pregnancy, kidnapping, and violent death than ever before. Terrified parents are offered the solution—Jesus.

But are the frightening claims actually true? Are our kids less safe and less moral than ever before? **Consider these statistics:**

- According to the U.S. Bureau of Justice Statistics, violent crime rates across the board have declined continuously since 1994, reaching the lowest level *ever* in 2005.[10]
- Teen pregnancy is on the decline. According the Guttmacher Institute's 2006 report, teen pregnancy rates are down 36 percent from 1990 to the lowest level in thirty years.[11]
- Child abduction rates—always infinitesimal—continue to fall. Rates of violent crime against children have fallen by nearly 50 percent since 1973. The child murder rate is the lowest in forty years.[12] Any given child is fifty

times more likely in any given year to die from a world-ending comet or meteor (1 in 20,000) than to be abducted by a stranger (1 in 1 million).[13]

So why do we fear unlikely things and ignore far greater risks? An article in *Scientific American Mind* summed up the psychological research:

- **We fear what our ancestral history has prepared us to fear,** like confinement, heights, snakes, spiders, and humans outside our tribe.
- **We fear what we can't control.** The car is less safe than the airplane, but our hands are on the steering wheel of one and not the other.
- **We fear things that are immediate** (strangers around us) more than the long term (global warming).
- **We fear threats readily available in memory.** Every plane crash, every child abduction, every home invasion is covered by the news media and takes on a significance far beyond the actual threat.[14]

We can provide our children the best security and the least fearful environment by assessing risks intelligently and refusing to give in to those who benefit from fear mongering and the sounding of moral alarms.

Q: Why is it so important for nonreligious parents to "come out"? Won't my child benefit from a lower profile?

A: One of our main goals as parents should be the creation of a saner world for our kids. One of the best ways nonreligious parents can do this is by working toward a world in which religious disbelief is no big deal. That's the goal, of course—not to dominate the culture, not to wipe religion off the map, but to simply make religious disbelief *no big deal.*

We can learn a great deal from the progressive movements that have preceded us. Racism becomes difficult to support once you know and love someone of a different race. Homophobia falls apart when you learn that your neighbor or your child is gay. The same is true for religious disbelief. Religious people are currently surrounded by closeted nonbelievers. This makes it possible for them to retain a caricature of the nonreligious as someone "out there," far away, wild-eyed and repugnant, alien and threatening. When instead they learn that sweet, normal cousin Susan doesn't believe in God, a powerful shift must take place to accommodate the new information.

Many nonreligious people think the shift will downgrade *them* in the eyes of the other person. After talking to literally hundreds of nonbelievers about their "coming out" experiences, I am happy to report that it generally works in reverse: Instead of downgrading the friend or relative, most religious people will upgrade, however slightly, their overall opinion of the nonreligious. Their caricature becomes less supportable when a face both known and loved is placed on it.

If every nonreligious person were to reveal her beliefs to those around her, gently and with a smile, the predominant cultural attitude toward religious disbelief would be profoundly altered overnight. Fear and mistrust would not change to instant approval by any means, but the simplistically drawn image of the nonreligious would necessarily become more complex, more nuanced, more accurate. It almost *always* goes better than you think it will. And it would go a long, long way toward allowing our children to think freely and independently about questions of religious belief.

Notes

1. A name second only to that of my actual college roommate, Phil Graves.

2. Yonish, Stephen, and David Campbell, "Religion and Volunteering in America," in Smidt, Corwin, *Religion as Social Capital* (Waco, TX: Baylor University Press, 2003).

3. Brooks, Arthur C., "Religious Faith and Charitable Giving," in *Policy Review* (October/November 2003).

4. Warren Buffett (#1), Bill Gates (#2 along with his wife Melinda, who is Catholic), and George Soros (#3). Cited in 50 Most generous philanthropists, *Business Week*. Accessed April 13, 2008, from *http://bwnt.businessweek.com/philanthropy/06/index.asp*

5. Text at *http://richarddawkins.net/article,903,n,n*. A very thoughtful reply is at *www.dailykos.com/story/2007/4/19/18451/0971*. Site accessed May 30, 2008.

6. Greg Epstein, the humanist chaplain at Harvard, hit the nail on the head when he said "Science and reason are important, but science and reason won't visit you in the hospital."

7. Full text at *www.firstunitariansociety.org/sermons0203/092202.htm#092202.htm*. Accessed July 11, 2008.

8. Fundamentalist Church of Jesus Christ of Latter Day Saints.

9. Gershoff, Elizabeth Thompson. "Corporal Punishment by Parents and Associated Child Behaviors and Experiences: A Meta-Analytic and Theoretical Review," *Psychological Bulletin, 128* (2002), 539–579.

10. *www.ojp.usdoj.gov/bjs/gvc.htm#Violence*

11. Accessed June 11, 2008, from *www.guttmacher.org/pubs/2006/09/12/USTPstats.pdf*

12. National Center for Juvenile Justice 2006 report. Accessed June 8, 2008, from *www.ojjdp.ncjrs.gov/ojstatbb/nr2006/downloads/chapter2.pdf*

13. "A fistful of risks," *DISCOVER Magazine* (April 1996), 82.

14. Myers, David G. "The Powers and Perils of Intuition," *Scientific American Mind* (June/July 2007), 48–51.

Recommended Films by Category

Recommended films with themes related to religious literacy, coming of age, and exploring death. Synopses and reviews available at Netflix (www.netflix.com) or the Internet Movie Database (www.imdb.com).

FILMS for RELIGIOUS LITERACY

	Age 4–7	7–11	11–14	14–18
Prince of Egypt (G)	✓	✓		
Joseph, King of Dreams (G)	✓	✓		
Kirikou and the Sorceress (NR)	✓	✓	✓	
Jesus Christ Superstar (G)	✓	✓	✓	✓
Fiddler on the Roof (G)	✓	✓	✓	✓
Little Buddha (PG)		✓	✓	✓
Heaven Can Wait (PG)		✓	✓	✓
Oh, God! (PG)		✓	✓	✓
The Mission (PG)		✓	✓	✓
The Message (PG)		✓	✓	✓
The Nativity Story (PG)		✓	✓	✓
Jason and the Argonauts (NR)		✓	✓	✓
Inherit the Wind (NR)			✓	✓
Gandhi (PG)			✓	✓

(continued)

FILMS for RELIGIOUS LITERACY (*Continued*)

	Age 4–7	7–11	11–14	14–18
Jesus Camp (PG-13)			✓	✓
The 10 Commandments (G)			✓	✓
Saved (PG-13)			✓	✓
Seven Years in Tibet (PG-13)			✓	✓
Kundun (PG-13)			✓	✓
Bruce Almighty (PG-13)			✓	✓
Evan Almighty (PG-13)		✓		✓
Romero (PG-13)				✓
Dogma (R)				✓
Jesus of Montreal (R)				✓
Schindler's List (R)				✓
Black Robe (R)				✓
Agnes of God (R)				✓

FILMS EXPLORING COMING of AGE ISSUES

	Age 7–11	11–14	14–18
To Kill a Mockingbird (NR)	✓	✓	✓
Remember the Titans (PG)	✓	✓	✓
Stand and Deliver (PG)	✓	✓	✓
Believe in Me (PG)	✓	✓	✓
Coyote Summer (G)	✓	✓	✓
Hairspray (PG)	✓	✓	✓
October Sky (PG)	✓	✓	✓
Searching for Bobbie Fisher (PG)	✓	✓	✓
Dead Poet's Society (PG)		✓	✓
Son of Rambow (PG-13)		✓	✓
Sixteen Candles (PG)[1]		✓	✓
Lean on Me (PG-13)		✓	✓
Mean Girls (PG-13)		✓	✓
Odd Girl Out (PG-13)		✓	✓
Dirty Dancing (PG-13)		✓	✓

FILMS EXPLORING COMING of AGE ISSUES (*Continued*)

	Age 7–11	11–14	14–18
Double Happiness PG-13		✓	✓
Forrest Gump (PG-13)		✓	✓
Pretty in Pink		✓	✓
Bend It Like Beckham (PG-13)		✓	✓
Mask (PG-13)		✓	✓
Hoop Dreams (PG-13)		✓	✓
Whale Rider (PG-13)		✓	✓
Real Women Have Curves (PG-13)		✓	✓
Juno (PG-13)			✓
Stand by Me (R)			✓
Good Will Hunting (R)			✓
Boyz N the Hood (R)			✓
Into the Wild (R)			✓
Billy Elliot (R)			✓
Thirteen (R)			✓
Muriel's Wedding (R)			✓
Mystic Pizza (R)			✓

FILMS EXPLORING DEATH and LOSS

	Age 4–7	7–11	11–14	14–18
Charlotte's Web (G)	✓	✓		
Mr. Magorium's Wonder Emporium (G)	✓	✓	✓	
Bambi (G)	✓	✓		
Brian's Song (G)		✓	✓	✓
Tuck Everlasting (PG)		✓	✓	
On Golden Pond (PG)		✓	✓	✓
My Girl (PG)		✓	✓	
Big Fish (PG-13)		✓	✓	✓
Edward Scissorhands (PG-13)		✓	✓	✓
Defending Your Life (PG)			✓	✓

(continued)

FILMS EXPLORING DEATH and LOSS (Continued)				
	Age 4–7	7–11	11–14	14–18
Dead Poet's Society (PG)			✓	✓
Stepmom (PG-13)			✓	✓
What Dreams May Come (PG-13)			✓	✓
Life Is Beautiful (PG-13)			✓	✓
Philadelphia (PG-13)				✓
My Life as a Dog (PG-13)				✓
Harold and Maude (PG)				✓
Wit (PG-13)				✓
Kolya (PG-13)				✓
Dead Man Walking (R)				✓
The Green Mile (R)				✓
The Meaning of Life (R)				✓
One True Thing (R)				✓
Ponette (NR)				✓
Schindler's List (R)				✓

Note

1. *Sixteen Candles* was rated just weeks prior to the creation of the PG-13 rating. If re-rated today, it would certainly be designated PG-13.

Lists of Principles

Lists of principles, procedures, values, and ideals referenced elsewhere in the book.

The Seven Principles of Unitarian Universalism

We, the member congregations of the Unitarian Universalist Association, covenant to affirm and promote:

- The inherent worth and dignity of every person.
- Justice, equity, and compassion in human relations.
- Acceptance of one another and encouragement to spiritual growth in our congregations.
- A free and responsible search for truth and meaning.
- The right of conscience and the use of the democratic process within our congregations and society at large.
- The goal of world community with peace, liberty, and justice for all.
- Respect for the interdependent web of all existence of which we are a part.

Steps to Seeking Forgiveness

Applying ethical philosophy to the practicalities of living. Includes contributions by Lois Kellerman, Don Montagna, and Jone Johnson Lewis.

Phase 1: Acknowledge wrong-doing

- **Clarify why a certain behavior was hurtful.** Without understanding the harmful effects of your behavior, it will be difficult to change. Attempt to understand the hurt or pain from the point of view of those who have been hurt, and try to understand the harmful effect on yourself.
- **Acknowledge to yourself and others that the behavior was a mistake.** Being able to acknowledge the mistake verbally is an important first step if the relationship is to be healed.
- **Express genuine sorrow to all those involved for the mistake you have made.** When you understand the harmful effects of your behavior, and can express that with true feelings of sorrow, you open up possibilities for change and for healing.

Phase 2: Make amends

- **Act out of a deep sense of honoring yourself and the other party involved.** Don't cater to postures of narrow defensiveness. It is courageous to face up to the harm you have done. Take the first step toward healing by being generous and proactive in your attempts to reconcile.
- **Find a "stroke" that is equal to your "blow."** Do this by asking the party that is hurt what you can do that is equally positive to balance the negative. This is ultimately only symbolic, since we cannot undo past harm. But it is a critical sign of goodwill and true remorse.
- **Make amends in a timely manner.** The longer you delay, the more wounds will fester. So act as swiftly as the processing of your feelings will allow.

Phase 3: Commit to change

- **Make a clear commitment to change your harmful patterns of behavior.** This may involve clarifying what kinds of events trigger your destructive responses and finding ways to avoid such situations or training yourself to respond differently.
- **Act visibly on your commitment.** Change involves not only words, but actions, such as appropriate counseling, courses in relationship skills, publicly asking for help in identifying your harmful patterns and support in your not acting on them.
- **Respect the process of change.** Acknowledge to yourself and others that it is hard to change, and that behaviors deeply imbedded do not disappear quickly. Don't condemn yourself for slipping, and don't condone your old ways or trivialize their harmfulness. Rather, accept the actual without losing sight of the ideal.

The Twelve Core Values of the St. Louis Ethical Society Sunday School

- Ethics is my religion.
- Every person is important and unique.
- Every person deserves to be treated fairly and kindly.
- I can learn from everyone.
- I am part of this earth; I cherish it and all the life upon it.
- I learn from the world around me by using senses, mind, and feelings.
- I am a member of the world community, which depends on the cooperation of all people for peace and justice.
- I can learn from the past to build for the future.
- I am free to question.
- I am free to choose what I believe.
- I accept responsibility for my choices and actions.
- I strive to live my values.

Affirmations of Humanism: A Statement of Principles

From the Council for Secular Humanism (*www.secularhumanism.org*)

- We are committed to the application of reason and science to the understanding of the universe and to the solving of human problems.
- We deplore efforts to denigrate human intelligence, to seek to explain the world in supernatural terms, and to look outside nature for salvation.
- We believe that scientific discovery and technology can contribute to the betterment of human life.
- We believe in an open and pluralistic society and that democracy is the best guarantee of protecting human rights from authoritarian elites and repressive majorities.
- We are committed to the principle of the separation of church and state.
- We cultivate the arts of negotiation and compromise as a means of resolving differences and achieving mutual understanding.
- We are concerned with securing justice and fairness in society and with eliminating discrimination and intolerance.
- We believe in supporting the disadvantaged and the handicapped so that they will be able to help themselves.
- We attempt to transcend divisive parochial loyalties based on race, religion, gender, nationality, creed, class, sexual orientation, or ethnicity, and strive to work together for the common good of humanity.

- We want to protect and enhance the earth, to preserve it for future generations, and to avoid inflicting needless suffering on other species.
- We believe in enjoying life here and now and in developing our creative talents to their fullest.
- We believe in the cultivation of moral excellence.
- We respect the right to privacy. Mature adults should be allowed to fulfill their aspirations, to express their sexual preferences, to exercise reproductive freedom, to have access to comprehensive and informed healthcare, and to die with dignity.
- We believe in the common moral decencies: altruism, integrity, honesty, truthfulness, responsibility. Humanist ethics is amenable to critical, rational guidance. There are normative standards that we discover together. Moral principles are tested by their consequences.
- We are deeply concerned with the moral education of our children. We want to nourish reason and compassion.
- We are engaged by the arts no less than by the sciences.
- We are citizens of the universe and are excited by discoveries still to be made in the cosmos.
- We are skeptical of untested claims to knowledge, and we are open to novel ideas and seek new departures in our thinking.
- We affirm humanism as a realistic alternative to theologies of despair and ideologies of violence and as a source of rich personal significance and genuine satisfaction in the service to others.
- We believe in optimism rather than pessimism, hope rather than despair, learning in the place of dogma, truth instead of ignorance, joy rather than guilt or sin, tolerance in the place of fear, love instead of hatred, compassion over selfishness, beauty instead of ugliness, and reason rather than blind faith or irrationality.
- We believe in the fullest realization of the best and noblest that we are capable of as human beings.

Forty Things You Can Do to Raise a Moral Child

From *Ethical People and How They Get to Be That Way* by Arthur B. Dobrin. Used by permission.

Feelings

Emotions Are the Groundwork of Morality

Tune into your child's feelings.

Comment on your own emotions.

Talk about how you think others may be feeling.

Read stories that are fanciful.

Sing to your children.

Reason

Feelings Need to be Guided by Reason

Give reasons why you approve or disapprove of your child's behavior.

Provide reasons for rules you want your child to follow.

Encourage your child to play with children of various ages.

Engage your children in reflective discussions by asking open-ended question.

Promote independent thinking.

Self-Esteem

Self-Respect Is a Prerequisite to Acting Morally

Treat your child with respect.

Express interest in your child's activities, projects, and dreams.

Help set goals and encourage your children to see them through.

Praise a task well done.

Give your child emotional and verbal support to stand against the crowd when necessary.

Discipline

Behavior Has Consequences

Be flexible—not arbitrary—in your discipline.

Don't use intimidation; never use ridicule.

Severity of punishment should be related to the severity of the wrongdoing.

Discipline with explanations.

Criticize in private.

Prejudice

Treating All People Fairly Is Fundamental to Morality

Examine your own biases.

Provide examples that counteract society's prejudices.

Don't allow biased or bigoted comments to go unchallenged.

Give your child books that show different kinds of people playing, working, and living together.

Talk about differences between people, but speak about them neutrally.

Values

Some Values Are More Important Than Others

Tell your children who you admire and why.

Live your life as you want your child to lead hers.

Show the importance of protecting the vulnerable.

Comment on compassionate behavior—let your child know that caring is an important value.

Let your children know what you value and why you value it.

Habits

Morality Is Learned Through Observing and Doing

Provide opportunities for your child to help others.

Give positive verbal feedback for being a good person.

Work with your child in community and volunteer service.

Expect and encourage good deeds from your children.

Help your children to keep promises.

Community

Morality Involves Other People

Talk about the TV shows, music, and movies your child sees and hears.

Get involved in your child's education.

Make family meals an important and regular occasion.

Encourage activities that involve your child with others.

Take an interest in the world outside your home.

INDEX

Other Titles of Help to Parents!

Parenting Beyond Belief: On Raising Ethical, Caring Kids Without Religion

Edited by Dale McGowan
Foreword by Michael Shermer, Ph.D.
Contributors include Richard Dawkins, Penn Jillette, Julia Sweeney, and Dr. Donald B. Ardell

It's hard enough to live a secular life in a religious world. And bringing up children without religious influence can be even more daunting. Despite the difficulties, a large and growing number of parents are choosing to raise their kids without religion. In *Parenting Beyond Belief*, Dale McGowan celebrates the freedom that comes with raising kids without formal indoctrination and advises parents on the most effective way to raise freethinking children.

With advice from educators, doctors, psychologists, and philosophers as well as wisdom from everyday parents, the book offers tips and insights on a variety of topics, from "mixed marriages" to coping with death and loss, and from morality and ethics to dealing with holidays. Sensitive and timely, *Parenting Beyond Belief* features reflections from such freethinkers as Mark Twain, Richard Dawkins, Bertrand Russell, and wellness guru Dr. Don Ardell that will empower every parent to raise both caring and independent children without constraints.
ISBN# 9780814474266   Paperback $17.95

ADD/ADHD Drug Free: Natural Alternatives and Practical Exercises to Help Your Child Focus

By Frank Jacobelli and L.A. Watson
Foreword by Dr. Jay Carter

ADD/ADHD Drug Free gives frustrated parents a long-awaited natural alternative. The first book to feature enjoyable, practical activities for children that will help them cope with their disorder by strengthening brain functioning, this life-changing guide shows parents, teachers, and counselors how they can improve learning and behavior effectively and without medication. Timely and thoroughly researched, this guide will help thousands of children become more focused and more successful in school and in life, without jeopardizing their health.
ISBN# 9780814400944   Paperback $15.00

Generation Text: Raising Well-Adjusted Kids in an Age of Instant Everything

By Dr. Michael Osit

Our children can't remember a time without computers, the Internet, and cell phones. Here's how to help them stay on track.

Parents who want to ensure that their children successfully develop key social skills, a healthy identity, and a strong work ethic need to make the right choices every step of the way. Clinical psychologist Dr. Michael Osit draws on his professional—as well as personal—experiences working with children and teens who have been challenged by unprecedented access to information, possessions, and temptation. Using case studies and examples, the book provides reasonable, down-to-earth strategies readers can use to address the unique issues faced by children surrounded by infinite choices . . . and very few limits.
ISBN# 9780814409329   Hardcover $22.00

Raising Gifted Kids: Everything You Need to Know to Help Your Exceptional Child Thrive

By Barbara Klein, Ph.D.

While it can be rewarding to raise an extremely bright child—quick, curious, sensitive, and introspective—it's also a daunting challenge. Parents need insight into their own motivations (as well as those of their children) and the courage and ability to make tough decisions about their child's development. *Raising Gifted Kids* will help parents understand and cope with the obstacles they face in raising a gifted child, and help them make the best choices for their son's or daughter's growth and happiness.
ISBN# 9780814473429   Paperback $16.95

When to Worry: How to Tell If Your Teen Needs Help—And What to Do About It

By Lisa Boesky, Ph.D.

When to Worry helps parents distinguish typical teenage behaviors from those that merit concern. It provides essential information on problematic teenage issues: mood swings, rebellion and defiance, school difficulties, teen depression, ADHD, alcohol and drug use, self-injury ("cutting"), low self-esteem, delinquency, learning disabilities, out of control teens, worries/fears and stress,

eating disorders, aggression, bipolar disorder, aspergers, teen suicide, trauma, and more. Parents learn how to recognize warning signs of important teen problems and are given specific "dos and don'ts" to decrease their teen's struggles and increase peace in the family home.
ISBN# 9780814473634   Paperback $17.95

Overcoming School Anxiety: How to Help Your Child Deal with Separation, Tests, Homework, Bullies, Math Phobia, and Other Worries

By Diane Peters Mayer, MSW

Seasoned psychotherapist Diane Peters Mayer has successfully treated hundreds of elementary school students suffering from anxiety about school. She shows parents how to deal with a wide variety of problems, from test and homework anxiety, to bullying, to fear of speaking up in class. Mayer also offers easy-to-learn techniques for children, including breathing and relaxation exercises, focusing techniques, and tips on proper diet and exercise that help relieve stress. Filled with real-life examples as well as proven advice for working with teachers, principals, and counselors, this is the only comprehensive guide that will enable every parent to help a child cope, build confidence, and succeed in school.
ISBN# 9780814474464   Paperback $16.00

Available at your local bookstore, online, or call 800-250-5308.
Savings start at 40% on bulk orders of 5 copies or more!
Save up to 55%!
Prices are subject to change.
For details, contact AMACOM Special Sales
Phone: 212-903-8316   E-Mail: SpecialSls@amanet.org